THE BOUNDARIES
OF THE HUMAN IN
MEDIEVAL ENGLISH LITERATURE

The Boundaries
of the Human in
Medieval English Literature

DOROTHY YAMAMOTO

OXFORD
UNIVERSITY PRESS

OXFORD
UNIVERSITY PRESS

Great Clarendon Street, Oxford OX2 6DP
Oxford University Press is a department of the University of Oxford.
It furthers the University's objective of excellence in research, scholarship,
and education by publishing worldwide in

Oxford New York

Athens Auckland Bangkok Bogotá Buenos Aires Calcutta
Cape Town Chennai Dar es Salaam Delhi Florence Hong Kong Istanbul
Karachi Kuala Lumpur Madrid Melbourne Mexico City Mumbai
Nairobi Paris São Paulo Singapore Taipei Tokyo Toronto Warsaw

and associated companies in Berlin Ibadan

Oxford is a registered trade mark of Oxford University Press
in the UK and certain other countries

Published in the United States
by Oxford University Press Inc., New York

British Library Cataloguing in Publication Data
Data available

Library of Congress Cataloging in Publication Data
Data available
ISBN–0–19–818 674–6

1 3 5 7 9 10 8 6 4 2

Typeset by Kolam Information Services Pvt Ltd, Pondicherry, India
Printed in Great Britain
on acid-free paper by
Biddles Ltd, Guildford and King's Lynn

In memory of R. J.

Preface and Acknowledgements

THIS BOOK HAD its genesis a long time ago when I listened to a lecture about *Sir Gawain and the Green Knight* in the Cambridge English Faculty and wondered who—or what—were the 'wodwos' Gawain fights with on his journey north. The definition in Tolkien and Gordon's glossary, 'satyrs, trolls of the forest', didn't seem to fit. I have several people to thank for keeping alive my interest in medieval literature and culture during the intervening years, and inspiring me to write about it. At Cambridge I was very fortunate to be taught by John Stevens and J. A. W. Bennett; later, at Oxford, Rosemary Woolf showed me the importance of painstaking research through her own meticulous example. When I enrolled as a Ph.D. student at Oxford Brookes University, and started to write the thesis on which this book is based, I was helped immeasurably by two exemplary—and complementary—supervisors: Douglas Gray generously shared his immense knowledge of medieval literature and suggested many new avenues to explore; while Rob Pope made sure that all those new leads did not result in an undisciplined tangle. Rob kept a watching brief on the thesis as it developed, and never lost faith in it, however snail-like its progress. He saw that it could—and should—be more than an investigation of the 'wild man', and continually prodded me to extend my boundaries and ask more questions. I know he will not mind me saying that he is the book's midwife. Helen Cooper examined the thesis with proper rigour and made several suggestions for improving it—I am very grateful for these, as I am for the reports on the book written by the Press's necessarily anonymous advisers, who pointed out what still needed doing and offered guidance about how to do it. I would also like to thank Elizabeth Stratford, who copy-edited the final draft of the typescript with thoroughness and tact.

I am grateful to the staff of the Bodleian Library, and the library of Oxford Brookes University for the help they have given me. The Humanities department of Oxford Brookes was a friendly and stimulating environment in which to work (right from the moment when someone, when he heard I was going to work on wild men, said, 'Ah, you've come to the right place, then . . .'), and I would like to thank all the people—students, colleagues, and support staff—who made it so. Thanks, too, to friends who generously combined their holidays with searching for carvings of wild men—especially to Elizabeth Knowles, who found several excellent specimens in East Anglia. My husband, Mike, and son, Alex, also joined in the hunt, and have helped and supported me in lots of other ways too.

Some of the material in Chapter 1, 'The Bestiary: Establishing Ground Rules', has appeared in 'Aquinas and Animals: Patrolling the Boundary', in Andrew Linzey and Dorothy Yamamoto (eds.), *Animals on the Agenda: Questions about Animals for Theology and Ethics* (SCM Press, 1998), 80–9, and parts of Chapter 6, 'A Reading of *The Knight's Tale*', in my article 'Heraldry and the *Knight's Tale*', *Neuphilologische Mitteilungen*, 93 (1992), 207–15.

Dorothy Yamamoto
Oxford
March 1999

Contents

x   *Contents*

Note on References, Translations, and Abbreviations

ALL quotations from Chaucer's works are from *The Riverside Chaucer*, ed. Larry D. Benson, 3rd edn. (Oxford, 1987). All quotations from *Sir Gawain and the Green Knight* are from *Sir Gawain and the Green Knight*, ed. J. R. R. Tolkien and E. V. Gordon, 2nd edn., rev. Norman Davis (Oxford, 1967). References to these works are usually included within the text. Translations not otherwise attributed are my own.

The following abbreviations have been used:

BL	British Library
BN	Bibliothèque Nationale
EETS	Early English Text Society
ES	Extra Series
JEGP	*Journal of English and Germanic Philology*
MÆ	*Medium Ævum*
MED	*Middle English Dictionary* (Ann Arbor, 1956–)
OS	Original Series
SS	Special Series
STS	Scottish Text Society

Introduction

MEDIEVAL CULTURE ABOUNDS in bodies. In the kind of pageant that we might idly allow to run through our minds, figures like the knight, the monk, and the ploughman appear in reassuring solidity, each encapsulating a whole way of life and its attendant values. Stranger bodies, too, catch our attention—perhaps the members of the 'monstrous' races who range the borders of the known world in the Hereford and Ebstorf maps, the disconcertingly hybrid creatures in manuscripts such as the Luttrell Psalter, or the weird foes met by the questing knights of romance—from Gawain's Green Knight to Malory's Blatant Beast. The 'body', in its exceedingly various manifestations, is one of our points of access to the medieval world—at once a lure and a conundrum.

Yet bodies, although each of us has one and, in Thomas Laqueur's words, only attains knowledge through 'that extraordinarily fragile, feeling, and transient mass of flesh with which we are all familiar',[1] are not simple things to deal with. Laqueur goes on to remind us that there is no straight path to a body—rather, finding out about bodies means exploring the ways in which particular sorts of bodies are generated by particular societies with their individual ways of looking at, and operating in, the world. There is no 'neutral' body, shorn of cultural meaning, which will come to our hands as a counter in the game. ' "The body" ', as Denise Riley puts it in her stimulating study of identity and gender, 'is not, for all its corporeality, an originating point nor yet a terminus; it is a result or an effect.'[2]

Such cautions are salutary, but they should not make us think that, because it is never possible to question a body apart from its cultural bonds, it is not worth framing questions in 'bodily' terms at all. In fact, research focusing on 'bodies' has proved an extremely

[1] Thomas Laqueur, *Making Sex: Body and Gender from the Greeks to Freud* (Cambridge, Mass., 1990), 12.

[2] Denise Riley, *Am I That Name? Feminism and the Category of 'Women' in History* (Basingstoke, 1988), 102.

fruitful area in the past few years, and has every sign of continuing to do so.[3] Here, the body is not so much an imponderable, more an exciting way of journeying. 'Thinking the body' can give one privileged access to a culture's ways of representing the world to itself, and of handling its own composing elements. For example, Peter Stallybrass and Allon White invoke the human body as a symbolic domain to analyse the ways in which a society deals with its periphery—with what it has coded as low, degraded, or aberrant. Those manifestations of the 'other', although in theory exiled from the centre, are apt to return in powerfully symbolic form, challenging and seducing through their fantasies of the forbidden. For example, in the fairs of the eighteenth and early nineteenth centuries, the 'pigmey' which 'walks upright and drinks wine' and 'the creature looking like a wild man' who 'politely removes his hat to the crowd' display manners which 'amusingly transgress, as well as reaffirm, the boundaries between high and low, human and animal, domestic and savage, polite and vulgar'.[4] And, comparably, the metaphorical proper names of Freud's patients 'Rat Man' and 'Wolf Man' are not randomly chosen, but spring from 'the terrors conjured up by semantic material from cultural domains (the slum, the forest) extraterritorial to their own constructed identities as socio-historical subjects'.[5] In a very different setting, Page duBois has explored the ways in which the 'bodies' of centaurs and Amazons, through their aberrancy, point towards the value given to a particular kind of identity in the world of the Greek polis. Both centaur and Amazon have bodies that differ from regular human bodies, and such visible difference serves as a sign that neither conforms to the rules by which the polis defines itself, as a single culture operating through 'an *internal* process of exchange',[6] expressed through marriage alliances. Neither centaurs nor Amazons can

[3] In the field of medieval studies, see especially, for its variety of topics and approaches, Sarah Kay and Miri Rubin (eds.), *Framing Medieval Bodies* (Manchester, 1994); also, L. Lomperis and S. Stanbury (eds.), *Feminist Approaches to the Body in Medieval Literature* (Philadelphia, 1993), and Caroline Walker Bynum, *Holy Feast and Holy Fast: The Religious Significance of Food to Medieval Women* (Berkeley and Los Angeles, 1987).

[4] Peter Stallybrass and Allon White, *The Politics and Poetics of Transgression* (London, 1986), 41.

[5] Ibid. 196.

[6] Page duBois, *Centaurs and Amazons: Women and the Pre-History of the Great Chain of Being* (Ann Arbor, 1991), 42.

marry—centaurs because their exaggerated sexuality runs counter to any restraining code, Amazons because they spurn male company—and so they are necessarily excluded from culture. Their bodies, openly displaying their unmarriageableness and shading into the alien and the monstrous, represent everything that has to be kept at bay if the polis, 'the terrain of [the Greek male's] existence',[7] is to retain its integrity.

The analogical model, typical of fifth-century speculation about difference—racial, sexual, species—defined the Greek male human in terms of a series of polarities which together articulated his nature. The others, that is, female, barbarian, and animal, were like spokes radiating from the hub of a wheel. At the center was the common element of each of the polarities, the center of the city and of culture, the graceful, civilized warrior of the classical frieze.[8]

What emerges powerfully from the studies by Stallybrass and White and duBois is that all bodies are not of equal value. Every society, including our own, sends out messages about the kind of body it is good to have. In the world of the polis it is better to be a poised male warrior than a hypersexual centaur. (It is also, of course, better to be a male than a female.) However, there are two complicating factors.

The first—perhaps not one that readily applies to centaurs and Amazons but one that will be investigated in the course of this book—is that individual bodies do not always stay the same. In the romance *Sir Orfeo*, when the king enters the wilderness in search of his lost wife Heurodis, he also acquires, or 'becomes', a different body.

> Al his bodi was oway duine
> For missays, and al to-chine.
> Lord! who may telle the sore
> This king sufferd ten yere and more?
> His here of his berd, blac and rowe,
> To his girdel-stede was growe.[9]

Does his altered body leave Orfeo's true identity untouched? And how does it impact upon his eventual return to his social milieu?

---

[7] Ibid. 95.   [8] Ibid. 129.
[9] *Sir Orfeo*, in A. C. Gibbs (ed.), *Middle English Romances*, York Medieval Texts (London, 1966), lines 247–52.

Questions such as these will be explored at length in the chapters below on Wild Men, but they also underlie the whole of my enquiry. For, if bodies can change, or be changed, then in what sense can a body truly 'speak' identity?

The second complicating factor concerns the relationship between differently valued bodies—between 'high' and 'low' in Stallybrass and White's terms or between centre and periphery in duBois's. This relationship is essentially a dynamic one, as Stallybrass and White convey through their use of a Freudian model in which the marginal returns, in the form of the eroticized fantastic, to haunt the individual consciousness. Their argument is that borders, margins, edges, are always the sites of the 'most powerful symbolic repertoires', since cultural identity itself 'is inseparable from limits'. It is 'always a boundary phenomenon and its order is always constructed around the figures of its territorial edge'.[10] Therefore, the 'centre' is forever in animated dialogue with the 'periphery': in fact, it can only maintain its full identity through activity of this kind.

Although neither Stallybrass and White nor duBois writes about medieval culture, the two models they suggest—of high/low, centre/periphery—bear a particular medieval resonance. 'High' and 'low' have obvious embodiment in a hierarchical society, in which, for instance, as in John of Salisbury's *Policraticus*, the ruler is imagined as the body's 'head' and the peasants as its labouring 'feet'.[11] Centre and periphery are illustrated in the Hereford world map, with its focal Jerusalem the site of a fully achieved humanity and its borders populated with a variety of visibly deviant forms. They are also thematically present in the world of romance, in which the knights, leaving their castle, move out into a wild and unpredictable environment in which normal laws do not apply and out of which strange bodies rise up to challenge them. (The establishment of this pattern also prompts its reversal, as at the opening of *Sir Gawain and the Green Knight*, when a being that is rightly of the margins suddenly makes its appearance in the central stronghold.)

---

[10] Stallybrass and White, *Politics and Poetics of Transgression*, 20, 200. Jonathan Dollimore employs very similar premises to answer the question 'why in our own time the negation of homosexuality has been in direct proportion to its cultural significance' (*Sexual Dissidence: Augustine to Wilde, Freud to Foucault* (Oxford, 1991), 28).

[11] John of Salisbury, *Policraticus*, ed. Clemens C. I. Webb (Oxford, 1909), 5. 2. 540b–c.

Ideas of the centre and the margins are explored by Michael Camille in his book *Image on the Edge*.[12] Analysing 'marginal art'—drawings in the borders of manuscripts, gargoyles and other architectural 'protrusions'—he finds it expressive of resistance to the 'official' culture of the primary text. That resistance is expressed through parody, typically through filling the borders with figures whose low status and/or questionable activities tilt at the pretensions of the more decorous centre. Thus, in a late thirteenth- or early fourteenth-century manuscript of the romance of *Lancelot del Lac*,

on the page where Hector is shown meeting a group of damsels and fighting with the Tercians in a two-tiered framed miniature, the *bas-de-page* has a knight firing his crossbow at the exposed behind of a crouching figure. Looking closely, we can see that in the underdrawing or sketch for the target figure, the arm was originally bent over to expose his buttocks, but the painter has changed this to make him point upwards to the miniature, as if drawing attention to the proper chivalrous activity of a knight depicted above.[13]

Here there is an appreciable difference between the centre and the margins, between what is 'proper' and what is not, but elsewhere Camille points to a more dynamic relationship in which neither term survives unaffected by the other:

In the works of art made for knights, marginal forms appear that respond to their fears of the lower orders, and to their wish to retain the signs of rank, blood, gesture and manners, all of which subjected their courtly bodies to a pseudo-spiritual code of ethical chivalric behaviour and, in turn, subjugated all other bodies beneath them. It was already a dream of a lost order. While they placed others in the margins, they themselves were already halfway there.[14]

Thus, interplay between centre and margins is itself subject to historical process—in Camille's example, by the decline of chivalry. Similarly, the Greek city-state eventually falls victim to the forces it had tried to exclude: the appearance of centaurs and Amazons among the figures on the Parthenon frieze declares that 'The

---

[12] *Image on the Edge: The Margins of Medieval Art* (London, 1992).
[13] Ibid. 106 and illus. 50; *Lancelot del Lac*, Beinecke Rare Book Library, Yale University, New Haven, MS 229, fo. 39ᵛ.
[14] Camille, *Image on the Edge*, 100.

aggression and monstrosity of these traditional enemies of civilization have become part of the city's most sacred space, and they operate continuously from inside'.[15]

Some of the people Camille finds in the margins of manuscripts could also be seen as 'marginal' in a wider social sense—archers, whose way of life had been condemned by the Second Lateran Council; jugglers, dancers, jongleurs, and musicians, whose roving instability troubled the forces of control; and beggars, whose marginality, as well as being geographical, might also be read in the physical deformities that prevented them from working for a living.[16] In his discussion of the portrayal of beggars, Camille acknowledges his debt to Bronisław Geremek's pioneering study, *The Margins of Society in Late Medieval Paris*.[17] Geremek, whose interest in deviance and the social response it stimulates links him in turn with writers such as Foucault, maps out a city in which the established world of work and familial alliances was interpenetrated by the alternative world of 'those groups whose way of life appeared abnormal, that is, did not respect the standards in force in society'.[18] Beggars, pimps, prostitutes, lepers, and criminals would all come into this category. Importantly, Geremek stresses that these 'marginal' people were not simply excluded from conventional society: instead, they were engaged in a ceaseless dialogue with it, sometimes aspiring to obtain, or retrieve, a place within it, at other times creating a fellowship of the inn or tavern which stood over against, but still fulfilled some of the same needs as, the conventional bourgeois family. Such activity made permeable the line between the world of work and the world of crime: 'the boundaries of these

[15]   duBois, *Centaurs and Amazons*, 67.

[16]   Camille, *Image on the Edge*, 107, 57–8, 116, 129–52, and illus. 69 (beggars on the bridges of medieval Paris). On archers see also Jacques Le Goff, *Medieval Civilization: 400–1500*, trans. J. Barrow (Oxford, 1988), 113, and on jongleurs Carla Casagrande and Silvano Vecchio, 'Clercs et jongleurs dans la société médiévale (xiie et xiiie siècles)', *Annales: économies, sociétés, civilisations*, 24/5 (1979), 913–28. Nurith Kenaan-Kedar makes a similar observation about the subjects of sculptured corbels on 12th-cent. French churches: 'people from the margins of society—jongleurs, acrobats, musicians, female drunkards, fools and beggars—predominate.' Interestingly, their faces and bodies are endowed with much more expression than their counterparts in the 'official' sculptural programme. ('The Margins of Society in Marginal Romanesque Sculpture', *Gesta*, 31/1 (1992), 15–24.)

[17]   Trans. Jean Birrell (Cambridge, 1987; first pub. Warsaw, 1971).

[18]   Ibid. 3.

classes were blurred and fluctuating, and the links between them strong.'[19]

Like Camille, Geremek lays emphasis on the bodily signs of marginality. In the teeming streets of a medieval city, where the criminal or the prostitute might rub shoulders with you, it was clearly important to have some way of telling who was of the edge and who was not. So, prostitutes had to wear clothing specified by law, sometimes of a particular colour or with a distinctive accessory such as a badge or a hood.[20] Beggars, too, were expected to be instantly recognizable, 'not only by their clothes, the natural indicator of their material condition, but even more by their physical appearance, which had to justify their requests for alms and demonstrate their incapacity for work'.[21] Yet here again it was not just a question of the official culture labelling and then 'reading' the passive bodies of its outcasts, for once more the dangerous lability of the body came into play. Prostitutes might masquerade as married women, beggars might fake their disabilities. Geremek even records cases of children being abducted and then mutilated so that they could excite sympathy and attract alms.[22]

High and low, centre and periphery, are key terms in this book, which explores a particular kind of marginality and its expression within medieval culture. Humans of course may be grouped according to their closeness to, or distance from, the centres of power and influence in their communities (and in Geremek's Marxist analysis it is integration into the world of work which gives a person social grounding). However, in another sense all humans occupy a central position simply by virtue of being human. According to the medieval world-view, man[23] is the high point of mortal creation, made by God in his own image and directed by him to 'have

[19] Ibid. 243.
[20] Ibid. 222–5; Barbara Hanawalt, 'At the Margins of Women's Space in Medieval Europe', in Robert R. Edwards and Vickie Ziegler (eds.), *Matrons and Marginal Women in Medieval Society* (Woodbridge, 1995), 7–8; Ruth Mellinkoff, *Outcasts: Signs of Otherness in Northern European Art of the Late Middle Ages*, 2 vols. (Berkeley and Los Angeles, 1993), i. 44.
[21] Geremek, *Margins of Society*, 301.
[22] Ibid. 203–4.
[23] Here and subsequently I intend the word 'man', when used in the sense of 'human', to keep touch with its overtones of gender. Some of the questions this gives rise to are explored in Ch. 9.

dominion over the fish of the sea, and over the fowl of the air, and over every living thing that moveth upon the earth' (Genesis 1: 29). Man, therefore, stands at the summit (and the centre), and beneath (and around) him lie all other animate beings. These—the animals—differ crucially from man in that they lack a reasoning soul and so cannot be held responsible for what they do. It is therefore entirely right that God has appointed man their governor, to direct, control, and exploit their bodies as he sees fit. As Aquinas puts it, quoting John of Damascus, 'irrational animals are not masters of their own actions: for they do not act, but are rather acted upon'.[24]

Animals proclaimed their lesser role in God's design through their bodily stance. They looked downwards, focusing on the things of this earth. 'All such animals', Albert the Great wrote, 'are prone to the ground, i.e. because of the weight of their head and the earthy character of their body, they tend to bear themselves in a horizontal plane, their innate heat being inadequate to maintain them in an erect posture.'[25] Conversely, man's upright posture was tangible evidence of his divine vocation, his orientation towards the things of the spirit.

Reasoning man, unreasoning beast: the difference, springing as it does from a divine fiat, ought to be clear cut. Yet there are complications, and these spring from the invocation of the body as a guarantor of identity. For, as Foucault and many others have shown, the body is perpetually the site of tensions, of competing discourses. On the one hand, it is the basic building block of any social structure, on the other it is potentially aberrant, rebellious, the playground of Freud's Id. It is also our expressive medium *par excellence*, and as such partakes of a dangerous lability. If men stand upright and beasts crawl on all fours, what are we to make of a man who copies a beast's posture? If he starts to live like an animal, does he forfeit his humanity?

Further, although man stands at the head of creation, he cannot divorce himself from the lower orders, for it is his degree of difference *from* them that constitutes his identity. Thus, the relations between high and low, centre and periphery, must always be char-

---

[24] 'bruta animalia non habent dominium sui actus: *non enim agunt, sed magis aguntur*': *Summa Theologiae*, IIa, q. 6, art. 2.

[25] *Man and the Beasts (De animalibus, Books 22–26)*, trans. James J. Scanlan (Binghamton, NY, 1987), 69.

acterized by a dynamic instability, as bodies of various kinds inter-
mingle, trade features, or try to articulate their ascendancy. It is this
dynamic instability that I set out to explore, intending to show that it
is richly productive of culture and that, following in Stallybrass and
White's footsteps, the 'most powerful symbolic repertoires [are
located] at borders, margins and edges, rather than at the accepted
centre of the social body'.[26]

I also try to bring together a number of subjects which have been
extensively investigated but usually in isolation from each other.
Animals themselves are a case in point—in their very variousness,
they are an inviting topic for anthologies, collections, conferences,
and symposia: however, that variety has tended to evoke a large
number of separate studies in place of an analytical overview.[27]
Similarly, the key medieval social practices of hunting and heraldry
have each generated a huge amount of literature, but not many
attempts have been made to ally them with other discourses involving the bodies of animals.

The first chapter is about the Bestiary, which I see as the text
providing the ground rules for the relationship between humans and
the animal kingdom. The next two chapters discuss birds and foxes,
exploring the sort of cultural play that is inspired by the bodies of
these creatures. In Chapters 4 and 5, which are about heraldry and
hunting respectively, the dynamic of human–animal involvement
becomes more complex, since these are enterprises involving raids
(both metaphorical and literal) upon the world of the non-human,
and an elaborate re-inventing of what is found there. Chapter 6,
about *The Knight's Tale*, draws together threads from the previous chapters and presents them in the specific context of a literary text.

Moving, again, in the direction of greater complexity, and deeper
interpenetration of centre and margins, the next two chapters are
about what is perhaps the most problematic of all medieval bodies—
that of the 'wild man' who seemed to straddle the boundary

---

[26] *Politics and Poetics of Transgression*, 20.

[27] Among recent collections are: Nona C. Flores (ed.), *Animals in the Middle Ages: A
Book of Essays* (New York, 1996); L. A. J. R. Houwen (ed.), *Animals and the Symbolic in
Mediaeval Art and Literature*, Mediaevalia Groningana, 20 (Groningen, 1997); Willene B.
Clark and Meradith T. McMunn (eds.), *Beasts and Birds of the Middle Ages: The Bestiary
and its Legacy* (Philadelphia, 1989); and Joyce E. Salisbury (ed.), *The Medieval World of
Nature: A Book of Essays* (New York, 1993).

between what was human and what was not. In the wild man the dividing line between the centre and the periphery seems to have vanished altogether. How can the prevailing discourse cope with him? The region he inhabits has always been one of absorbed speculation, and also of profound anxiety, since his presence within culture suggests that the membrane between humanness and otherness is frighteningly permeable—that there might, in fact, be circumstances in which men might *lose* their humanity, and revert, or sink, to the level of beasts. In the eighteenth century, writers and thinkers focused upon this question through the cases of so-called 'wild' children, who had apparently grown up without any human contact at all. Was there some inalienable human characteristic which had survived in these children? Or were they truly indistinguishable from the animals which were sometimes thought to have reared them?[28] In Chapters 7 and 8 I discuss medieval wild men in their social and historical context and attempt to show how 'the intensifying grid of the body'[29] serves once more to bring contemporary debates about humanness into focus.

Chapter 9 is about women and the margins, and gathers together some of the questions that have hovered over the preceding chapters. One of these is obviously, why so many wild men and so few wild women? What part does gender play in constructions of 'wildness'? Are women in some sense 'of the edge' anyway? It is certainly possible to argue that a scheme that places 'man' at the centre of things does so in both senses—that women, despite being humans, are not accorded either the symbolic or the practical dignity of centrality within medieval culture. Geremek's description of his marginal people as those who 'did not belong to the society of estates because in the hierarchy of rank, honour and respect they were defined only negatively'[30] could well be read as applying to women *tout court*. The 'body' that stands for the organicity of the received social order in John of Salisbury's *Policraticus* is, after all,

---

[28] See e.g. Maximilian Novak, 'The Wild Man Comes to Tea', in Edward Dudley and Maximilian E. Novak (eds.), *The Wild Man Within: An Image in Western Thought from the Renaissance to Romanticism* (Pittsburgh, 1972), 183–221; Harlan Lane, *The Wild Boy of Aveyron* (London, 1979); Lucien Malson, *Wolf Children* (London, 1972); Roger Shattuck, *The Forbidden Experiment: The Story of the Wild Boy of Aveyron* (London, 1980).

[29] Stallybrass and White, *Politics and Poetics of Transgression*, 26.

[30] *Margins of Society*, 2.

male and not female.[31] In Chapter 9 I consider these questions, and take a new look at themes I have already presented. Of course, I do not aim to deal with the whole subject of the marginality of women within medieval culture; nevertheless, I hope that the argument I present may make some contribution to that important debate.

[31] As pointed out by Michael Camille in his Tomas Harris Lecture on the History of Art, 'Picturing the Body Politic in the Middle Ages', given at London University, 21 Jan. 1992.

CHAPTER ONE

The Bestiary:
Establishing Ground Rules

WHAT DOES IT mean to be human? The answers we give to that question will determine the way our society draws up its codes of rights and obligations. They will affect our actions towards those whose possession of full humanity appears problematic, for whatever reason—unborn babies, for example. Should 'human rights' perhaps be extended to creatures which are close to us in biological terms? The authors of *The Great Ape Project* propose a Declaration on Great Apes (a category that includes human beings) which would incorporate three basic principles: the right to life, the protection of liberty, and the prohibition of torture.[1] Is that mere sentimentality, or does it indicate a deeper unease and uncertainty about the line that marks us off from the rest of animate creation?

The debate about who is human and who is not, and in what, precisely, humanity consists, is not a new one. Typically, it focuses upon 'markers' such as language. 'Parle, et je te baptise', the Cardinal de Polignac is supposed to have said to a chimpanzee in the Jardin de Roi in Paris in the eighteenth century. In the twentieth century numerous experiments have been carried out to discover whether or not chimpanzees really can 'talk'—that is, manipulate linguistic counters or use a gestured code such as American Sign Language. The jury is still out: some researchers express their disappointment at the apes' inability to progress beyond the level of a 2-year-old human child, while others find evidence of genuine creativity in their unprompted 'signing'. 'Before they can fly, apes must jump, insist commentators who believe that the linguistic gulf

[1] Robert Wokler, review of Paola Cavalieri and Peter Singer (eds.), *The Great Ape Project: Equality Beyond Humanity* (London, 1993), *Times Literary Supplement* (17 Sept. 1993), 6.

between man and beast has already begun to vanish. To jump is not to embark on flight, the doubters retort...'[2] The case, perhaps, will never be conclusively decided, for what, after all, *is* language? Another way of looking at the conversing chimps would be to see them as only one among a host of examples of the projection of humans' own fascination with language into the circumambient animal world. From the intricacies of birdsong to the sounding of blue whales across miles of ocean, it could be said that there is hardly a corner where we do *not* find 'language' in one form or another.[3]

The animal world, indeed, is never simply 'there', unaffected by our own cultural enterprises. We are continually remaking it in our own image, and using it as a resource to speak about the things that matter to us. We, at the centre, traffic with the periphery in all sorts of ways, and are certainly ready, when it suits our interests, to blur lines and make barriers permeable. Twelfth-century theologians debated whether Jews might not be animals rather than humans, since their rejection of Christ showed that they lacked the faculty of reason.[4] In fact, the attribution of animal traits to groups seen as alien or inferior is a theme running through medieval culture, surfacing in the gibe about men with tails that is alluded to in the *Speculum stultorum* and in names like the 'horsebread' that was baked for poor people, as well as dogs and horses, to eat.[5]

Comparisons with animals might be used to degrade, but they could also be used to enhance status. In the well-known miniature of Sir Geoffrey Luttrell in the Luttrell Psalter, the warhorse on which he is mounted obviously contributes to his prestige. The coat it wears is patterned with the Luttrell arms, and the crest

---

[2] S. Zuckerman, 'Apes Я Not Us', *New York Review of Books* (30 May 1991), 43–9.

[3] The sounds made by blue whales 'are not voiced indiscriminately. They may well represent a simple form of communication', William C. Cummings, in Joan McIntyre (ed.), *Mind in the Waters* (New York, 1974), 137. Also: 'The creatures in the cartoon film *Antz* aren't pure fantasy. New research suggests that ants are not only better workers than us—they can talk, too', Donald Michie, 'Look who's talking', *Independent on Sunday* (15 Nov. 1998), 8.

[4] See Anna Abulafia, 'Bodies in the Jewish–Christian Debate', in Sarah Kay and Miri Rubin (eds.), *Framing Medieval Bodies* (Manchester, 1994), 124 and n. 7; and, for the attribution to Jews of animal features such as tails and horns, Joshua Trachtenberg, *The Devil and the Jews: The Medieval Conception of the Jew and its Relation to Modern Antisemitism* (New Haven, 1943; repr. Cleveland, 1961), 44–53.

[5] See Nigel Wireker, *Nigel de Longchamps: Speculum stultorum*, ed. John H. Mozley and Robert R. Raymo (Berkeley and Los Angeles, 1960), 159, n. to lines 1533–8; and C. Dyer, *Standards of Living in the Late Middle Ages* (Cambridge, 1989), 57.

between its ears matches the crest on the helmet Sir Geoffrey is receiving from his attendant wife. It has been absorbed into the chivalric design, and even the bits of its natural body that show through, shod hooves and bared teeth, underscore the consonance of its intentions with those of its owner.[6] Why is it, though, that association with certain animals is an admirable thing and with others quite the opposite? Why does a man sitting on a horse 'mean' something different from a man sitting on a cow—or on a donkey?

The answer lies in the way we have divided up the animal world, inscribing it with correspondences and differences, stocking it with our own values and concerns. As the naturalist Stephen Jay Gould puts it, 'all forms of human relationship with animals must record (at the least) human hopes and preferences imposed upon nature, or (at most) elaborate metaphors of human society read into the lives of animals'.[7] As *our* world is based on endless fine discriminations, so the animal world is conceived as a mirroring system of affinities and antipathies. These elements obviously vary between cultures—for example, dogs are kept as pets in Britain but are eaten in Korea—but this variation itself exposes the arbitrariness of the system, the extent to which it is absolutely a human construction. The category of 'vermin' is a case in point: the word has unpleasant overtones and—perhaps partly through its root, Latin *vermis*, worm—evokes masses of small, creeping creatures invading, and threatening, our living-space. The young reveller in *The Pardoner's Tale* claims to be plagued by 'vermin that destroyed him by nighte' (line 572), and readily persuades an apothecary to sell him the deadliest poison he can find so that he can get rid of them. We would agree with him that rats are vermin—but are surprised, if not shocked, to hear whales and seals (which at present, in Britain, have broadly positive associations) referred to in the same way:

Professor Ola Flaaten, economic adviser to the Norwegian govern-ment . . . described fish-eating whales and seals as vermin to be kept

---

[6] BL MS 42310, fo. 202ᵛ. See Janet Backhouse, *The Luttrell Psalter*, The British Library (London, 1989), 5 and fig. 1. See also Simon Schama, on the significance of the bison to the Lithuanian-Polish cult of knighthood, as a formidable foe that symbolizes the indomitable courage of its hunters: *Landscape and Memory* (London, 1995), 37–53.

[7] Review of Harriet Ritvo, *The Animal Estate*, in *New York Review of Books* (3 Mar. 1988), 7.

down as their equivalents were on game estates. The worst offenders were the minke whale and the harp seal.[8]

In the medieval world, the Bestiary is a key text for exploring how the relations between humans and animals were construed. Its popularity and widespread dissemination are undoubted: M. R. James, who studied nearly all the extant copies, described it as 'one of the leading picture-books of the twelfth and thirteenth centuries in this country', ranking it, in this respect, with 'the Psalter and the Apocalypse'.[9] Over forty Bestiaries produced in England survive today, and many of these are illustrated with pictures of its animals, birds, fishes, and reptiles. The iconography associated with the Bestiary was both widely dispersed and enduring. This is shown not only in the number of the manuscripts themselves but in the appearance of Bestiary images in such books as the early fourteenth-century Queen Mary's Psalter[10] or the artists' pattern-book now in the Pepysian Library, Magdalene College, Cambridge, where, in one picture, the lion reliably roars to wake its new-born cub.[11] Two related early sixteenth-century picture-books, the Helmingham Herbal and Bestiary and Bodleian MS Ashmole 1504, preserve a number of traditional images, such as the tiger fooled by the reflection of her cub in the mirror thrown to her by the hunter.[12] None of the manuscripts I have mentioned has any accompanying written identification, suggesting that, even in the latest, the meaning of the pictures was well understood. There is also evidence to suggest that the words of the Bestiary had equal currency. A well-known instance is Chaucer's allusion to 'Physiologus' (the ultimate source of the Bestiary text) in *The Nun's Priest's Tale*, when he compares the

---

[8] 'Norwegian call to stem "whale pest"', *Guardian* (25 June 1990), 24. For attempts by 18th- and 19th-cent. British naturalists to establish 'vermin' as an objective category, see Harriet Ritvo, *The Platypus and the Mermaid, and Other Figments of the Classifying Imagination* (Cambridge, Mass., 1997), 38–9, 192–4.

[9] *The Bestiary, being a reproduction in full of the manuscript Ii. 4. 26 in the University Library, Cambridge*, Roxburghe Club (Oxford, 1928), 1.

[10] Facsimile reproduction: *Queen Mary's Psalter*, introd. Sir George Warner (London, 1912).

[11] fo. 19ᵛ; facsimile reproduction: *An English Medieval Sketchbook, No. 1916 in the Pepysian Library, Magdalene College, Cambridge*, ed. M. R. James, Walpole Society, No. 13 (Oxford, 1925).

[12] *Two East Anglian Picture Books*, ed. Nicholas Barker, Roxburghe Club (London, 1988).

sweet singing of Chauntecleer with the mermaids' song.[13] Richard Rolle draws on Bestiary material in his discussion of the bee and the stork (which he confuses with the ostrich),[14] while John Morson and G. R. Owst have demonstrated its importance, respectively, to the Cistercians and to vernacular preachers in search of exempla.[15] Even today we talk about 'halcyon days' (from the calmness of the sea while the halcyon broods its eggs) or 'licking someone into shape' (after the bear, who moulds the bodies of its premature and shapeless cubs).

It is not necessary here to trace the detailed history of the Bestiary, from its beginnings in the Greek *Physiologus*, written some time between the second and the fourth centuries, probably in Alexandria, to the greatly expanded text current in thirteenth- and fourteenth-century England.[16] Briefly, in the original *Physiologus* animals, birds, and stones were used to illustrate points of Christian doctrine. The core text was augmented, most importantly with extracts from Isidore of Seville's *Etymologiae*, and, in the twelfth century, in England, underwent a major reshaping when the medley of its subjects was classified according to the divisions—animals, birds, reptiles, fish—in the *Etymologiae*, book 12. At the same time yet more material was drawn in—for example from Rabanus Maurus and from Gerald of Wales (on the birds of Ireland).

That account is obviously oversimplified, but it may mislead in another, more important, respect by suggesting that the Bestiary is a closed text—an 'inventory of animals', as T. H. White's publisher describes his translation of a twelfth-century Bestiary.[17] That characterization—Bestiary as catalogue—has been the dominant one

---

[13] *The Nun's Priest's Tale*, lines 3271–2 and n. See also L. A. J. R. Houwen, 'Flattery and the Mermaid in Chaucer's *Nun's Priest's Tale*', in Houwen (ed.), *Animals and the Symbolic in Mediaeval Art and Literature*, Mediaevalia Groningana, 20 (Groningen, 1997), 77–92.

[14] *English Writings of Richard Rolle*, ed. H. E. Allen (Oxford, 1931), 54–6. See also Kenneth Sisam (ed.), *Fourteenth Century Verse and Prose* (Oxford, 1921), 215 n.

[15] John Morson, 'The English Cistercians and the Bestiary', *Bulletin of the John Rylands Library*, 39 (1956), 146–70; G. R. Owst, *Literature and Pulpit in Medieval England*, 2nd edn. (Oxford, 1961), 195–204. See also Debra Hassig, *Medieval Bestiaries: Text, Image, Ideology* (Cambridge, 1995), 176.

[16] For the development of the Bestiary, see Florence McCulloch, *Mediaeval Latin and French Bestiaries* (Chapel Hill, NC, 1962); F. N. M. Diekstra, 'The *Physiologus*, the Bestiaries and Medieval Animal Lore', *Neophilologus*, 69 (1985), 142–55.

[17] T. H. White, *The Book of Beasts* (London, 1954).

among present-day writers, and it is easy to see why, since the work's main appeal lies in its idiosyncratic portraits of the individual beasts, whose charm White certainly enhances in his annotated version.[18] However, I believe we need to treat the Bestiary as more than a viewing gallery of weird and wonderful creatures. We need, in short, to see ourselves there too, for the Bestiary is a text that speaks vitally about bodies of all kinds—ours included—and that lays down the ground rules for that intercourse between human and animal worlds whose subtleties will be explored in the rest of this book.

First, it is easy to forget that it is not always clear what the limits of a Bestiary 'text' are. T. H. White admitted that he treated his chosen manuscript selectively, summarizing 'in one longish footnote' its section on trees and skating even more quickly over the following section, 'a remorseless catalogue of about 170 parts of the human body, with their function and derivation of their names'.[19] Both these sections, together with the concluding section on man (which did attract White's interest), appear quite commonly in Bestiary manuscripts: their integrity with the 'animal' part of the text is shown by their source (Isidore's *Etymologiae*) and by their shared characteristic of starting with the origin of the name in question.[20] If we allow them into our view, these extra parts certainly expand our idea of what a Bestiary may be; however, most modern writers have followed White in either ignoring them or minimizing their relevance. Florence McCulloch excludes them from her authoritative study of the Bestiary tradition,[21] while Richard Barber, in his translation of the Bestiary in MS Bodley 764, chooses not to include the section on trees with which it concludes (this manuscript lacks the sections on man). Barber also intervenes occasionally in the 'animals' section, pruning some of the scriptural examples: 'the

---

[18] See e.g. Nona C. Flores (ed.), *Animals in the Middle Ages: A Book of Essays* (New York and London, 1996), p. x: 'Like the *Physiologus*, the Bestiary was a compilation of accumulated folklore, legend, pseudoscience, and rudimentary scientific observation of *an assortment of real and imaginary animals*' (my italics).

[19] White, *Book of Beasts*, 219.

[20] The etymologies too derive from Isidore. See Ernst Curtius, 'Etymology as a Category of Thought', in his *European Literature and the Latin Middle Ages*, trans. Willard R. Trask (London, 1953), 495–500.

[21] McCulloch, *Bestiaries*, 35: 'The long sections on Trees and the Ages of Man, both from Isidore and forming the concluding divisions of many bestiaries, will not be included in this study.'

effect', he writes, 'is perhaps to redress the balance of natural history, morality and mystical meaning in favour of natural history.'[22] Such decisions are justified as far as presenting a book for a general readership is concerned (a further deciding factor must have been that these later sections are usually unillustrated). However, the overall effect has been to 'close off' the Bestiary text as a straightforward catalogue of animals. We need to re-complicate it, to treat it as the focus for questions about the whole relationship between humans and the rest of creation. I have already mentioned the overlooked 'extra' sections it includes: another line of enquiry (outside the scope of this book) would be to discover which other texts are characteristically associated with the Bestiary in manuscripts. For example, the first of the two Bestiaries in Bodleian MS Douce 88 also contains a section of animal fables and one on the Deadly Sins. The second Bestiary begins with a description of the 'monstrous races' (with pictures), and ends with a list of classical monsters such as Cerberus and the Centaur.[23] Inclusions like these strengthen my argument that the Bestiary animals are best studied as part of a more extensive web of meaning.

No two Bestiaries are exactly the same, but, on the other hand, a great deal of material is repeated, unchanged, in Bestiary after Bestiary. In what follows, I concentrate on a group of five Bestiaries: St Petersburg State Public Library MS Lat. Q. v. V. I;[24] the Alnwick Castle Bestiary;[25] Bodleian MS Ashmole 1511;[26] MS Bodley 764;[27]

---

[22] *Bestiary* (an English version of MS Bodley 764, with all the original miniatures reproduced in facsimile), trans. and introd. Richard Barber (London, 1992), 15.

[23] See Otto Pächt and J. J. G. Alexander, *Illuminated MSS in the Bodleian Library, Oxford*, vol. iii (Oxford, 1973), nos. 487, 524. Debra Hassig makes some interesting suggestions about how the reception and readership of Bestiaries may be deduced from the kinds of texts bound in with them: *Medieval Bestiaries*, 172 and 261–2 n. 23.

[24] Henceforth *P*. Facsimile reproduction: *The Medieval Bestiary*, text and commentary by Xenia Muratova, trans. Inna Kitrosskaya (Moscow, 1984). There is a good selection of illustrations from this and the next four Bestiaries in Hassig, *Medieval Bestiaries*.

[25] Henceforth *Aln*. (Hassig, *Medieval Bestiaries*, refers to it as the Northumberland Bestiary.) Reproduction: *A Thirteenth-Century Bestiary in the Library of Alnwick Castle*, ed. E. G. Millar, Roxburghe Club (Oxford, 1958).

[26] Henceforth *Ash*. See Xenia Muratova, 'Workshop Methods in English Late Twelfth-Century Illumination and the Production of Luxury Bestiaries', in Willene B. Clark and Meradith T. McMunn (eds.), *Beasts and Birds of the Middle Ages: The Bestiary and its Legacy* (Philadelphia, 1989), 53–68.

[27] Henceforth *B*. See n. 22 above.

and Cambridge University Library MS Ii. 4. 26.[28] These span the twelfth and thirteenth centuries and, with their fine illustrations, represent the high point of Bestiary production in England. I also refer to John Trevisa's *On the Properties of Things*, his translation into English of Bartholomaeus Anglicanus' *De proprietatibus rerum*, which includes a large amount of Bestiary material and must have contributed to its widespread dissemination.

Several Bestiaries start not with an animal at all but with an account of the Creation story from Genesis. In the Alnwick Castle Bestiary, for instance, illuminations on successive folios depict the Fall of the Angels; God's creation of heaven and earth, and trees; of sun, moon, and stars; birds and fishes; animals, and Adam and Eve. After God has rested on the seventh day, Adam is shown giving names to the animals. Robed, to show the God-like nature of his task, he holds a long scroll, and stands between two crowned women, identified by E. G. Millar as the Nous and Natura of Bernard Silvestris' *De mundi universitate*.[29] The picture is of an ordered universe, whose primal patterning flows from God and is interpreted and sustained by man. God makes the major divisions— night from darkness, day from night, water from dry land—and man, through his power of name-giving, confirms each partition of reality. In the Ashmole Bestiary the magnificent illustrations, with the creatures set against a background of glowing gold, make the theme of division even more explicit than it is in the accompanying text: on folio 6^v, for example, the beasts created on the sixth day are shown in four tiers that correspond to broad categorizations of kind. Ungulates—sheep, goat, ox, horse, and deer, each with hooves clearly detailed—are on the lowest level; above them are two carnivores—a lion and a dog; above these again are small animals—hare, cat, and squirrel, each sitting up on its haunches; while at the top is the anomalous elephant.

The theme of orderly partition is maintained in the discussions of the individual creatures. Following Isidore, these have been divided into four-footed beasts, birds, fishes, and reptiles, and each of these groups is seen as self-contained, distinguished from the others by its way of moving and its association with a particular element. So, beasts run on the earth, birds fly in the air, fish swim in water, while

---

[28] Henceforth *C*. See n. 9 above.   [29] *Aln*, p. 17.

reptiles crawl along the ground. Accordingly, the bat is classed among the birds, while the flightless ostrich is frequently included among the animals.[30]

As living creatures derive a part of their identity from the element they inhabit, so they reflect the patterning of the natural world in their bodily forms and in their behaviour. The sea becomes calm when the halcyon broods her eggs,[31] while the ostrich delays producing hers until she can see the Pleiades appearing in the sky.[32] The liver of the mouse grows bigger and smaller with the waxing and waning of the moon.[33] Most impressively of all, the Phoenix, in its self-immolation and revivification, enacts the resurrection of Christ, a truth as undeniable as the seasons or the tides.[34] The vital point is that the Phoenix, like those other creatures that reproduce the constancies of nature in their bodily rhythms, has no conscious knowledge of the facts it represents—its actions are performed 'without the benefit of reason' ('sine exemplo et sine rationis perceptione'). It is as if it has been programmed by God, from creation, with the same commands that operate throughout the natural universe. And this program is run not for its own benefit but for the benefit of those who observe, and understand. Birds are there to teach man, the Bestiarist remarks, not the other way round.

Just as animals unconsciously echo truths about the scheme of creation in their bodies and in their behaviour, so their instinctive methods of organizing themselves communally have implications for human society. This is especially the case with birds and fishes, groups which are distanced from humans by their mastery of a different element and so can be thought of more readily 'in the round'. For example, the Bestiarists often point out the ways in which the differentiated communities of fish under the sea reflect those in the world above. Fish are compared with cattle—the names of both (*pisces, pecus*) are said to derive from their habit of browsing

---

[30] e.g. in *Aln* and *P*. In one of Marie de France's *Fables* a bat first swears allegiance to the king of the beasts but then breaks his vow and joins the kingdom of the birds: *Die Fabeln der Marie de France*, ed. Karl Warnke (Halle, 1898), no. 23. Uncertainty about the bat's proper status persisted into the 19th cent.: see Ritvo, *Platypus and the Mermaid*, 46.

[31] *Aln*, fo. 35; *Ash*, fo. 67ʳ; *B*, fo. 69ᵛ; *C*, fos. 35ᵛ–36ʳ; *P*, fos. 50ᵛ–51ʳ.

[32] *Aln*, fo. 24ᵛ; *Ash*, fo. 52ᵛ; *B*, fo. 67ʳ; *P*, fo. 35ᵛ.

[33] *Aln*, fo. 33ʳ; Ash, fo. 35ᵛ; *B*, fo. 51ʳ; *C*, fo. 28ᵛ; *P*, fo. 46ʳ.

[34] *Ash*, fos. 68ʳ–69ʳ; *B*, fo. 70ʳ⁻ᵛ; *C*, fo. 36ᵛ; *P*, fos. 61ᵛ–62ᵛ. See Hassig, *Medieval Bestiaries*, 72–83.

in flocks (*a pascendo*)—while a popular illustration at the start of their section plays on this idea of a mirror world beneath the waves, showing fish with the foreparts of horses, goats, carnivores, and so on.[35]

As well as physically reflecting the world above, fish present various aspects of human social behaviour in an idealized form. We are told, for example, that they maintain bonds with one another of absolute purity and fidelity. They preserve an untainted descent ('pura et inviolata successio') and are totally innocent of adultery with strange fish.[36] They also embody—literally—the ultimate expression of love, quite beyond human capacity. Humans are satisfied with kisses, but fish open up their whole insides ('aperire viscera') when danger threatens their young. Parents and children share a single body ('in corpore uno vivere') until it is safe for the young to venture out again.[37] The Bestiarists also point out that, as well as forming a perfect society, fish are ideally attuned to their environment. They do not seek to live without water, or to be separated from their parents' company.[38] It is their nature that they die at once if they are taken from the sea. In the fishes' world, harmony with nature and harmony with one another are intimately linked. A contrast with the way humans organize themselves, and behave, is always implied, and is often made explicit, as when the Bestiarist follows his praise of the sexual purity of fish with a condemnation of the human habit of adultery, and of the practice of deliberately cross-breeding animals to produce hybrids.

Birds, too, present images of the ideal society. The hoopoe cares for its parents when they grow old, preening their feathers, keeping them warm, and cleaning their eyes. 'It looks as if it were saying to its father and mother: "Just as you worked hard to nourish me, I am going to do the same for you".'[39] Storks show the same solicitude, and are also models of dutiful child-rearing, incubating their eggs so

---

[35] *Aln*, fo. 48^r; *Ash*, fo. 86^r; *B*, fo. 106^r; *C*, fo. 54^r; *P*, fo. 72^v. *P* also has an illustration showing four fish-pigs (*porcus marinus*, fo. 69^v).

[36] *C*, fo. 56^v; *P*, fo. 71^v.

[37] *C*, fo. 56^{r-v}.

[38] *C*, fo. 57^v: 'Vivere pisces sine aqua non querunt, nec a sue parentis consortio separari.'

[39] *Ash*, fo. 61^r; *B*, fo. 61^{r-v}; *C*, fo. 38^r (trans. White, *Book of Beasts*, 131); *P*, fo. 50^v. An illustration in Bodleian MS Laud misc. 247, fo. 145^r has the young birds feeding their parent with bunches of grapes. See also Hassig, *Medieval Bestiaries*, 93–103.

tirelessly that they lose their own feathers.[40] The crow accompanies its young when they learn to fly, and takes care to lay in a store of food for them.[41] By contrast, human mothers show untimely eagerness in weaning their children, or even refuse to suckle them at all. Abortion, and the exposure of unwanted babies, are mentioned as further examples of shameful human practices.

If birds such as the hoopoe and the stork exemplify family life at its best, cranes show how military society should be properly organized. They fly in correct formations, led by a pathfinder who reproves the ones lagging behind. At night, the cranes post sentries to give warning of danger, each holding a stone between its claws to keep itself awake. It is stressed that the efficacy of the birds' professional discipline is grounded in the bonds of affection between them. 'There is no dereliction of duty, because there is natural affection. There is a safe watch, because there is free choice.'[42]

With the bees, classed among birds in the Bestiaries, there is scope for an extended description of a model commonwealth.[43] Bees share everything, apportioning food, work, and recreation with perfect equity. They live freely under a king, who dispenses justice and to whom they give their unquestioning allegiance. Their whole polity is bound by the confines of the hive, and within this every bee fully discharges the tasks required of it. Even bees who have broken the rules inflict their own punishment upon themselves, dying by their own stings. As bees have attained equilibrium in their social relationships, so they are blessed with extraordinary fertility and spared the pains of childbirth. Trevisa writes: 'Also maydenhede of body wiþouten wemme is comyn to hem alle, and so is burþe also, for þey beþ nouȝt imedlid wiþ seruyse of Venus noþir resolued wiþ lecherie noþir ibrosed wiþ sorewe of birþe of children. And ȝit þey bringiþ forþ swarmes of children.'[44] The picture is rounded out with an

---

[40]   *Ash*, fo. 61^r; *B*, fo. 62^{r-v}; *C*, fo. 34^{r-v}; *P*, fo. 50^v.

[41]   *Ash*, fo. 70^v; *B*, fo. 79^v; *P*, fo. 54^{r-v}.

[42]   *Aln*, fo. 34^{r-v}; *Ash*, fos. 57^v–58^r; *B*, fo. 62^{r-v}; *C*, fo. 33^r (trans. White, *Book of Beasts*, 112). The sentry-crane, with the stone between its claws, was a popular subject for illustration: it appears, for example, in *Ash*, *B*, *C*, and *P*, in Queen Mary's Psalter (fo. 123) and occasionally in wood-carvings in churches (see M. D. Anderson, *Animal Carvings in British Churches* (Cambridge, 1938), 50–1, 81 (list of examples), and no. 28).

[43]   *Aln*, fos. 38^v–40^r; *Ash*, fos. 75^v–77^r; *B*, fos. 89^r–91^r; *C*, fos. 43^v–45^r; *P*, fos. 57^r–59^r. Bestiary illustrations reinforce this theme: see Hassig, *Medieval Bestiaries*, 52–61.

[44]   *On the Properties of Things*, 3 vols. (Oxford, 1975–88), i. 611.

emphasis on cleanliness: bees remove the bodies of the dead from their hive and are careful to avoid bad odours. The Bestiarists appear to acknowledge that such self-regulating harmony is not to be found in any proximate human society when they draw their comparisons with the bees' practices from the semi-mythical countries of the far east and north: Persia, India, and Sarmatia.

Birds and fish, therefore, present various aspects of a perfected pattern of living, in which each individual acknowledges its place within the social and physical environment, and maintains and cherishes the bonds that unite it with its fellows. The crucial point is that it is the bodily identity of each creature, God's imprint upon it at the moment of creation, that determines its behaviour. Incapable of exercising intelligent choice, each animal is still led, by virtue of its physical idiosyncrasy, to adopt an admirable lifestyle. So, the way in which fishes are able to shelter their young inside their mouths becomes, interpreted, an image of complete parental devotion. The upright stance of the cranes speaks for their disciplined military behaviour. Even the bees, who, because of their sophisticated social structure, might perhaps be expected to exercise rational judgement in their choice of a king, are guided by unmistakable physical signs: 'With bees, the king is naturally endowed with special qualities, as his large and handsome body shows.'[45]

The validity of the ideals that the animals of the Bestiary present therefore depends upon their physical integrity. The stability of bodily form is linked to the stability of the moral universe. The fact that, in general, the bodies of animals do *not* observably change, in turn becomes the rationale for preserving existing roles and functions within human society. This extends to stability of place, as in the popular saying (scorned by Chaucer's Monk) that a monk who leaves his cloister is like a fish out of water. Gower, in the fourth book of his *Vox Clamantis*, expands upon the theme:

> Non foris a claustris monachus, nec aqua fore piscis
> Debet; tu nisi sis, ordo, reversus eis.
> Si fuerit piscis, qui postpositis maris undis
> Pascua de terra querat habere sua,
> Est nimis improprius piscis sibi ponere nomen,
> Debeo set monstri ponere nomen ei.
> Sic ego claustrali dicam, qui gaudia mundi

[45] Trans. Barber, *Bestiary*, 179; C, fo. 44[r].

Appetit et claustrum deserit inde suum
Non erit hic monachus set apostata iure vocandus,
Aut monstrum templi quod notat ira dei.[46]

The sea is the proper habitat of a live fish, and the monastery is the right home for a monk. Just as the sea will not keep dead fish, so the monastery casts out evildoing monks. A fish ought not to be out of the water, nor ought a monk to be away from his cloisters, unless you return to them, O monk in holy orders. If there were a fish that forsook the waters of the sea to seek its food on land, it would be highly inappropriate to give it the name of fish; I should rather give it the name of monster. Such shall I call the monk who yearns for worldly delights and deserts his cloister for them. He should not rightly be called a monk but a renegade, or what God's wrath brands as a monster of the Church.

Of course, the Bestiary's readings of the bodies of animals are thoroughly infused with the social and cultural preoccupations of its time. It is *because* there is concern about the politics of the family and conventions of child-rearing that birds and fish are imaged in that particular way. The bodies of the creatures are manipulated so that they 'speak' a chosen message—one has only to think of birds of prey, which feed the oldest chick preferentially and allow it to harry its siblings to death, or of coots, which reduce the number of their offspring through selective bullying or starvation, to realize that there is no *intrinsic* connection between birds and good parenting.[47] In other words, humans and human concerns are the hub around which the text as a whole revolves. Far from being primal foci of identity, the animals of the Bestiary reflect, in their forms, the fears and hopes of their historical moment.

Each individual creature takes its bearings from man. One way of picturing this would be to place man at one end of a continuum and space the other animals along it, at varying distances from him. Such a gradation is an established part of Bestiary tradition. In Trevisa's words, the beasts closest to man are those which 'acordeþ to mannes complexioun, as lambren, kydes, schiepe, and swyn among tame, hertes and hyndes, bukkes and roes among wilde bestes'.[48] These are

---

[46]   *The Complete Works of John Gower*, ed. G. C. Macaulay, 4 vols. (Oxford, 1899–1902), vol. iv: *The Latin Works*, 4. 281–90. The translation is by Eric W. Stockton, *The Major Latin Works of John Gower* (Seattle, 1962), 171–2.

[47]   David Attenborough, *The Life of Birds* (London, 1998), 266, 264.

[48]   *Properties*, ii. 1104. Trevisa's categorization of animals has obvious affinities with the scheme proposed by Edmund Leach, which I discuss below, in Ch. 5.

the animals that have been most thoroughly assimilated to human usage: not only is their flesh nourishing and easily digestible but other parts of their bodies serve a valuable purpose too. When the horse, the goose, and the sheep in Lydgate's poem debate about which of them is most useful to man, they do not discuss whose service is intrinsically the most worthwhile but offer up their bodies as examples of total assimilability.[49] So the goose claims that its grease is good for gout, its feathers for making arrows, its down as a filling for pillows and mattresses, while even its droppings when they are burnt can be used as a cure for burns. Last—but by no means least—geese are delicious to eat. Trevisa describes the lamb in similarly comprehensive terms: its meat, skin, and wool are all of value, its 'drytte' fertilizes the land, and its hooves and horn are medicinal.[50]

Another category of animals are not entirely contrary to man's complexion, and can be made use of, but with strong qualifications. 'And somme beþ vnliche to mannes kynde þat þey beþ not al contrarie nouþer poysoun, as hirchons, hares, and foxes and oþer bestes with fleissh of heuy smylle. For of suche bestes comeþ worste norisshynge for mannes body.'[51] Finally, there are the creatures that are quite alien to man, 'as þaddre *tyrus* and oþere serpentes . . . attur-coppes and scorpiouns'.[52] The gulf between serpents and certain insects, on the one hand, and man on the other is often expressed by extremes of humours—serpents are usually said to be excessively cold[53] (although Trevisa says they embody too much heat).

The category of Bestiary serpents is a distinctive and interesting one. For a start, its members are far more diverse and highly coloured than anyone's experience of actual reptiles could possibly suggest. There is a prevailing emphasis on the frequently mysterious ways in which serpents are able to injure people. The basilisk has a fatal odour;[54] the hypnale induces a deadly sleepiness;[55] jaculus, a flying serpent, launches itself from a tree upon any creature passing

---

[49] John Lydgate, 'The Debate of the Horse, Goose, and Sheep', in *Minor Poems*, ed. H. N. MacCracken, Part II, EETS os 192 (1934), 539–66.

[50] *Properties*, ii. 1114.

[51] Ibid. 1104.

[52] Ibid.

[53] *Aln*, fos. 59ᵛ–60ʳ; *B*, fo. 100ʳ; *C*, fo. 51ᵛ; *P*, fo. 88ʳ.

[54] *Aln*, fo. 54ᵛ; *Ash*, fo. 79ʳ; *B*, fo. 93ᵛ; *C*, fo. 47ʳ⁻ᵛ; *P*, fo. 80ᵛ.

[55] *Ash*, fo. 81ʳ; *B*, fo. 96ᵛ; *C*, fo. 49ʳ; *P*, fo. 88ʳ.

underneath;[56] the venom of the syren is so fierce that the victim dies before even feeling the pain of the bite;[57] the serpent dipsa is so tiny that it cannot be seen, yet its bite too causes instant death.[58] Although attempts have been made to find real origins for the fabulous reptiles of the Bestiary, even for the two-headed amphisbaena,[59] it is clear that the category has a collective significance beyond any actual identifications. Serpents seem to represent all the uncomprehended dangers of the natural world—the traumas and diseases that can destroy the human body with terrifying speed and inevitability. Their association with the unknown is partly expressed by their location in the mysterious lands of the East—in Arabia, Arcadia, in desert places or on the banks of the Nile—and partly too by the way they seem to challenge, or even elude, the scope of human perception: some hide, some move incredibly fast, some are too tiny even to be seen. At the same time the injuries these creatures inflict are frighteningly real: the basilisk induces hydrophobia;[60] dipsa or situla makes people die of thirst;[61] emorroris, so called because it sweats blood, causes haemorrhage;[62] seps destroys the bones within the body.[63] As Isidore of Seville writes, in the introduction to his section on serpents, which passed into Bestiary tradition, 'There are as many poisonous snakes as there are different kinds of snake and as many deadly snakes as there are colours among them' ('quorum tot venena, quot genera; tot pernicies, quot species; tot dolores, quot colores habentur').[64] Serpents, at the far end of the continuum from man, perhaps avenge their degree of alienation by the disturbingly potent threats they pose to the integrity of the human body.[65]

---

[56] *Aln*, fo. 59ʳ; *Ash*, fo. 82ᵛ; *B*, fo. 98ᵛ; *C*, fo. 50ᵛ; *P*, fo. 87ʳ.   [57] Ibid.

[58] *Aln*, fo. 59ʳ⁻ᵛ; *Ash*, fo. 82ᵛ; *B*, fo. 98ʳ; *C*, fo. 50.

[59] G. C. Druce, 'The Amphisbaena and its Connexions in Ecclesiastical Art and Architecture', *Archaeological Journal*, 67/268 (Dec. 1910), 285–317; summarized in White, *Book of Beasts*, 177 n. 2.

[60] *B*, fo. 93ᵛ; *C*, fo. 47ʳ.

[61] *Ash*, fo. 81ʳ; *B*, fo. 96ᵛ; *C*, fo. 49ʳ.

[62] *C*, fo. 49ʳ; *Aln*, fo. 57ʳ.

[63] *Aln*, fo. 59ʳ; *Ash*, fo. 82ᵛ; *B*, fo. 98ᵛ; *C*, fo. 50ᵛ; *P*, fo. 87ᵛ.

[64] *Etymologiae*, bk. 12: *De animalibus*, in J.-P. Migne, *Patrologia Latina*, vol. 82, col. 442; quoted in *Aln*, fo. 55ʳ; *B*, fo. 92ᵛ (trans. Barber, *Bestiary*, 182); *P*, fo. 80ᵛ.

[65] Although it does contain one allegorized 'good' serpent, whose habit of crawling through a crevice in a rock to shed its old skin is compared to the sinner who rejuvenates himself by following the commandments of Christ, the Bestiary's serpents are generally

The Bestiary also incorporates another pattern—one of move-ment, or, more precisely, of aspiration. Man, we are told, derives his name, *homo*, from *humo*, mud, yet he alone among creatures pos-sesses a rational soul, which raises him from his base, earthly origins to an awareness of God. For this reason he also bears the Greek name *anthropos* to signify that he has been 'lifted up'.[66] Trevisa writes:

Antropos is to menen 'arered vp' for þe spirit is arered vp by gouernaunce to þe contemplacioun of God his makere. Þerfore þe poete seiþ:

> Pronaque cum spectent animalia cetera terram
> Os homini sublime dedit, celumque videre
> Iussit et erectos ad sidere tollere vultus.

Þe menynge is þis: oþir bestis lokeþ donward to þe erþe, and God 3af to man an hi3e mouþ and hete hym loke vp and se heuen, and he 3af to men visagis arerid toward þe sterres. Also a man schal seche heuen and nou3t putte his pou3t in þerþe and be obedient to þe wombe as a best.[67]

Man looked up, but beasts, fettered by their animal natures, looked down towards the ground. However, the individual animals in the Bestiary often exemplify particular virtues or vices, and, to the degree that they are associated with spiritual values, so their gaze is lifted towards the sky. Xenia Muratova, discussing the St Petersburg Bestiary, writes: The movements and eyes of the animals, either

---

associated with evil qualities. The dragon, the largest of all of them (*C*, fos. 46ᵛ–47ʳ), is compared to the Devil— echoing the identification of the serpent with the Devil which stems from the Genesis story. Common, too, in medieval literature is the tradition that the serpent in the garden of Eden disguised itself as a woman to appeal to Eve: see e.g. *The Chester Mystery Cycle*, ed. R. M. Lumiansky and David Mills, 2 vols., EETS SS 3, 9 (1974, 1986), i. 21, lines 193–5: 'A manner of an edder is in this place | that wynges like a bryde shee hase | feete as an edder, a maydens face'; Nona C. Flores, '"Effigies Amicitiae . . . Veritas Inimicitiae": Antifeminism in the Iconography of the Woman-Serpent in Medieval and Renaissance Art and Literature', in Flores (ed.), *Animals in the Middle Ages: A Book of Essays* (New York, 1996), 167–95. Gower's story of Adrian and Bardus (*Complete Works*, vol. ii: *The English Works, Confessio Amantis*, 5. 4937–5162) features a grateful serpent; interestingly, Gower has made his serpent female (it is male in the analogues to the tale in Nigel Wireker's *Speculum stultorum* and Matthew Paris's *Chronica majora*). Perhaps Gower wanted his readers to associate this 'grete gastli Serpent' with the Devil and his powers of deception, before overturning expectation and revealing a deeply moral beast.

[66] *C*, fo. 64ʳ.

[67] *Properties*, i. 90–1. The idea that man looked upward while beasts looked down to the ground was a medieval commonplace: it appears, for instance, in Chaucer's ex-hortation to 'Vache' in his balade 'Truth': 'Forth, pilgrim, forth! Forth, beste, out of thy stal! | Know thy contree, look up, thank God of al . . .' (lines 18–19).

associated with Christ or expressing spiritual aspirations, are directed upwards, to the heavens. Such are the panther . . . the ostrich . . . the doves . . . while the eyes of the dragon, hiding in the hole, are directed downwards, to the earth.'[68] She also draws attention to the particularly expressive quality that the illustrator of this manuscript has given to the eyes of his subjects: 'big, elongated . . . with a stretched brow-line'.[69] Spiritual identity looks out through these selectively humanized features.

While some animals are raised in the scale, others sink below the surface of the earth itself. In response to the captivating scent of the panther, a figure of Christ after his resurrection, most of the animals in the picture in the St Petersburg Bestiary stand rapt, their upward gaze signalling their acknowledgement of spiritual truth.[70] Only the dragon buries its head in its burrow underground ('fugit in cavernis terre').[71] To be associated with the regions under the earth, the places farthest removed from the heavens, is to shun the light in a metaphorical as well as in a literal sense. Trevisa, in his section on natural features, describes *spelunca* as 'a dyche or an holownesse vndir erþe', and goes on to remark: 'Also suche places [ben couenable] to hidynge and wonnynge of wylde bestes to don þerinne hoore and unclennes and to wonnynge and bydynge of serpentes and of oþer bestes.'[72] Animals linked with vice or uncleanness in the Bestiary are therefore often located underground: so the asp lurks in its hole to avoid hearing the song of the charmer. Its hole, the Bestiarist explains, symbolizes carnal desires, and the song the asp is hiding from is the call of heaven.[73] Foxes, too, are creatures of the lower regions, and illustrations in many Bestiaries show them peeping out from their earths.[74] The strong association between a subterranean habitat and uncleanness or sin also means that animals that are not naturally underground dwellers are sometimes placed there

---

[68] Muratova, *Medieval Bestiary*, 43. Cf. also Hassig, *Medieval Bestiaries*, 51: 'creatures representing good in the Bestiaries are often positioned in the upper portion of the picture space, facing right, while the evil creatures are relegated to the lower spaces and frequently face left.'

[69] Ibid. 44.

[70] *P*, fo. 2ʳ. There are similar pictures in *Aln*, fo. 16ᵛ; *Ash*, fo. 13ʳ; *B*, fo. 7ᵛ.

[71] *Aln*, fo. 16ᵛ; *Ash*, fo. 13ʳ; *B*, fo. 7ᵛ; *C*, fo. 4ᵛ.

[72] *Properties*, ii. 724.

[73] *Aln*, fo. 56ʳ; *B*, fo. 96ᵛ; *P*, fo. 84ʳ⁻ᵛ.

[74] See e.g. *Aln*, fo. 10ᵛ; *C*, fo. 16ʳ; *P*, fo. 12ᵛ.

because of the qualities that have been assigned to them. In Caxton's translation of the Middle Dutch version of the *Roman de Renart*, the fox, whose own 'castle' of Maleperduys is full of twisting subterranean passages, penetrates a chamber deep in the earth to find it occupied by a huge she-ape and her offspring, 'byslabbed and byclagged to their eres in her own dong'.[75]

The Bestiary, then, is a work that enacts the relationship between animals and man. The bodies of its creatures are shaped by the stress of human needs and desires—in a way, much as their real-life domestic counterparts had their physical features altered by years of managed breeding.[76] Man stands both above the Bestiary, as the divinely appointed controller of its teemingly active population, and also centrally within it, since each animal derives its identity from its relationship with him and has been created to contribute in some way to his profit or pleasure. 'Man appears . . . as contemplator who is ready to learn a lesson from everything around him', Xenia Muratova writes,[77] while Trevisa numbers the various practical ways in which animals may be of use to man. As well as providing him with food, some are made to serve him (horses, asses, and camels), others to amuse him (apes, marmosets, parrots), others so that he might recognize his infirmity (fleas and lice), and others to frighten him so that he might call upon God for help (lions, tigers, bears).[78]

However, any ordered system means that there must be boundaries between the different categories—the sort of demarcation visually expressed in the tiers of animals shown in some of the illuminations of Creation. Where there are boundaries, and borderline areas, there is always a danger of frontiers being crossed and categories becoming mixed, with formlessness or hybridization the result. The Bestiary text is concerned with this kind of liminality. Since it presents a model of total orderliness, incorporating stability of habitat as well as stability of form, its anxiety over creatures who

---

[75] William Caxton (trans.), *The History of Reynard the Fox*, ed. N. F. Blake, EETS os 263 (1970), 94. The bond between the underground, wickedness, and excremental filth was a strong one, and is discussed in more detail in Ch. 3 below.

[76] J. Clutton-Brock, *Domesticated Animals from Early Times*, British Museum (London, 1981), 22–5.

[77] *Medieval Bestiary*, 70.

[78] *Properties*, ii. 1110.

breach the boundaries sometimes appears as repudiation of the areas in which they live—which are described as physically marginal, neither one thing nor the other. For instance, of the four kinds of tortoises, the third is said to live 'filthily' (*lutarie*) in marshy areas (*in ceno et palude*), unlike the others, which inhabit the land, the sea, and flowing rivers.[79] Trevisa writes of the frog, another 'borderline' animal, that it is 'watery and morische, cryinge and slymy, wiþ a grete wombe and ysplekked þervnder and is venemous and abhominable þerfore to men and most yhated. And boþe in water and in londe he lyueþ.'[80] He uses the same concatenation of details to express his disgust for the swine. This beast too 'froteþ and walweþ in drytte and in fenne and dyneþ in slyme and bawdeþ himself þerwiþ and resteþ in stynkyng place. Oracius seiþ þat "þe sowe is frende to fenne and to pluddes" and þerfore swyn be accompted foule and vnhoneste.'[81] *Slyme, slymy*—these words, describing the mingling of water and solid matter, figure anomaly. So too does the description of the frog's markings as *ysplekked*: spots and stipples and mixed colours are often associated with deceitfulness or other bad qualities. For example, the hybrid leopard of the Bestiary, born from the union of a lion and a pard, is compared to the Antichrist of Revelation, its coat densely spotted with evil, while the magpie, with its *flekked* plumage, is often portrayed as a wretched chatterer who can only parody true speech.[82]

If the boundaries between categories of animals are permeable, what of the line between animals and humans? Humans, although they occupy a specially privileged niche within creation, cannot bar out the non-human world, which constantly impinges on them through the senses. Through eating and drinking, in particular, as Bakhtin recognizes, 'man tastes the world, introduces it into his body, makes it part of himself'.[83] Perhaps that is why the Bestiarists report that a serpent will die if it swallows the spittle of a fasting

---

[79] *C*, fo. 59[v].

[80] *Properties*, ii. 1242–3.

[81] Ibid. 1237. See also ii. 1250; *B*, fo. 37[v].

[82] *B*, fo. 10[r]. In Nigel Wireker's *Speculum stultorum* the Augustinians, in their black and white habits, are compared to both the leopard and the magpie, in a context that makes it obvious the author is hinting at their hypocrisy (ed. cit. 81–2). On the magpie, see Ch. 2, below.

[83] Mikhail Bakhtin, *Rabelais and his World*, trans. Hélène Iswolsky (Bloomington, Ind., 1984), 281.

man[84]—to build up its defences the body has to become a fortress, sealed from invading contamination. Bakhtin also identifies the sexual act as a time when the body's self-enclosed integrity is at risk, when 'the confines between bodies and between the body and the world are overcome: [when] there is an interchange and an inter-orientation'.[85] In the Bestiary there is an awareness of how, at such a moment, the inner world of thought and spirit and the outer world of physical phenomena may become interpermeable. It is pointed out, for example, that pigeon breeders deliberately mingle beautifully coloured pigeons among their flocks, so that the females, catching sight of these, may give birth to similar chicks. However, what is felicitous for pigeons may prove disastrous to humans: pregnant women are warned not to look at any of the most disgusting animals (*turpissimos animalium*), such as monkeys or dog-headed apes, in case their children should turn out to resemble them.

For such is said to be the nature of females that whatever they view, or even if they imagine it in the mind during the extreme heat of lust while they are conceiving, just so do they procreate the progeny. Animals in the act of venery translate images from outside inward, and, fertilized by the imaginary figure, they transform the apparition into a real quality.[86]

The Bestiary's meticulous deployment of categories therefore throws up the problem of anomaly—not just as an intellectual

---

[84] *C*, fo. 52. Also: 'The spyttle of a man fastyng sleeth comynly the spyncoppe [spider] & the tode yf it touche them' (*Caxton's Mirrour of the World*, ed. Oliver H. Prior, EETS ES 110 (1913), 100.

[85] Bakhtin, *Rabelais*, 317.

[86] *C*, fo. 27[v] (translation from White, *Book of Beasts*, 89–90); also *Ash*, fo. 35[v], *B*, fo. 49[v]. Gerald of Wales tells the story of a queen who looked so long at the picture of a negro in her bedroom that she gave birth to a black baby (*Itinerarium Kambriae*, ed. James F. Dimock, Rolls Series, 21, vol. vi (London, 1868), bk. 2, ch. 7). (The belief that what females took in through their eyes could influence the form of their subsequent offspring was still current in the 19th cent.: see Ritvo, *Platypus and the Mermaid*, 112–13.) The antifeminist bias of both Gerald of Wales's story and the Bestiary text is obvious: in the latter it is at least hinted that the woman is to blame, since her receptivity to external images is linked to her libidinous fantasizing. For medieval views of female sexuality in general, and the association of the woman's pleasure with conception, see Joan Cadden, *Meanings of Sex Difference in the Middle Ages: Medicine, Science, and Culture* (Cambridge, 1993), esp. 134–65. The Bestiary text manifests antifeminism elsewhere too: for example, the viper, 'whose story once stood for filial ingratitude and the failings of the Pharisees, later also acquires the lesson that women should put up with brutish husbands' (ibid. 51; see also White, *Book of Beasts*, 170–1); while the iconography of the 'fire rocks' often alludes to Eve's responsibility for the Fall (see Hassig, *Medieval Bestiaries*, 116–28).

irritant, a crease upon the page, but as a rogue agent apt to undermine the whole carefully designed system. Not even the dividing
line between humans and animals is safe from its insinuating power.
Some of the stranger portraits in the Bestiary could actually be seen
as studies in anomaly—experiments in how far one can go before all
sense of form and coherence is lost. The hyena, for instance, changes
sex from male to female ('and is þerfore an vnclene beste'), has an
adder's neck and a rigid spine which it cannot bend, imitates the
human voice to lure men out and prey on them, and feeds upon
dead bodies in graves.[87] It is almost impossible to see *any* individual
animal, even a mythical one, in the midst of all these impacted
details. Instead the portrait says something about the dangers written
into the Bestiary's structure—it is a kind of fearful summation of all
that anomaly could be.

Animals in the Bestiary act in the ways dictated to them by the
bodily identity given to them by God at their creation. Each part of
an animal is stamped with its particular individuality, and expresses
the affinities and antipathies that characterize its place in the whole
design. Trevisa writes about the wolf:

And so I haue yradde in a booke þat a strenge ymade of a wolues gutte ydo
among harpe strenges ymade of þe guttes of scheep destroyeþ and corrumpeþ hem, as an egle feþer ydo amonge coluere feþeres pilieþ and
gnaweþ hem if þey ben ylefte togidres longe in oon place, as he seiþ.[88]

The system therefore combines extreme diversification with extreme individuation. Creatures are what they are, unchangeably.
Each occupies its own niche in the world of nature, bound to
express particular aspects of physical and spiritual reality, and bound
into unalterable relationships both with other animal species and
with man. We might contrast present-day views of nature, in which
all animals, humans included, continually adapt their behaviour to
meet the varying stresses and challenges of a frequently unpredictable environment.

All organisms are ultimately concerned to pass on their genes to the next
generation. That, it would seem to a dispassionate and clinical observer, is
the prime objective of their existence. In the course of achieving it they

---

[87]   *Aln*, fo. 12^v; *Ash*, fos. 17^v–18^r; *B*, fo. 15$^{r–v}$; *C*, fo. 9$^{r–v}$; *P*, fo. 16^r; Trevisa, *Properties*,
ii. 1210–11. See also Hassig, *Medieval Bestiaries*, 145–55.

[88]   *Properties*, ii. 1222.

must face a whole succession of problems as they go through their lives. These problems are fundamentally the same whether the animals are spiders or squirrels, mice or monkeys, llamas or lobsters. The solutions developed by different species are hugely varied and often astounding. But they are all the more comprehensible and engaging for they are the trials that we also face ourselves.[89]

Yet whatever the differences between our thoughts about nature and those of the Bestiarists, animals have continued to carry 'examples for the mind as well as food for the body... not only loads but principles'.[90] In the next two chapters I discuss how two particular groups of animals—birds and foxes—are made to play out an especially elaborate metaphorical role.

[89]   David Attenborough, *The Trials of Life* (London, 1990), 10.
[90]   Review of Francis Klingender, *Animals in Art and Thought*, in *New Society* (25 Nov. 1971), 1043.

CHAPTER TWO

Birds:
The Ornament of the Air

'To Þe ournament of þe eire parteneþ briddes and foules, as Beda seiþ', Trevisa writes,[1] and, as we have seen, birds, creatures of a particular element, are treated in the Bestiary as a self-contained and distinctive form of creation. Physically, birds are not at all like us, and yet there is a persistent tradition of thought which aligns bird society and bird mores closely with our own. Claude Lévi-Strauss, for example, suggests that it is precisely *because* birds are so different from humans that they can be permitted to resemble them, and he goes on to identify the constituent parts of this likeness/unlikeness:

Birds are given human christian names in accordance with the species to which they belong more easily than are other zoological classes, because they can be permitted to resemble men for the very reason that they are so different. They are feathered, winged, oviparous and they are also physically separated from human society by the element in which it is their privilege to move. As a result of this fact, they form a community which is independent of our own but, precisely because of this independence, appears to us like another society, homologous to that in which we live: birds love freedom; they build themselves homes in which they live a family life and nurture their young; they often engage in social relations with other members of their species; and they communicate with them by acoustic means recalling articulated language.[2]

---

[1] *On the Properties of Things*, 3 vols. (Oxford, 1975–88), i. 596.

[2] 'Si, plus aisément que d'autres classes zoologiques, les oiseaux reçoivent des prénoms humains selon l'espèce a laquelle ils appartiennent, c'est q'ils peuvent se permettre de ressembler aux hommes, pour autant que, précisément, ils en diffèrent. Les oiseaux sont couverts de plumes, ailés, ovipares, et physiquement aussi, ils sont disjoints de la société humaine par l'élément où ils ont le privilège de se mouvoir. Ils forment, de ce fait, une communauté indépendante de la nôtre, mais qui, en raison de cette indépendance même, nous apparaît comme une société autre, et homologue de celle où nous vivons: l'oiseau est épris de liberté; il se construit une demeure où il vit en famille et

It is intriguing to see how consonant such a passage is with Trevisa's description of bird behaviour, five centuries earlier:

Among alle bestis þat ben in order of generacioun, briddes and foules [folwen] most honest[ee] of kynde. For by order of kynde males seche femalis wiþ bisynesse and loueþ hem whanne þey beþ ifounden and fiʒtiþ and puttiþ hem to perile for ham and beþ ioyned to ham onliche, as it were by couenaunt and loue weddynge, and norischiþ and fedeþ onliche briddes þat þey getyn. . . . And briddes and foules gendrynge kepiþ couenable tyme, for in springinge tyme whanne þe generacioun comeþ inne, briddes crien and singen. Males drawen to companye of females and preyen iche oþir of loue and wowiþ by beckes and voys, and makeþ nestis and leggiþ eyren and bringiþ forþ briddes. And whanne þe briddes beþ igendrid þey fediþ and noirischiþ ham and bringiþ hem vp.[3]

Although both writers present themselves as dispassionate observers, each 'sees' bird behaviour in terms dictated by his contemporary milieu. Trevisa's (male) birds contend with their rivals in love like knights in a medieval romance, while Lévi-Strauss's more bourgeois individuals are at once lovers of freedom and devotees of home and family. More subtly, Trevisa's text mirrors anxieties about the legitimacy of children in its assertion that birds 'norischiþ and fediþ onliche briddes þat þey geten', while Lévi-Strauss's exhibits its author's key preoccupation with language ('la langue articulé').[4] To achieve his picture, each author screens out those aspects of bird behaviour which would not sit well with his model: the cuckoo is an obvious counter-example to Trevisa's emphasis upon legitimate succession, while Lévi-Strauss passes over the mating habits of birds such as the dunnock, which opts for polygamy or monogamy according to the food resources in its territory.[5]

---

nourrit ses petits; il entretient souvent des rapports sociaux avec les autres membres de son espèce; et il communique avec eux par des moyens acoustiques qui évoquent la langue articulé' (Claude Lévi-Strauss, *La Pensée sauvage* (Paris, 1962), 270–1; trans. as *The Savage Mind* (London, 1966), 204).

[3] Trevisa, *Properties*, i. 597–8.

[4] That preoccupation appears, for example, in the reference at the start of the passage to the names we give to birds. The names of dogs, cattle, and horses are discussed in similar terms in the pages immediately following.

[5] 'Nor is this the complete list of variations in the sexual partnerships made by dunnocks. Sometimes two males will share two females, each mating with two partners. In other circumstances, two males will share three females. The inventive dunnocks are able to modify their behaviour to ensure that they produce the maximum number of

For both writers, in fact, birds represent an ideal society, in which the problems currently facing their human counterparts have been resolved in a harmonious way. That idealizing strand is strongly present in medieval presentations of birds: more interestingly, what is also present is a playful awareness of the attendant incongruity. Writing about Chaucer's *Parliament of Fowls*, J. A. W. Bennett acknowledges that poem's typically medieval alliance of human and bird worlds—'How closely the medieval mind paralleled the behaviour of birds and men'[6]—but his proposal of parallelism does not quite capture the nuance of that relationship. It is more a relationship of *homology*, in which similar functions and properties are manifested through extremely different physical structures. It is a homologous relationship that Lévi-Strauss identifies, and that Trevisa points to when he allows that, even though birds may court each other like true human lovers, they are forced to conduct their wooing not with lips but with 'beckes'. Social congruence coexists with emphatic physical divergence, and much medieval writing about birds takes its cue from the paradoxical imagery of the body that this generates. Bennett argues that, in the *Parliament*, we completely accept the female eagle in human terms, 'without . . . any incongruity';[7] I think, rather, that we are intended to catch the joke when Nature plants a decorous kiss not on lips or cheek but on her 'bek' (line 378).

To begin with, though, we need to establish the contours of that 'ideal society' that medieval birds represent. For ideals are socially generated, and typically privilege one mode of living over another. In fact, the depiction of birds in medieval culture consistently foregrounds and rationalizes the 'noble' life: the cultivated lifestyle of the powerful and prosperous few.

The different species of birds are frequently arranged in a hierarchy that replicates that of human society. Aristotle had divided birds into groups according to their eating habits,[8] and medieval texts continue this tradition by according pride of place to eagles, hawks, and other birds of prey. In the Bestiary, the eagle, which

young that their particular territory can support' (David Attenborough, *The Trials of Life* (London, 1990), 306).

[6] J. A. W. Bennett, *The Parlement of Foules* (Oxford, 1957), 154–5.
[7] Ibid. 153.
[8] *Historia animalium*, VIII. iii, 592b–593b.

soars to the circle of the sun to renew its youth, is foremost among the birds; while in Robert Holcot's *Super libros sapientiae* birds of prey generally are aligned with the nobility.[9] Gerald of Wales describes a wall-painting in the castle at Winchester executed on the orders of Henry II: it was to show the king himself as a royal eagle, pecked and harried by four eaglets representing his trouble-some sons.[10] Alexander Neckam tells the story of a goshawk which killed an eagle by means of a trick and was condemned by the king to be hanged for committing treason against its lord, even though it had acted in self-defence. Elsewhere Neckam extends his analogy between bird ranks and human ranks, likening the raven to mem-bers of the clergy (because of its black vestments) and the watchful cock to preachers of the Church. He makes the cuckoo, which sings *affer, affer* ('bring, bring'), a symbol of avarice.[11] Chaucer, of course, develops the whole conceit in particularly elaborate fashion in the *Parliament.*

Just as birds like the eagle and the hawk are made to represent those of high status in human society, so they are associated with the kinds of experience thought to be the preserve of the nobility. Love, and the behaviour allied to it, is the prime example. In Chaucer's *Squire's Tale*, Canacee, the daughter of the Tartar king Cambyuskan, walks out one morning with her attendants and listens to the birds singing:

> But nathelees it was so fair a sighte
> That it made alle hire hertes for to lighte,
> What for the seson and the morwenynge,
> And for the foweles that she herde synge.
> For right anon she wiste what they mente
> Right by hir song, and knew al hire entente.   (395–400)

The fact that Canacee can understand what the birds are saying is part of the tale's magical atmosphere, but it also suggests that her experience and theirs are enclosed within the same exclusive sphere—birds and princess share an elevated appreciation of love and of its discourse.

---

[9] Lectio lxvb.

[10] *De principis instructione*, ed. George F. Warner, Rolls Series, 21, vol. viii (London, 1891), dist. III, cap. 26 (pp. 295–6).

[11] *De naturis rerum*, ed. Thomas Wright, Rolls Series, 34 (London, 1863), chs. 24 (goshawk), 61 (raven), 75 (cock), 72 (cuckoo).

The distressed peregrine falcon whom Canacee rescues is without doubt a member of the same circle. She shrieks and swoons and mutilates herself in the way that the queen Heurodis does in *Sir Orfeo*. She also complains loudly against the faithless lover who has deserted her. Yet Chaucer continually reminds us that her body is the body of a bird. Canacee and the falcon might appear to be in perfect accord, but their bodies tell another story as they act out a delicately comic sub-plot to the tale's high matter of love and betrayal. Absorbed in pity for the falcon's plight, Canacee stands beneath the tree, ready to catch her in her lap when she drops from the bough, but the moment of rescue is deferred by the princess's long and graciously wrought speech of welcome; when (it is tempting to write 'so that when') the falcon finally does fall, she misses the proffered soft landing and hits the ground hard:

> Tho shrighte this faucon yet moore pitously
> Than ever she dide, and fil to grounde anon,
> And lith aswowne, deed and lyk a stoon . . . [12]   (472–4)

Despite Canacee's willing sympathy, where bodies are concerned she and the falcon appear to be slightly out of sync with one another. Elsewhere, too, Chaucer makes play with the falcon's double identity as both bird and wronged noblewoman: she was born and fostered, for instance, 'in a roche of marbul grey' (line 500)—the description of her natural habitat enlivened by the princely 'marbul'.

When the falcon herself comes to speak of her tribulations, there is further playful ambiguity:

> And ever in oon she cryde alwey and shrighte,
> And with hir beek hirselven so she prighte
> That ther nys tygre, ne noon so crueel beest
> That dwelleth outher in wode or in forest,
> That nolde han wept, if that he wepe koude,
> For sorwe of hire, she shrighte alwey so loude.   (417–22)

Although, on the surface, these lines seem to emphasize the pathos of the falcon's situation, they in fact embody a double denial of it. A tiger would have wept to hear her if it *could* weep—but it is

---

[12] The point about the 'missed catch' has been made by Harry Berger, Jr., 'The F Fragment of the *Canterbury Tales*: Part I', *Chaucer Review*, 1 (1966), 91, and by John P. McCall, 'The Squire in Wonderland', ibid. 106.

extremely doubtful whether tigers can weep at all.[13] What is more, such animals live in the wild forest, far away from the fragrant parkland through which Canacee has been walking, so that even a provisionally pitiful tiger would have been well out of earshot.

The dance of ambiguity continues when the falcon describes the demeanour of her faithless lover when she pledged him her love:

> Anon this tigre, ful of doublenesse,
> Fil on his knees with so devout humblesse,
> With so heigh reverence, and, as by his cheere,
> So lyk a gentil lovere of manere,
> So ravysshed . . .   (543–7)

The tercelet is 'ful of doublenesse' in more senses than the one the falcon intends. Obviously he has no knees on which he can fall.[14] And how *could* he be like 'a gentil lovere of manere', given the radical difference between bird bodies and human bodies? The falcon has not just been deceived by the base behaviour of a particular individual—by unthinkingly aligning bird 'manners' with human ones, she has doomed her venture from the start.

What in *The Squire's Tale* is a finely comic exploration of incongruity takes on a note of poignancy in Gower's tale of Ceyx and Alcione in his *Confessio Amantis*. When the bodies of husband and wife are turned into living halcyons, the narrator first celebrates the birds' joyous recognition of each other, and their reunion. However, as he moves into detailed description of their actions, it becomes clear that their new form makes it impossible for them to express their love in fully human terms:

> Hire wynges bothe abrod sche spradde,
> And him, so as sche mai suffise,
> Beclipte and keste in such a wise,
> As sche was whilom wont to do:
> Hire wynges for hire armes tuo
> Sche tok, and for hire lippes softe
> Hire harde bile, and so fulofte
> Sche fondeth in hire briddes forme,

---

[13] For the tiger's traditional attributes, see Melvin Storm, 'The Tercelet as Tiger: Bestiary Hypocrisy in the *Squire's Tale*', *English Language Notes*, 14 (1976–7), 172–4.

[14] E. T. Donaldson writes: 'it is hard to believe that the creator of Chauntecleer and Pertelote could with a straight face describe a hawk as a "tigre" who falls on his knees to his love' (*Chaucer's Poetry*, 2nd edn. (New York, 1975), 1086).

> If that sche mihte hirself conforme
> To do the plesance of a wif,
> As sche dede in that other lif;
> For thogh sche hadde hir pouer lore,
> Hir will stod as it was tofore,
> And serveth him so as sche mai.[15]

The essentially human pieties of 'that other lif'—the wife's loving attention to her husband's needs—hover over this latest change. Alcione yearns to do everything for Ceyx that she once did, but there is now no way in which this is possible. Wings are not arms, and beaks are not at all like lips—*softe* and *harde* emphasize the contrast.

Chaucer and Gower both exploit the discordances that arise when bird world and human world are brought together under the aegis of romantic love. Gower goes further, however: in his tale of Tereus he lays bare the unspoken gender bias which has long been a part of the same tradition. The analogy between the courtly, male lover and the 'noble' bird of prey—whether eagle, falcon, or tercel—is a thoroughly conventional one, running from Andreas Capellanus to Shakespeare (Romeo is a 'tassel gentle', II. iii. 159) and beyond.[16] However there is a problematic side to such imagery, for there must come a point at which the qualities associated with hawk or eagle: the strength, speed, and intrepidity bodied forth in Troilus's eventual possession of Criseyde—

> What myhte or may the sely larke seye,
> Whan that the sperhauk hath it in his foot   (3. 1191–2)

—shade into something less praiseworthy: into rapacity and ultimately into violent assault. The progression is implicit in the word *ravine*, which refers both to the general class of birds of prey (the 'fowls of ravine') and to robbery with violence or actual rape.[17] The imagery therefore comes to be enlisted in the service of a particular viewpoint: the speed of the descent obliterates any sense of struggle, or suffering, and the voice of the victim—the feminine— remains unheard.

---

[15] *The Complete Works of John Gower*, ed. G. C. Macaulay, 4 vols. (Oxford, 1899–1902), vol. ii: *The English Works*, 4. 3102–15.

[16] See Bennett, *Parlement*, 155 and n. 1.

[17] *MED ravine* n., 1, 3.

It is this elision of the feminine that Gower challenges when he gives us the story of Tereus in Book 5 of the *Confessio Amantis*. Genius tells the story to Amans as an illustration of the vice of Ravine, and there is already, in his prefatory words, a hint of that unhappy commingling of essences that will figure so crucially in the tale itself:

> Nou list, mi Sone, and thou schalt hiere,
> So as it hath befalle er this,
> In loves cause hou that it is
> A man to take be Ravine
> The preie which is femeline.   (5. 5546–50)

Although the man, the assailant, is human here, his victim, the 'preie', has already begun to shade into a different form. What is implicit in *preie* becomes disturbingly explicit when the narrator describes Tereus's rape of his wife's sister, Philomela:

> And sche was of to litel myht
> Defense ayein so ruide a knyht
> To make, whanne he was so wod
> That he no reson understod,
> Bot hield hire under in such wise,
> That sche myhte noght arise,
> Bot ley oppressed and desesed,
> As if a goshauk hadde sesed
> A brid, which dorste noght for fere
> Remue...   (5. 5637–46)

The passage is vivid and powerful because the details of Philomela's suffering have *not* been subsumed into the dominant image of a hawk swooping down on its victim. The fact that she is unable to 'arise' is inappropriate to a bird seized on the wing—instead it reminds us of her real, human identity. So does *oppressed*, which conveys the heavy weight of Tereus's body on top of hers. By setting bird bodies against human ones, Gower has taken apart the conventional metaphor. In a tale in which women overcome the constraints of a literal, and savage, silencing, it is entirely fitting that, at this initial level, he should have provided a way for the victim to register her own experience.[18]

[18] In Ovid's tale (*Metamorphoses*, bk. 6) Tereus is compared to an eagle, seizing a hare in its crooked talons. Philomela is a 'frightened lamb', and a trembling dove (Loeb edn.,

The drawing of a circle of 'noble' lovers, to which the category of 'noble' birds corresponds, presupposes another, devalued kind of consciousness beyond its bounds. Outside the 'mewe' which Canacee constructs for the sorrowing falcon, there are pictures painted of

> alle thise false fowles;
> As ben thise tidyves, tercelettes, and owles;
> Right for despit were peynted hem bisyde,
> Pyes, on hem for to crie and chyde.   (647–50)

Similarly, in Lydgate's *Temple of Glas* the lady prays that jealous people who speak ill of her might be despised by all lovers,

> ryght as a-mong foulys
> Ben Iayis, Pyis, Lapwyngis & these Oulys.[19]

In human terms, these are the 'goosissh poeple' who, according to the narrator of *Troilus and Criseyde*, cannot be expected to understand the exalted purpose behind the lovers' secretive behaviour (3. 584). It is their voices we hear in the motley chorus of the 'lower' sorts of birds in *The Parliament of Fowls*, who reject the ideals of self-denying devotion proposed by the eagles:

> 'I seye I rede hym, though he were my brother,
> But she wol love hym, lat hym love another!'   (566–7)
>
> 'Ye queke,' seyde the goos, 'ful wel and fayre!
> There been mo sterres, God wot, than a payre!'   (594–5)

The noble tercelet has a quick response to such pragmatism, and his words explicitly link demeaned social status with congenitally narrowed experience:

> 'Now fy, cherl!' quod the gentil tercelet,
> 'Out of the donghil cam that word ful right!
> Thow canst nat seen which thyng is wel beset!
> Thow farst by love as oules don by lyght:
> The day hem blent, ful wel they se by nyght.
> Thy kynde is of so low a wrechednesse
> That what love is, thow canst nouther seen ne gesse.'   (596–602)

---

1. 325). The pathos is reduced because the victim's identity is divided among several creatures; Gower concentrates, tellingly, on a single image.

[19] John Lydgate, *The Temple of Glas*, ed. J. Schick, EETS ES 60 (1891), stanza 25c, lines 6–7. (These additional stanzas are included in four MSS of the poem.)

The tercelet stresses that the duck and the goose really are the lowest of the low by his allusion to the 'donghil' where they live. According to him, their lack of fine discrimination in matters of love is inevitable, given their rank in society. They are no more able to expand their vision than the owl is able to see properly by day.

Lydgate's early poem 'The Churl and the Bird' wittily embroiders on this theme of nobly enhanced experience winning out over mere 'dunghill' vision.[20] The poem starts by presenting the ordered and graded universe of the Bestiaries:

> Eglis in the ayer hihest to take their fliht,
>> Power of leones on the grounde is sene,
> Ceedre of trees hihest is of sight,
>> And the Laurel of nature is ay grene,
>> Of floures all Flora, goddes & queene,
> Thus of al thyng ther been dyuersites,
> Some of estat, & som of low degrees.   (22–8)

The representative of nobility is the bird who lives in a fresh laurel tree in the churl's garden. Its gentility is shown in its appearance—its 'sonnysh fetheris brihter than gold wer'—and in the classical decorum which leads it to sing both at the setting of 'Phoebus' and at the dawn rising of 'the Queen Alceste'. The action of the poem revolves around the tricks the bird plays upon the churl, who catches her and puts her in a cage, threatening to pluck and roast her unless she sings for him. Even though the bird has been imprisoned, she refers to herself as a 'mayster'—'It sitt a mayster to have his liberte' (line 166)—implying the superior qualities she in fact demonstrates in the course of the story. If the churl sets her free, she offers to give him 'Thre greete wisdames' worth more than 'al the gold that is shett in thi coofre' (line 161). The churl agrees, and she delivers her wise sayings, which turn out to be: don't be too credulous, don't desire the impossible, and don't sorrow too much

---

[20] *Minor Poems*, ed. H. N. MacCracken, Part II, EETS os 192 (1934), 468–85. The story appears in the *Gesta Romanorum* and in the *Disciplina clericalis* of Petrus Alfonsus (see Derek Pearsall, *Lydgate* (London, 1970), 198); for Lydgate's probable source, see Neil Cartlidge, 'The Source of John Lydgate's *The Churl and the Bird*', *Notes & Queries*, 242/1 (Mar. 1997), 22–4. The poem evidently had a wide currency, as the number of MSS and early printed versions testifies (ed. cit. 468). Skelton may be alluding to it in *Speke Parott* when he credits Parott with concealing in parable 'maters more precious than the ryche jacounce' (*The Complete English Poems*, ed. John Scattergood (Harmondsworth, 1983), no. XVIII, line 366).

over treasure you have lost. She then tells the churl he was a fool to let her go, since she carries in her body a stone with magical properties which would have been his if he had held on to her. However, it is useless to tell a churl about precious stones:

> 'Ech þing drawith vn-to his semblable:
>> Fissh in the sea, bestis on the stronde,
> The eyr for fowlis of nature is covenable,
>> To a plowman for [to] tyle his londe,
>> And to a cherl, a mookfork in his honde;
> I lese my tyme any moor to tarye,
>> To telle a bovir of the lapidarye.'   (260–6)

The bird's insults are maliciously shafted—the mention of the 'lapidarye' is a particularly disdainful thrust—so that we might imagine the churl weeps as much from social chagrin as from material disappointment. The bird immediately charges him with forgetting everything he has just been taught. She had warned him not to be too credulous, yet he had believed that she could carry a precious stone weighing more than an ounce inside her when her whole body does not weigh so much:

> 'All my body weieth nat vn vnce,
>> How myht I than have in me a stoon,
> That peisith more than doth a grett iagounce?'   (316–18)

She also reminds him that she told him not to sorrow for what he had lost and not to desire what is impossible. However, she concludes, it is pointless to try to teach a churl 'termys of gentilnesse'. Churls can never attain the commanding perspective enjoyed by beings like the little bird, who understand and appreciate all the fine distinctions upon which the world's order rests:

> 'All oon to the a ffaucoun & a kyte,
>> As good an oule as a popyngay,
> A donghyl doke, as deynte as a snyte;
>> Who serveth a cherl hath many a carful day.
>> Adieu, Sir Cherl, farwell, I flye my way;
> I cast me nevir hensforth, my levyng,
> Aforn a cherl anymore to syng!'   (358–64)

The bird's total appropriation of the narrative is shown by the fact that, by the end of the poem, it is *she*, not the churl, who is said to have been annoyed and discomfited by what has happened. She has spent a 'carful day' in unappreciated service. Her conceptual and experiential dominance is symbolized by her final flight out of the churl's reach after her gratuitously rude, mock-heroic farewell to him.

In 'The Churl and the Bird' the centre traffics with the periphery, asserting that it lacks an essential kind of knowledge about the way the world works, and allying this with liminal aspects of the body itself (the duck on its dunghill, the churl with a 'mookfork' in his hand). (The argument of the periphery, which breaks through in *The Parliament of Fowls,* is of course that such 'knowledge' is itself illusory and, more, a positive impediment to the real business in hand.) We might well conclude that bird world and human world in Lydgate's poem speak with a single voice, and that their message is the same as the merlin's riposte to the cuckoo in the *Parliament,* 'Go, lewed be thow whil the world may dure!' (line 616). However, this would be to miss out on some of the poem's subtlety, for the particular piquancy of the joke against the churl derives not from the *identity* of birds and humans but from the *difference* between the two. The reason why the bird's story about the jacinth *has* to be a fiction is that she is, physically, a bird, and a very small one at that. She simply could not carry a stone of that size in her body. So, the churl is doubly trounced—for forgetting both that birds are socially congruent to humans (he should therefore have realized that a 'noble' bird which parades its learning in songs to the classical gods would easily be able to outwit a peasant), and that they are physically divergent. In the end it is he who is caught in the lime-twigs, while the little bird, mistress of discourse, flies free.

In Lydgate's poem, the bird's song is one of the markers which identify it as a member of the nobility. Birdsong is an important part of the discourse concerning birds in medieval texts, and, in keeping with the minutely graded universe of the birds themselves, is subjected to exhaustive social scrutiny. The underlying model is one of creative variety versus mindless monotony, the former an image of the multifarious richness of experience that is alleged to characterize the noble way of life. The singing of birds (that is, the *right* kind of singing) both gives pleasure in itself and underscores the justness of noble preoccupations—for birds always sing about love. So, in Chaucer's *Legend of Good Women,* a whole chorus of little birds appear (cousins, surely, to the bird in Lydgate's poem), and 'despise' the fowler—'The foule cherl'—in their song (lines 122–5). They go on to display their courtly status by singing 'Layes of love, that joy it was to here' (line 140).

In Chaucer's *Manciple's Tale*, birdsong again plays a vitally expressive role. At the outset of the tale, the god Phoebus is presented as the 'flour of bachilrie', 'fulfild of gentillesse'. Fittingly, the crow he has tamed can imitate human speech flawlessly, and sing far better than any nightingale (lines 130–8). However, the plot of the story turns upon Phoebus's wife's rejection of all his noble qualities in favour of someone who is not in any respect his equal:

> A man of litel reputacioun,
> Nat worth to Phebus in comparisoun.   (199–200)

The sordid nature of their affair is brought out by animal comparisons, such as the she-wolf's choice of 'The lewedeste wolf that she may fynde' (line 184) as mate, and by the Manciple's use of the word *lemman*. (In apologizing for it, of course, he only succeeds in drawing attention to it.)[21] When the crow reveals the adultery by crying *Cokkow*, Phoebus kills his wife, and then smashes his weapons—arrows and bow—and his 'mynstralcie', harp and lute, 'gyterne and sautrie' (line 268). He thus destroys those instruments which have 'spoken' of his noble way of life through their varied and pleasurable melody. At once he regrets what he has done, and, now convinced of his wife's innocence, he turns upon the crow:

> And to the crow he stirte, and that anon,
> And pulled his white fetheres everychon,
> And made hym blak, and refte hym al his song,
> And eek his speche, and out at dore hym slong
> Unto the devel, which I hym bitake;
> And for this caas been alle crowes blake.   (303–8)

Phoebus's descent from noble discourse to the demotic is mirrored in these lines: in the monosyllabic *slong*, and 'Unto the devel', which presumably echoes the curse with which the crow is sent on his way. In most of the analogues to the tale, the point of the story is simply

---

[21]   For Chaucer's emphasis on the sordidness of the affair, see Richard Hazelton, '*The Manciple's Tale*: Parody and Critique', *JEGP* 62 (1963), 1–31; John P. McCall, *Chaucer among the Gods: The Poetics of Classical Myth* (University Park, Pa., 1979), 129–31.

the crow's change in colour from white to black: Chaucer himself seems to have inserted the taking away of his song, as well as Phoebus's breaking of his musical instruments.[22] Both the crow and Phoebus lose their melody, as both forfeit the myriad delights of their former way of life. Each is left with only one note to sing.[23]

As the essence of 'noble' birdsong is variety, so the birds at the bottom of the heap produce no more than a single, endlessly repeated call. The narrator in *The Parliament of Fowls* reminds us how irksome this is to listen to:

> The goos, the cokkow, and the doke also
> So cryede, 'Kek kek! kokkow! quek quek!' hye,
> That thourgh myne eres the noyse wente tho.   (498–500)

The little bird in 'The Churl and the Bird' also refers to the uninspired, monotonous tones of the cuckoo:

> 'And semblably in Aprill and in May,
>   Whan gentil briddis make most melodie,
> The cookkow syngen can but o lay,
>   In othir tymes she hath no fantasye.'   (344–7)

Base notes equate to base behaviour—the cuckoo is, notoriously, a 'glotoun' (*Parliament of Fowls*, 610) and the 'mortherere of the heysoge on the braunche' (line 612).[24]

However, in Clanvowe's *The Cuckoo and the Nightingale* the cuckoo with its unembellished song is treated more equivocally, as part of a playful critique of romantic love.[25] The narrator, 'olde and vnlusty' (line 37), is lying half asleep and half awake when he hears the 'foule voyse' (line 94) of the cuckoo. He then hears the

---

[22] See Britton J. Harwood, 'Language and the Real: Chaucer's Manciple', *Chaucer Review*, 6 (1972), 268–79.

[23] In Dunbar's poem '[To the King]' ('Schir, ȝit remember as befoir...'), the poet, pleading for preferment and complaining of those who win undeserved favours, draws a similar comparison between debased social status and harsh, unpleasing birdsong when he writes of the magpie who tries in vain to sing like the nightingale: 'The pyat withe the pairtie cote | Feynȝeis to sing the nychtingale note, | Bot scho can not the corchet cleiff | For hasknes of hir *carleche* throte' (*The Poems of William Dunbar*, ed. James Kinsley (Oxford, 1979), no. 42, lines 16–19; my italics).

[24] The boring, unvaried nature of the cuckoo's song was proverbial: see B. J. Whiting, *Proverbs, Sentences, and Proverbial Phrases from English Writings Mainly Before 1500* (Cambridge, Mass., 1968), C600.

[25] *The Works of Sir John Clanvowe*, ed. V. J. Scattergood (Cambridge, 1975), 35–53. Subsequent references to the poem are included in the text.

nightingale sing, and, in a straight 'lift' from *The Squire's Tale*, realizes that, in his tranced state, he can understand

> that the briddes ment,
> And what they seyde, and what was her entent.[26]   (109–10)

Each bird then defends its own song and attacks that of its rival. The cuckoo, for example, asserts:

> 'For my songe is bothe trewe and pleyn,
> Al thogh I can not breke hit so in veyne,
> As thou dost in thy throte, I wote ner how.
>
> And euery wight may vnderstonde me,
> But, nyghtyngale, so may they not the,
> For thou has mony a nyse queynte crie.
> I haue herd thee sey "ocy! ocy!"
> Who myght wete what that shulde be?'   (118–25)

By calling its song *pleyn*, the cuckoo both linguistically co-opts the word *trewe* as an ally and relates its music to that of 'plainsong', concerning the virtues of which, as opposed to polyphony, there was then an active debate.[27] The cuckoo hints that the nightingale's sophisticated trilling in fact refers to the arcana of erotic play—*queynte* surely bears a sexual meaning, and exemplifies the poet's witty juxtaposition of bird and human bodies. The 'plain' cuckoo professes not to understand what is being sung about, but this is mock naïvety, delivered with a knowing wink to the poem's audience. The part he *does* understand, 'ocy! ocy!', 'kill! kill!', he stolidly deconstructs. The nightingale explains that she wishes all those who refuse to serve the god of love were dead, but the cuckoo points out that this is hardly fair, since love itself makes a person unhappy—the choice offered therefore appears to be either permanent misery or death. The nightingale has no logical answer to this, merely diatribe:

> 'What!' quoth she, 'thou art out of thy mynde.
> How maist thou in thy cherles herte fynde
> To speke of loves seruauntes in this wyse?'   (46–8)

---

[26] *The Squire's Tale*, 399–400. Scattergood does not record this parallel in the notes to his edition.

[27] Ed. cit., n. to lines 118–20. Scattergood also quotes *A Midsummer Night's Dream*, III. i. 134: 'The plain-song cuckoo gray'.

She can only respond by hurling back the insult crafted by the little bird in 'The Churl and the Bird', but with considerably less skill. In the end, the nightingale breaks down weeping, and appeals to her patron, the god of love, for help. No help is forthcoming, and the narrator himself has to step in, throwing a stone at the cuckoo, who flies away.

> And euermore the cukkow as he fley,
> He seyde, 'Farewel, farewel, papyngay.'
> As thogh he had scorned, thoghte me.
> But ay I hunted him fro tre to tre
> Till he was fer al out of syght away.   (221–5)

The narrator does not cut a very impressive figure here. Not only does he fail to hit the cuckoo, who appears to flit teasingly from tree to tree rather than flap away in fright, but, according to popular lore, throwing stones at the cuckoo meant that one was likely to sing that bird's song, that is, become a cuckold.[28] The cuckoo's mocking departure marks its exit from the poem—but as it retreats, does it also relinquish its hold upon human meaning? The narrator hears the word *papyngay* (in itself a pert refocusing of human as bird), but he is not sure he has caught the tone: '*As thogh* he had scorned, *thoghte me.*' Does the cuckoo 'speak' and deliver a cruel but accurate rebuke, or does it merely produce noise, which the narrator, in his receptive state, relates to his own sad experiences in love? The question is left open, as is the final outcome of the contest. The birds the nightingale summons to deliver a verdict for her against 'that foule false unkinde bird' (line 270) in fact postpone making any decision until they can all come together in a parliament, presided over by the eagle. Here the eagle will either give a judgement or arrange some kind of accord between the opposing parties. The poem neatly plays with notions of birds and humans and their disparate bodily experiences, and, despite its obvious borrowings, is a more subtle and skilfully wrought piece of work than has sometimes been allowed.[29]

---

[28] For examples, see Whiting, *Proverbs*, C603.

[29] For discussions of *The Cuckoo and the Nightingale*, see W. A. Davenport, 'Bird Poems from *The Parliament of Fowls* to *Philip Sparrow*', in Julia Boffey and Janet Cowen (eds.), *Chaucer and Fifteenth-Century Poetry*, King's College London Medieval Studies, 5 (London, 1991), 68; Thomas Honegger, *From Phoenix to Chauntecleer: Medieval English*

In Clanvowe's poem, the cuckoo's unvarying song was offered as a proof of its openness and honesty. Elsewhere, the repetitive nature of birdsong—and most of it does consist of endlessly repeated phrases—is used as the vehicle for homiletic truths which must be said over and over again to have their effect. Several poems in the early fifteenth-century commonplace book of Richard Hill feature birds, who sometimes repeat a moral lesson that becomes the refrain of each verse: 'Timor mortis conturbat me', 'Assay a frend or þou haue nede'.[30] In one poem, the constant chant of *Revertere* is set against the wild and ranging flight of the narrator's hawk, which represents his unsatisfied thirst for 'worldly pursuit and youthful liberty'.[31]

> This hawke of yowth ys high of porte,
>   And wildnes makyth hym wyde to fle,
> & ofte to fall in wykyd thowght,
>   And than ys best: 'Revertere.'[32]

Not all birds repeat the same notes over and over again: another group produce sounds with at least some of the variety of human speech. Jays and magpies were often kept as pets:[33] both birds naturally 'chatter' and can be taught to mimic certain words. However, there is never any sense behind what they are saying: they are simply copying what they have heard. Because their 'speech' is so clearly derivative, it is often equated with various kinds of discourse that writers wish to devalue. 'Beleue nou3t yn þe pyys cheteryng; | Hyt ys no trouþe, but fals beleuyng', Robert Mannyng warns in *Handlyng Synne*, alluding to the bird's role in popular superstition as the harbinger of important events,[34] while the magpie appears as the spreader of malicious rumours in both *The House of Fame* and *Troilus*

Animal Poetry, Swiss Studies in English, 120 (Tübingen and Basle, 1996), 138–44; and A. C. Spearing, *Medieval Dream-Poetry* (Cambridge, 1976), 176–81.

[30] *Songs, Carols, and other Miscellaneous Poems from Balliol MS 354, Richard Hill's Commonplace Book*, ed. Roman Dyboski, EETS es 101 (1907), nos. 4, 57.

[31] Davenport, 'Bird Poems', 73.

[32] *Songs, Carols*, no. 73, lines 29–32.

[33] John Paston III wrote to his brother about his disappointment with a 'talking' magpie: 'I sye the pye and herd it spek, and be God it is not worthe a crowe. . . . Be God, it wer shame to kep it in a cage.' *Paston Letters and Papers of the Fifteenth Century*, ed. Norman Davis, 2 vols. (Oxford, 1971, 1976), i. 584 (no. 356).

[34] *Robert of Brunne's Handlyng Synne*, ed. F. J. Furnivall, EETS os 119, 123 (1901), lines 355–6.

and Criseyde.[35] Magpies are quite often given a specifically female identity: Mannyng refers to his bird as 'she', and a late fifteenth-century commonplace book lists as its three 'claterars' 'A pie, A iai, A woman'.[36] Chaucer's 'magpies' are typically those self-assured, sexually assertive women who walk abroad in their finery, deliberately challenging men's gaze. His Wife of Bath, remembering the days when she paid back her fourth husband for his philandering with her own innocent, but highly provocative, 'cheere', describes her young self as 'ful of ragerye, | Stibourn and strong, and joly as a pye' (lines 455–6), while the miller Simkin's wife in *The Reeve's Tale*, parading on holy days in her red gown (with her husband attired to match), is as 'peert as is a pye' (line 3950).[37] The bird's various features—its jaunty manner, eye-catching plumage, raucous 'chattering', and possibly its liking for bright trinkets—come together to form, for men, an apt and compendious image of a certain kind of woman.[38]

Invoking the 'speech' of magpies and jays also means positing the existence of a 'true' speech which these mindless mimics fail to attain. In *Piers Plowman*, the rich who hoard their wealth and refuse to share it with others are warned that Christ will turn a deaf ear to their pleas:

> Thouȝ he crye to Crist þanne wiþ kene wil, I leue
> His ledene be in our lordes ere like a pies chiteryng.[39]

Valid prayer has to issue from integrity of life. In Chaucer's *General Prologue*, the narrator shows us the divide between genuine and spurious learning when he likens the Summoner's bogus Latin, the 'fewe termes...two or thre, | That he had lerned out of som decree' (lines 639–40), to the 'Watte' spoken by a tame jay. Jays appear again in *The Canon's Yeoman's Tale*, when the teller compares

---

[35] *House of Fame*, lines 703–4: 'alle the pies | In al a realme, and alle the spies'; *T&C* 3. 526–7: 'Dredeles, it cler was in the wynd | Of every pie and every lette-game.'

[36] *A Common-Place Book of the Fifteenth-Century*, ed. L. T. Smith (London, 1886), 12.

[37] See also *The Shipman's Tale*, 209: 'And forth she gooth as jolif as a pye.'

[38] In Jehan Le Fèvre's antifeminist *Les Lamentations de Matheolus* (ed. A.-G. Van Hamel, 2 vols., Paris, 1892, 1905) a woman is described as 'more gossipy than a magpie' (quoted in Alcuin Blamires (ed.), *Woman Defamed and Woman Defended* (Oxford, 1992), 183).

[39] William Langland, *Piers Plowman: The B Version*, ed. George Kane and E. Talbot Donaldson, rev. edn. (London and Berkeley, 1988), 11. 254–5.

men's futile attempts to penetrate the mysteries of alchemy with
these birds' nonsensical jargoning:

> Philosophres speken so mystily
> In this craft that men kan nat come therby,
> For any wit that men han now-a-dayes.
> They mowe wel chiteren as doon jayes,
> And in hir termes sette hir lust and peyne,
> But to hir purpos shul they nevere atteyne.   (1394–9)

Old January in *The Merchant's Tale* is

> al coltissh, ful of ragerye,
> And ful of jargon as a flekked pye.
> The slakke skyn aboute his nekke shaketh
> Whil that he sang, so chaunteth he and craketh.   (1847–50)

Although January might like to think of himself as 'al coltissh, ful of
ragerye', the assonance of *flekked . . . slakke . . . nekke* means that we
link him most closely with the particoloured magpie, which can
chatter away but never endow its speech with true content. That
would certainly be the verdict of May, who 'preyseth nat his
pleyyng worth a bene' (1854).

Finally, Gower, in the first book of his *Vox Clamantis*, written in
response to the rising of 1381, characterizes the leader of the rebels,
Wat Tyler, as a 'jay' ('quodam Graculus avis, anglice Gay, qui
vulgariter vocatur Watte'—apparently alluding to the fact that
'Wat' was a name often given to pet birds).[40] Gower takes a
doom-laden view of the divisions within society breaking down
and terrible chaos resulting, and conveys his feelings through his use
of hideous mutations of animal forms. His wild multitude of misshapen monsters is addressed by the 'jay', who goads them to
violence. Gower's aim, through this personification, is to discount
Tyler's argument, by equating it with the nonsensical prattle of a
tamed bird. Tyler as jay is not even credited with originating his own
speech, for he is described as 'well instructed in the art of speaking'
('edoctus in arte loquendi', 1. 681), implying that others have taught
him what he now declaims. He is dangerously unrestrainable: no

---

[40]   *Complete Works*, vol. iv: *The Latin Works*, 1. 679 ff. See n. to ch. 9 in the translation
of the poem by Eric W. Stockton, *The Major Latin Works of John Gower* (Seattle, 1962),
352. Subsequent references to the *Vox* are included in the text; the English versions are
Stockton's.

cage could keep him at home ('Quem retinere domi nulla catasta potest', I. 682). Gower toys provocatively with physical details that align bird and man even more closely:

> Vox fera, trux vultus, verissima mortis imago,
> Eius in effigiem tanta dedere notam. (I. 687–8)

A harsh voice, a fierce expression, a very faithful likeness to a death's head—these things gave token of his appearance.

Gower tries to ensure that when we see Tyler we see the pitiless visage of a predator (for the metaphor has widened to include other kinds of birds) and that when we hear him we hear no more than jangling discordancy. His aim is both to deny Tyler autonomy, and to make him, in his mindlessness, an object of terror.

Thus the world of birds, in medieval literature, is the subject of endlessly creative manipulation. It is perhaps an acknowledgement of that manipulation that there is often an attempt to bring into view all the birds that there are. Clanvowe's birds hasten off to bring their fellows together in a full assembly (and they include at least one bird, the eagle, who is not a native of the woodland glade where the narrator has been dreaming); the birds in 'The Harmony of Birds', a mid-sixteenth-century macaronic poem, who sing verses from the *Te Deum*, cluster 'as thycke | As sterres in the skye';[41] while the dreamer who listens to *La Messe des oisiaus* remarks, 'Nobody ever saw so many birds in his life.'[42] Like the galaxies above, the bird world, sparkling and diverse, extended as far as the eye could see, but it *could* be compassed and understood, interpreted like a complicated—but not a complex—code.

The crowning touch is to make the birds themselves responsible for the regulation of divisions in their ranks—to make them, in other words, the authors of their own story. Nature in *The Parlia-*

---

[41] *Two Early Renaissance Bird-Poems*, ed. Malcolm Andrew (Washington, 1984), lines 20–1.

[42] Jean de Condé, *La Messe des oisiaus*, trans. B. Windeatt, *Chaucer's Dream Poetry: Sources and Analogues* (Woodbridge, 1982), 104. Cf. also 'every foul . . . | Of every kynde that men thynke may': *Parliament of Fowls*, lines 310–11. J. A. W. Bennett suggests that the grouping together of many different *kinds* of birds is a specifically 14th-cent. practice (*Parlement*, 21).

ment of Fowls appeals to such an innate sense of precedence when she presents to the assembly

> The tersel egle, *as that ye knowe wel,*
> The foul royal, above yow in degre . . .   (393–4, my italics)

while Lydgate, in *The Temple of Glas,* describes the birds who symbolize gossiping ill-wishers as naturally despised by other birds:

> Had in despit, ryght as a-mong foulys
> Ben Iayis, Pyis, Lapwyngis & these Oulys.

The mobbing of the owl by smaller birds is mentioned in *The Owl and the Nightingale* and was a popular subject for manuscript illuminations—in effect, it is a reassuring example of the birds policing their own categories.[43]

This chapter has explored various treatments of birds and their world and how it interacts with the human one. There are, of course, many more literary works featuring birds which I have not discussed, but I hope that the themes explored so far will also help to illuminate these other texts.[44] There is also, of course, a wealth of material in the visual arts which I can do no more than mention here. Birds appear in illustrations of the Apocalypse,[45] in the delightful quarries in church windows,[46] in manuscripts such as the

---

[43] *The Owl and the Nightingale,* ed. E. G. Stanley (London, 1960), lines 1625–30. Pictures of birds mobbing an owl appear in some Bestiary MSS (e.g. MS Bodley 764, fo. 73); in Bodl. MS Rawlinson poet. 223, fo. 5^r; in the Amesbury Psalter, fo. 13^r; and in an East Anglian Book of Hours in the Walters Art Gallery, Baltimore (MS W. 105, fo. 10^v). There are roof-bosses of the scene at Exeter, Sherborne, Norwich, and Wells (C. J. P. Cave, *Roof Bosses in Medieval Churches* (Cambridge, 1948), 73 and pl. 206), and an illustration in the Lisle Psalter (BL MS Arundel 83, fo. 14^r) shows a man crouching in a bush using a live (or stuffed?) owl to lure a variety of small birds to him.

[44] *The Nun's Priest's Tale* is an obvious example, as are Richard Holland's *Buke of the Howlat* (*Longer Scottish Poems, i: 1375–1650,* ed. Priscilla Bawcutt and F. J. Riddy (Edinburgh, 1987), 43–84) and Skelton's *Speke Parott* and *Phyllyp Sparowe* (*Complete English Poems,* ed. Scattergood, nos. VII, XVIII). See also the late 15th- or early 16th-cent. 'Parliament of Birds' (ed. Andrew in *Two Early Renaissance Bird-Poems*), in which the birds gather in a parliament to bring their complaints against the predatory hawk.

[45] For examples see Francis Klingender, *Animals in Art and Thought to the End of the Middle Ages,* ed. Evelyn Antal and John Harthan (London, 1972), 402–13.

[46] See Christopher Woodforde, 'Some Medieval English Glazing Quarries Painted with Birds', *Journal of the British Archaeological Association,* 3rd ser. 60 (1944), 1–11.

'Bird Psalter', the Alphonso Psalter, and the Sherborne Missal,[47] and on richly embroidered vestments (the famous *opus Anglicanum*).[48] Mechanical birds, which sang upon command, also fascinated the medieval imagination, and are found in the exotic courts of the East visited by Mandeville and the conqueror Alexander.[49] In Lévi-Strauss's well-known phrase, birds truly were *bonnes à penser*. They were also, of course, *bonnes à manger*, and the diversely subtle techniques involved in their preparation for the table provide another perspective on their total assimilability to human needs.[50] 'Here it nediþ onliche to knowe,' Trevisa writes,

þat among oþir kynde of beestis generalliche foules ben more pure and liȝt and noble of substaunce and swift of meuynge and scharp of siȝt, of fleische of good digestioun and good sauor and turnynge into fedinge and holsom.[51]

[47] 'Bird Psalter' (Fitzwilliam Museum, Cambridge, MS 2–1954) and Alphonso Psalter (BL MS Add. 24686): see G. Evelyn Hutchinson, 'Attitudes towards Nature in Medieval England: The Alphonso and Bird Psalters', *Isis*, 65 (1974), 5–37; Sherborne Missal: see J. A. Herbert, *The Sherborne Missal*, Roxburghe Club (Oxford, 1920; most of the birds—several labelled with their English names—are between pp. 363 and 393).

[48] e.g. on the 'Cope of the Passion' (*c.*1300) now in the cathedral of St Bernard de Comminges: A. G. I. Christie, *English Medieval Embroidery* (Oxford, 1928), 127, pls. lxxvi–lxxx.

[49] Porus, king of India, has birds with beaks and claws of gold: 'And ay, when Porus liste, thir fewles thurgh craft of music walde synge after þaire kynde askede & was' (*The Prose Life of Alexander*, from the Thornton MS, ed. J. S. Westlake, EETS OS 143 (1913), 64–5). At the Great Khan of Cathay's court, Mandeville sees 'pecokes of gold and many other maner of dyuerse foules alle of gold and richely wrought and enameled. And men maken hem dauncen and syngen clappynge here wenges togydere and maken gret noyse' (*Mandeville's Travels*, ed. M. C. Seymour (Oxford, 1967), 157).

[50] See *Two Fifteenth-Century Cookery Books*, ed. Thomas Austin, EETS OS 91 (1888); W. E. Mead, *The English Medieval Feast* (London, 1931), esp. pp. 87–92. The splendid 'peacock feast' with which Robert Braunche regaled Edward III in 1349 is commemorated on his brass in St Margaret's church, King's Lynn: see Nikolaus Pevsner, *The Buildings of England: North-West and South Norfolk* (Harmondsworth, 1962), pl. facing pl. 64. From a later date, but still interestingly evocative of the themes in this chapter, are the remarks of Baldassare Pisanelli, a doctor in 16th-cent. Bologna, quoted by Piero Camporesi: 'Warblers cause peasants to become consumptive. They are not to be given to them, but shall be served to company of quality' (*Bread of Dreams: Food and Fantasy in Early Modern Europe*, trans. David Gentilcore (Cambridge, 1989), 169).

[51] *Properties*, i. 601–2. Perhaps there were some exceptions: 'Al maner of smale Byrdes be good and lyght of dygestyon, excepte sparowes, whiche be hard of dygestyon' (Andrew Boorde, *A Compendyous Regyment, or a Dyetary of Helth* (1542), ed. F. J. Furnivall, EETS ES 10 (1870), 270).

CHAPTER THREE

The Fox:
Laying Bare Deceit

IF BIRDS ARE of the air, medieval foxes are of the earth, earthy. They occupy a very different role. My purpose in this chapter is not to recapitulate Reynard scholarship in general. The field is far too wide, and much of it has already been covered in works like Kenneth Varty's pioneering iconographical study.[1] In addition, I have reserved my discussion of the fox as a hunted animal for Chapter 5. What I pursue here is the sort of 'body' that is assigned to the fox and the way it is used in various imaginative constructions.

The fox, Trevisa tells us, 'is a stynkynge beste and corrupte and corrumpeþ ofte þe places þat he wonyeþ inne contynualliche and makeþ hem bareyne'. Trevisa also describes how, when the fox is chased by hounds, it swings its tail, loaded with urine, at them, and the smell is so disgusting that the hounds afterwards leave it alone.[2] In Caxton's translation of the *Roman de Renart*, Reynard uses the same trick to blind his enemy, the wolf Isengrim, in their final contest.[3] The link between foxes and excrement was a pervasive one, for the Master of Game, in his hunting manual, tells how a fox

---

[1] Kenneth Varty, *Reynard the Fox: A Study of the Fox in Medieval English Art* (Leicester, 1967). See also Varty, 'The Death and Resurrection of Reynard in Medieval Literature and Art', *Nottingham Mediaeval Studies*, 10 (1966), 70–93; 'The Pursuit of Reynard in Mediaeval English Literature and Art', *Nottingham Mediaeval Studies*, 8 (1964), 62–81; 'Reynard the Fox and the Smithfield Decretals', *Journal of the Warburg and Courtauld Institutes*, 26 (1963), 347–54; and, for the Bestiary fox, Debra Hassig, *Medieval Bestiaries: Text, Image, Ideology* (Cambridge, 1995), 62–71. For the literary background of the Reynard stories, see R. Bossuat, *Le Roman de Renard* (Paris, 1957); J. Flinn, *Le Roman de Renard dans la littérature française et dans les littératures étrangères au Moyen Age* (Toronto, 1963), esp. pp. 673–88 for the currency of stories in England.

[2] *On the Properties of Things*, 3 vols. (Oxford, 1975–88), ii. 1263–4.

[3] William Caxton (trans.), *The History of Reynard the Fox*, ed. N. F. Blake, EETS OS 263 (1970), 99. Earlier, Isengrim complained that Reynard had blinded his children by pissing in their eyes (pp. 12–13).

will defecate in order to put the greyhounds off the scent.[4] Iron-ically, in Henry of Lancaster's *Livre de seyntz medicines*, which com-pares the sins that lurk in the human heart with a family of foxes skulking in their earth, it is the fox's stink that eventually gives him away: 'Et les renars ont tiel nature q'ils puent tresforte, siqe les chiens de tant meultz les chacent et preignont' ('And it is the nature of foxes that they smell very strongly, so that the dogs are better able to chase and catch them').[5]

The fox is thus associated with smell, the most primitive of the senses, and that smell, repugnant and polluting, surrounds it like a force field, keeping humans at bay. Foxes were also linked with darkness, the underground (as we have seen in Chapter 1), with evil, and with the Devil himself. 'Lowrence come lourand, for he lufit neuer licht', Henryson writes, in his fable of 'The Fox, the Wolf, and the Husbandman', conflating the predator's natural preference for the hours of darkness with its intrinsically evil, 'light-shunning' nature.[6] In another of his fables, 'The Fox, the Wolf, and the Cadger', a pedlar hails the apparently dead body of the fox lying in the middle of the road:

> 'Heir lyis the Deuyll', quod he, 'deid in ane dyke;
> Sic ane selcouth sau I not this seuin ʒeir.' (2063–4)

The fox's russet coat also prompted comparisons with Judas, the arch-betrayer, who was traditionally red-haired.[7] With so much evidence for the fox's vile and depraved nature, we might well expect the characteristic attitude towards it to be Bertilak's when he apologizes to Gawain for bringing nothing better back from his third day's hunting than 'þis foule fox felle—þe fende haf þe godez!' (line 1944).

---

[4] Edward, second Duke of York, *The Master of Game*, ed. W. A. and F. Baillie-Grohman (London, 1904), 36.

[5] Henry of Lancaster, *Le Livre de seyntz medicines*, ed. E. J. Arnould, Anglo-Norman Text Society, no. 2 (Oxford, 1940), 104.

[6] *The Poems of Robert Henryson*, ed. Denton Fox (Oxford, 1987), line 2294. Subse-quent references are given in the text. For the fox as devil, see L. Réau, *Iconographie de l'art chrétien*, 6 vols. (Paris, 1955–8), i. 111; *The Middle English 'Physiologus'*, ed. Hanneke Wirtjes, EETS OS 299 (1991), lines 261–312 (*Natura wulpis, Significaciones*), esp. 301–2: Ðe deuel is tus ðe [fox] ilik, I Mið iuele breides & wið swik . . .'.

[7] See e.g. *Le Roman de Renart*, ed. Jean Dufournet and Andrée Méline, 2 vols. (Paris, 1985), Branch II, lines 1065 ff.; Ruth Mellinkoff, *Outcasts: Signs of Otherness in Northern European Art of the Late Middle Ages*, 2 vols. (Berkeley and Los Angeles, 1993), i. 150–4.

However, medieval foxes in general could not be so easily relegated to the periphery. After exclaiming over the 'selcouth' of the dead fox in the road, Henryson's Cadger continues:

> 'I trou 3e haue bene tussillit with sum tyke,
> That garris 3ou ly sa still withoutin steir.
> Schir Foxe, in faith, 3e ar deir welcum heir;
> It is sum wyfis malisone, I trow,
> For pultrie pyking, that lychtit hes on 3ow.'   (2065–9)

The miracle of the Devil lying dead in a ditch is briskly undercut with images of a far homelier nature: the farmyard 'tyke' who has worried the fox to death, the wife who has cursed him for his 'pultrie pyking'. The reversal is signalled by the way the Cadger now greets the fox as a friend, displacing its uncanny powers on to the ill-wishing housewife. In the same vein, the Cadger quickly starts to think about the warm mittens he can make out of the fox's pelt. This inflow of the ordinary, the day-to-day, is entirely characteristic of a society in which real foxes were continually meddling with human attempts at subsistence—breaking into farmyards by day as well as by night,[8] and stealing precious chickens, ducks, and geese. Their entanglement in this intimate world is summarized in the image of the woman with her distaff pursuing the escaping fox, which appears over and over again in art as well as in literature.[9]

The fox is therefore an animal of the periphery which is at the same time inextricably meshed in the dealings of everyday life. It is this paradox which provides the key to its significance. For the fox, the arch-deceiver, becomes a way of articulating the presence of deceit, of false-seeming, within the various institutions of society.

How to recognize deceit, the debased reality beneath the outward dress, was a problem that continually exercised the medieval imagination.[10] If certain gestures or accoutrements confirmed one

---

[8] The fox in *The Nun's Priest's Tale* steals into the widow's yard by night (line 3218), but is still there, ready to make his capture, when it is 'passed undren of the day' (line 3222).

[9] e.g. 'Malkyn, with a dystaf in hir hand' (ibid. 3384). For illustrations of the scene, see e.g. BL MS Roy. 10 E IV (the Smithfield Decretals), fo. 175ʳ (reprod. in Varty, 'Reynard the Fox and the Smithfield Decretals', pl. 39). Many other examples are listed in Lilian M. C. Randall, *Images in the Margins of Gothic Manuscripts* (Berkeley and Los Angeles, 1966), 288: 'Woman and fox'.

[10] The difficulties involved in reading character and disposition from the outward appearance of bodies (as the science of Physiognomy attempted to do) are discussed in a

in a particular social role or social order—the penitent's kneeling position, the monk's tonsure, the knight's emblazoned shield, perhaps even the housewife's distaff—what would happen if a person simply copied those gestures or adopted those accoutrements: in effect crafted themselves a body to fit? Learning how to 'read' a deceitful body was a difficult skill. The fox's body might be thought of as a primer in that art, for in both stories and pictures there is always a point at which it is fully disclosed to the reader or viewer, so that its true foxiness becomes apparent. The fox in Henryson's 'The Trial of the Fox', brought to answer charges before the court of the lion, first tries to disguise himself in human fashion by pulling his hood down over his eyes. However, unmistakable bodily signs reveal that he is actually a pitiless killer:

> Thy gorrie gumis and thy bludie snout;
> The woll, the flesche, 3it stikkis on thy teith . . .   (1084–5)

In William Caxton's translation of the Middle Dutch version of the *Roman de Renart*, this theme of deceit and how one may see through it is explicitly addressed. Ironically, it is Reynard himself who puts the matter most clearly: 'For ther lyue many in the world that seme otherwise outward than they be withinne. I wolde that god shewde openly euery mans mysdedes and alle theyr trespaces stoden wreton in theyr forehedes.'[11] And he goes on, with sublime ingenuousness, 'I can not flatre, I wil allewey shewe openly my heed' (p. 63). At least the second half of that statement carries a kind of truth: the trouble is that the animals in *Reynard the Fox* are so blinded by their own lusts and vices that they fail to recognize that 'heed' when it is right in front of them.

The narrator of *Reynard the Fox* begins with an explanation of how a reading of his tale may prove useful in real life:

In this historye ben wreton the parables, goode lerynge, and dyuerse poyntes to be merkyd, by whiche poyntes men maye lerne to come to the subtyl knoweleche of suche thynges as dayly ben vsed and had in the counseyllys of lordes and prelates gostly and worldly, and also emonge marchauntes and other comone peple. And this book is maad for nede and

---

stimulating article by Robert Pope, 'A Sly Toad, Physiognomy and the Problem of Deceit: Henryson's *The Paddok and the Mous*', *Neophilologus*, 63 (1979), 461–8.

[11] Caxton, *Reynard*, 62. Subsequent references are given in the text. I have imposed a modern system of punctuation in quotations.

prouffyte of all god folke As fer as they in redynge or heerynge of it shal mowe vnderstande and fele the forsayd subtyl deceytes that dayly ben vsed in the worlde, not to thentente that men shold vse them but that euery man shold eschewe and kepe hym from the subtyl false shrewis that they be not deceyuyd. Thenne who that wyll haue the very vnderstandyng of this mater, he muste ofte and many tymes rede in thys boke and ernestly and diligently marke wel that he redeth. For it is sette subtylly, lyke as ye shal see in redyng of it, and not ones to rede it... (p. 6)

According to the narrator, deceit is everywhere—among religious men as well as among secular, among lords as well as among common people—and to survive in this world a person needs to be able to recognize it and deal with it, without being tainted by it himself. This skill he will acquire by poring over the stories in this book, which will only yield their full meaning after they have been read and studied many times. Tongue-in-cheek the narrator may be, but the tales that follow amply fulfil his promise of 'subtyl' matter (a word that is emphasized through constant repetition in the quoted passage).

The plot of *Reynard the Fox* revolves around the efforts of various animals to bring the fox back with them to the court of the lion so that he can stand trial for his crimes. The fox invariably eludes their devices, neatly snaring them by means of their own weaknesses and returning triumphant to his own stronghold of Maleperduys, which, with its 'so many by or side holes' (p. 47), is itself an image of his own multifarious resources. All the time, he counters supposedly higher modes of discourse with a basic, often brutal, earthy reality.

One discourse that comes under attack is that of religion. The religious milieu was a particularly rich one for the fox to exploit, since it relied so heavily on an iconic currency. Kenneth Varty describes a real-life burlesque in which the French king Philip the Fair had men dress up as foxes in order to poke fun at the pope Boniface VIII: 'First the actor would chant the epistle for the day as if he were an ordinary priest, then he would put on a mitre and then a pontifical tiara. Dressed like this he would run after men pretending to be hens and geese.'[12] In *Reynard the Fox* the burlesque is carried a stage further, for appeal is made to features of the fox's own, idiosyn-

---

[12] Varty, *Reynard the Fox*, 58.

cratic body. For example, when Reynard is accused of disguising himself in order to pick off Chauntecleer's numerous sons and daughters, his ally Grymbart the badger defends him in these terms: 'he eteth no more than ones a day, he lyueth as a recluse, he chastiseth his body and wereth a sherte of heer . . . [He] hath bylded a cluse.' All these details are true, but this simply goes to show that appearances can deceive. If the fox, who *appears* to be a religious hermit, is in fact no such thing, how does one 'read' a corresponding *human* body?

This juxtaposing of two contrasting modes of discourse, the spiritual and the physical, perhaps helps to explain the many apparently cruel disfigurings and mutilations which feature both in *Reynard the Fox* and in the Reynard tradition in general and seem to have been an important part of that tradition's popular appeal. The fox mocks Bruin the bear, who has just wrenched himself free from the cleft tree-trunk in which he had trapped himself when he delved into it for promised honey: 'In to what ordre wille ye goo that were this newe hode, were be ye a monke or an abbot. He that shoef your crowne, hath nyped of your eeris; ye haue lost your toppe and don of your gloues' (p. 18). The bear, according to the fox, has allowed himself to be tonsured and has taken off his gloves, badges of his secular identity. In fact, in struggling to get free the bear has scalped himself and torn the skin off his paws: the text expatiates on his pain and disfiguring bloodiness. Later, Reynard will depart on a pretend pilgrimage to Rome carrying a pilgrim's bag made from the bear's skin, and shoes skinned from the feet of Isengrim and his wife (pp. 43–4). To a modern reader, such jokes are distressingly brutal. Yet perhaps that violence is a product of the collision between high and low, as a privileged iconic language falls victim to the fox's earthy demotic. The bear has been mutilated so that, with his scalped head and bared hands, he looks like a monk or an abbot—but perhaps the religious man in turn is guilty of an excision, a forgetting of that primary bodiliness upon which everything else rests. A discourse that tries to establish itself in opposition to the body and its needs will always be open to this kind of assault.

Another tale that plays upon this theme is that of Tibert the cat. Reynard uses Tibert's love of mice to lure him into the priest's barn, where a trap has been set for him. Tibert is cornered by the priest and the priest's 'wife' and only manages to escape by clawing off one of the priest's testicles.

The foxe stode wythoute to fore the hole and herde alle thyse wordes, and lawhed so sore that he vnnethe coude stonde, he spack thus al softly, dame Iulock be al stylle and lete your grete sorowe synke. Al hath the preest loste one of his stones it shal not hyndre hym he shal doo wyth you wel ynowh ther is in the world many a chapel in whiche is rongen but one belle. (pp. 22–3)

In one mocking phrase, Reynard links the illicit sexual activity of the priest with the holy rites that are heralded by the ringing of the bells in the chapel. The passage illustrates a further characteristic of the tales in *Reynard the Fox*: as well as being about *actions*, frequently of the most audacious kind, they are also about *language* and the role it plays in revealing, or occluding, the truth.

The fox is the supreme master of language: he alone among the characters is multi-voiced, able to employ a variety of different registers and address a range of different listeners. Here, his words of 'comfort' to the priest's wife, dame Iulock, are not in fact directed at her but at us, the audience, who are invited to share in the joke. The fox's mediating role appears in this passage in his proleptic laughter; in a misericord in Bristol illustrating the story it is shown by his actual presence on the scene: instead of standing outside the barn listening to the kerfuffle (as the text relates), he is inside, a grinning figure planted four-square next to the priest's wife—a small, malevolent master of ceremonies.[13] When, later, the fox manages to convince the king and his court that he is truly penitent and ready to undertake a pilgrimage to seek pardon for his sins, we hear him talking to himself in a way that is strikingly at odds with his outward demeanour: '[he] wente and shewde hym outeward wysely. But he laughed in his herte that alle they brought hym forth whiche had a lytyl to fore been with hym so wroth' (p. 45).

The problem for the other animals is how to deal with this protean manipulation, for, as the rabbit and the rook lament, Reynard 'can bywrappe and couere his falshede, that his wordes seme as trewe as the gospel' (p. 67). Sometimes, too, he switches to another language in order to confuse: he opens his 'confession' to Grymbart in Latin (p. 25), and is immediately told to speak in English so he can be understood.[14] By contrast, we often see the fox's opponents

[13] Illustrated ibid., pl. 49.
[14] The fox also begins his defence at the court of the lion with the (garbled) Latin phrase, 'In nomine pater, criste, filij' (p. 29).

exposed as poor players of the language game, content to bandy worn-out counters which bear no relation to the real situation. The bear, urged by the fox not to eat too greedily of the honeycombs in the cleft tree, responds with a complacent cliché which his behaviour immediately contradicts: 'wene ye that I were a fole: mesure is good in alle mete' (p. 15). It is not only cliché that signals poverty of linguistic resource, but any kind of learned formula in which unthinking trust is placed. Before he sets out on his doomed quest for the fox, the bear boasts to the lion, who has warned him to beware of Reynard's feints: 'what good lord late it allone: deceyueth me the foxe, so haue I ylle lerned my casus [elementary lesson, ABC]. I trowe he shal come to late to mocque me' (p. 12). A similar joke features in the story of the trick played by the mare upon Isengrim the wolf. The wolf wants to eat the mare's foal, and is told by her that its price is written on the sole of her foot, which he is invited to inspect. He launches into a boastful account of his great learning: 'I can weel frenshe latyn englissh and duche, I haue goon to scole at oxenford I haue also wyth olde and auncyent doctours ben in the audyence and herde plees . . . ' (p. 59). None of this apparent erudition saves him from being severely kicked in the face by the mare, to the delight of the fox, who asks him what the writing was: 'I trowe it was cantum, for I herde you synge me thoughte fro ferre.'

The fox is infinitely more inventive and flexible in his use of language than his opponents are, but the difficulty for them does not stop there. He is also a prolific story-spinner, and weaves his stories out of the very elements his victims present him with, running rings around the controlling discourse as he does so. The tactic is shown in his attack on Cuwart the hare, which the panther relates to the assembled court:

he [Reynard] promysed to Cuwart and sayde he wold teche hym his credo, and make hym a good chapelayn, he made hym goo sytte bytwene his legges and sange and cryde lowde Credo. Credo: my waye laye ther by there that I herde this songe. Tho wente I ner and fonde maister reynard that had lefte that he fyrst redde and songe and bygan to playe his olde playe. For he [Reynard] had caught kywaert by the throte, and had I not that tyme comen he sholde haue taken his lyf from hym like as ye hiere may see on kywaert the hare the fresshe wounde yet . . . (p. 8)

Reynard, the good singing teacher, solicits intimate contact with his pupil's body so that he can school it to produce the right sounds.

The throat, through which the song of the 'litel clergeon' rises in *The Prioress's Tale* (line 548), was the key to good performance: it might suffer damage if an untrained singer forced a note too vigorously. Cuwart's throat does indeed suffer damage—but not in quite that way.[15]

In a later episode, Reynard manages to convince the king and queen of the existence of hidden treasure: although these jewels are purely imaginary, they have an appreciable effect upon the king and queen's behaviour—crucially, their behaviour *towards* Reynard: 'And by cause he had made them to vnderstonde that he had sente these Iewellis to them, though they neuer had them, yet they thankyd hym. And prayd hym to helpe that they myght haue them' (p. 88). Perhaps most impressive of all is the fox's ability to re-present an event so that we, his audience, are seduced through his wit into accepting it on his own terms. The re-reading of the priest's misfortune at the claws of Tibert is one example: another occurs in the final combat between Reynard and Isengrim, when the fox consoles his opponent for having one of his eyes scratched out: 'For whan ye here after shal slepe ye nede not to shette but one wyndowe where another muste shette two' (p. 102).

How, then, can one defend oneself against the fox, with his disconcerting ability to hijack the very fictions in which he appears? Part of the answer is provided by the narrator of *Reynard the Fox*, in terms accessible to those dutiful ideal readers the text itself calls into being: to see clearly and act wisely, one must avoid giving in to unreasoning passions and appetites. The animals who fall victim to the fox invariably do so because a vice such as greed, pride, or anger has clouded their judgement. The bear is trapped in the tree-trunk through his lust for honey, Tibert is caught in the priest's snare through his hunger for 'fat mice'. Bellyn the ram is persuaded to carry 'letters' to the king (actually, the hare's head inside a bag) because he is vain and avid for recognition: 'I shal be in the court gretly preysed whan it is knowen that I can so wel endyte and make a

---

[15] For medieval singing lessons, see Bruce W. Holsinger, 'Pedagogy, Violence, and the Subject of Music: Chaucer's *Prioress's Tale* and the Ideologies of "Song"', in Wendy Scase, Rita Copeland, and David Lawton (eds.), *New Medieval Literatures 1* (Oxford, 1997). Several marginal illustrations show Cuwart scanning his music-sheet while the fox, sitting behind him, appreciatively nibbles on his ear (Randall, *Images*, XL. 193–5).

lettre' (p. 49). That is not the whole answer, though, and the fox's double-dealing remains, dyed into the fabric of the tales about him. To unpick it one would have to unravel the entire fiction, and then there would be no *roman*, no speech at all.

In Henryson's fables of the trickster fox, this ambiguity is explored with marvellous subtlety. As in Caxton's retelling, the fox provides an earthy counterpoint to the discourse of spirituality. In 'The Fox and the Wolf', he begins by lamenting the usual fate of thieves such as himself, and, roundly accusing his 'cankerit conscience', resolves to make his confession to 'Freir Volff Waitskaith', newly come from the cloister. The details of the fox's confession closely follow actual practice: like a genuine penitent, he removes his hood, sinks humbly to his knees, and opens his account with the traditional *Benedicite*.

> 'Weill,' quod the volff, 'sit doun vpon thy kne.'
> And he doun bair-heid sat full humilly,
> And syne began with 'Benedicitie'. (691–3)

The fox has already greeted the wolf as a holy confessor:

> 'ȝe ar the lanterne and the sicker way
> Suld gyde sic sempill folk as me to grace;
> ȝour bair feit and ȝour russet coull off gray,
> ȝour lene cheik, ȝour paill and pietious face,
> Schawis to me ȝour perfite halines.' (677–81)

The wolf bears all the superficial signs of 'perfite halines': his feet are (naturally) bare, his (literal) hairshirt is rough and shaggy, and his face is pale and drawn (because of his perpetual hunger—the mainspring of the action in several of the stories about him). Once again, an idiosyncratic body becomes the focus of play upon the theme of deceit. Skilled reading is needed to disentangle appearance from reality, and then again, what if this seeming confessor were human...?

Freir Volff Waitskaith duly hears the fox confess to the killing of hens and lambs, and imposes a penance on him: he is to give up eating meat until Easter. (At the fox's plea, this is then reduced: he may now eat meat, but only twice a week.) The fox makes his way to the seashore, where he rejects the idea of catching fish (which would be permitted him) and instead seizes a kid, 'baptizing' it by ducking it in the water and declaring 'Ga doun, schir Kid, cum vp, schir Salmond agane' (line 751). Given this bare outline of the plot, we would read the fable as a parody of religious practices, and cast the fox as the arch-joker, busily burlesquing the spiritual ideals that these practices represent. However, Henryson subtly complicates our response in several ways.

First, given the presence of a completely bogus confessor, we might expect the fox's confession to be cram-full of lies. We are in fact invited to anticipate this with the description of his preparation, which invokes the kind of masquing disguise (the hood) we have met before, and caps it with the forthright adjective 'traitor':

> Seand this volff, this wylie tratour tod
> On kneis fell, with hude in to his nek...   (670–1)

However, what the fox confesses is all completely true. He is entirely honest both about what he has done (killing hens and lambs) and—equally important in confession—about the thoughts he has harboured in his mind:

> 'For to repent my mynd can not concluid,
> Bot off this thing, that I haif slane sa few.'   (703–4)

Asked by the wolf if he has any intention of amending his behaviour in the future (repentance, and a firm commitment to reform, were essential to the giving of absolution), he continues:

> 'And I forbeir, how sall I leif, allace,
> Haifand nane vther craft me to defend?
> Neid causis me to steill quhair euer I wend:
> I eschame to thig, I can not work, 3e wait,
> ðit wald I fane pretend to gentill stait.'   (707–11)

Again, this is no more than the truth, as we are drawn to acknowledge by the complicitous *3e wait*. The fox plays nicely on the word 'craft', often used (by humans) to refer to his own thieving activities: there really is 'nane vther craft'—no useful, productive skill—that he would be able to learn. Defined, and confined, by his body, there is no 'wirk', in the human sense, that he could conceivably be made to do. And if the things he *can* do are denied him, he will simply not survive.

When we see the fox standing on the beach contemplating the waves, the vivid description of their furious surging means that we empathize with his fear and bafflement, and realize how impossible it is for him to become a 'fischar':

> Bot quhen he saw the walterand wallis woude,
> All stonist still in to ane stair he stude . . .   (736–7)

Hemmed around with prohibitions, the fox responds in the one way that will guarantee his survival: in grabbing the kid, he takes the controlling discourse by the scruff of its neck. Now he is making it speak in *his* terms. Of course, his triumph doesn't last, for the goatherd, coming upon Lowrence warming his full belly in the sun, quickly shoots an arrow through him. Yet it is the fox who has the last word, and that word points back to the witty confusion of discourses he has accomplished in his fable:

> 'Me think na man may speik ane word in play,
> Bot now on dayis in ernist it is tane.'   (770–1)

During the course of the story, we have not been allowed to distance ourselves from the fox and his experiences. Now his farewell message invites us to consider the very way we have been reading his tale. Like Caxton's Reynard, Henryson's Lowrence makes a play for the role of narrator, insinuating himself into the actual devices of the fiction in which he appears. And of course what he says is genuinely challenging to human notions of superiority and difference: how can we blame him for shunning honest labour and establishing himself on the periphery when his body dictates to him that he should do exactly that? The narrator of *Reynard the Fox* uses a similar argument to explain his hero's magnetic attraction to hens: 'he coude not refrayne hym self: *that whiche clevid by the bone myght not out of the flesshe*, though he shold be hanged, he coude not lete the lokyng after the polayll as fer as he myght see them' (p. 28; my italics).

   In Henryson's fable of 'The Fox, the Wolf, and the Husbandman' play with the fox's identity continues as he takes his place within a miniature social system. This system's gradations are marked by forms of address, for, as Denton Fox points out, 'The wolf uses the familiar *thou* in speaking to both the fox and the husbandman; the husbandman uses the respectful *ȝe* to both the wolf and the fox; the fox uses *ȝe* to the wolf, but *thou* to the husbandman.'[16] This use of language appears to mirror established social proprieties

---

[16] Ed. cit. 303, n. to line 2316.

(although of course it inverts the usual order by placing the beasts above the man), but in reality it is not based on any model of precedence—however peculiar—but on sheer brute domination. The husbandman is daunted by the sudden appearance of the wolf in front of his plough-oxen: he 'worthit sumdeill agast' (line 2257) and, after the wolf's challenge to him, 'wes in ane felloun fray' (line 2261). The respectful 'Schir' with which he begins his speeches to the wolf is therefore an attempt to mollify him, and implies fear at being in a dangerous situation rather than ingrained deference to a social superior.

However, although the husbandman is consigned to the bottom of the heap by the fox and the wolf, in the wolf's argument that he should keep his 'promise' and surrender his oxen he is treated as though he were a lord or a king, whose word might justly be expected to have binding force:

> 'Weill,' quod the volff, 'I hecht the, be my hand,
> ðone carlis word as he wer king sall stand.'   (2250–1)

He goes on to batter at the husbandman's resistance with words that evoke the ideals of truth and loyalty, qualities that any lord must possess:

> 'Carll,' quod the volff, 'ane lord, and he be leill,
> That schrinkis for schame, or doutis to be repruuit—
> His sau is ay als sickker as his seill.
> Fy on the leid that is not leill and lufit!
> Thy argument is fals, and eik contrufit,
> For it is said in prouerb: ' "But lawte
> All vther vertewis ar nocht worth ane fle." '   (2280–6)

The husbandman bases his defence on the fact that he is *not* a lord or a king and may therefore make assertions and then deny them without penalty:[17]

> 'Schir,' said the husband, 'remember of this thing:
> Ane leill man is not tane at halff ane taill.
> I may say and ganesay; I am na king.
> Quhair is ðour witnes that hard I hecht thame haill?'   (2287–90)

---

[17] For evidence that the husbandman's argument is a valid one, see Craig McDonald, 'The Perversion of Law in Robert Henryson's Fable of The Fox, the Wolf, and the Husbandman', *MÆ* 49 (1980), 244–53.

This is the cue for the fox, who has been lurking in the thicket, to appear. He promptly gets himself appointed arbiter, 'iuge amycabill' (line 2310), and takes a bribe of several fat hens from the husbandman, promising in return to make his 'querrell sure' (line 2334). To the wolf he offers, in place of the oxen, a delicious 'cabok', a 'somer cheis, baith fresche and fair' (line 2355), and the wolf, after a token show of reluctance, asks to be taken to see it. The husbandman thankfully makes his escape, and the fox and the wolf start off on their journey together. Meanwhile the day, which had begun with the early rising of the husbandman, turns to darkness, 'neir midnycht and mair' (line 2377), the naturally active time for both animals.

The fox and the wolf's 'noble' identity is scrupulously maintained through their travelling. A line such as

> Throw woddis waist thir freikis on fute can fair   (2376)

beautifully preserves this double vision of them, for in it the two beasts making their way (of course) on foot, and instinctively shunning human habitations, momentarily become warriors, like Gawain, penetrating the sort of uncharted wilderness that is traditionally the testing ground for knightly virtues. The parody is marvellously detailed, in its mimicking of the alliterative long line, and in its introduction of the word *freikis*, whose primary allusion is to the old heroic tradition.[18] The place that these 'senȝeours' are heading for is, moreover, a 'manure place' (line 2387)—although the fox's interest in it is limited to the 'draw well' in its grounds. When they have arrived, Lowrence keeps up the feudal fiction by suggesting to the wolf that the 'caboik' he can see suspended in the water in the well is of such surpassing quality that it 'Micht be ane present to ony lord or king' (line 2398).

The 'cheese' in the well provides a brilliant consummation to the story's action. To begin with, of course, it is rather a come-down for a noble 'senȝeour' such as the wolf to lust after a 'cabok':

> 'Ƃone wer mair meit for sic ane man as me.'   (2403)

The fox goes on to hymn the 'cabok' in terms that wittily conflate its regal image and homely, down-to-earth reality. It is as perfectly round as a great lord's seal, but at the same time it resembles a turnip

---

[18] See *MED*, *freke* n., examples of usage cited under sense (a), 'a brave man, a warrior, a man-at-arms'.

because of its white colour and is so heavy that in trying to pull it up he has lost the nails from his toes. The play is upon notions of substance: seen two-dimensionally the 'cabok' is like a seal, but when the fox tries to grasp it it is suddenly apprehended mightily in the round. And of course the crowning joke is that there is no delectable cheese at all, simply the moon's reflection in the water—an illusion to which the greedy wolf falls prey with satisfying predictability.

Solidity and vacancy, substance and illusion—these are the themes that run through the tale. What is especially impressive is their particular embodiment in its language. For instance, the words *leill* and *seill* occur several times. Straightforwardly, like true coin, they should convey value, referring as they do to the quality of loyalty and to the instrument which is the pledge of it. However, in the course of the narrative both words are emptied of meaning—*leill* through its misuse by the wolf, who does not know the first thing about personal honour or fidelity, and *seill* through its application to the illusory cheese, which lacks substance entirely. Also linked in the chain of assonance is the word *taill*. It is upon the fox's tail that the wolf and the husbandman make their pledge to abide by his decision:

> The volff braid furth his fute, the man his hand,
> And on the toddis taill sworne thay ar to stand.   (2313–14)

However, they could hardly have made a worse choice of body-part, for, as I mentioned at the beginning of the chapter, the fox habitually uses his urine-soaked tail to blind his foes, by swinging it in their faces.[19] The *taill*, therefore, is the very opposite of a guarantee of good faith—the word joins with *leill* and *seill* in its subversive implications.

In the fable as a whole, the body is invoked several times as the substantive pledge behind verbal promises. The husbandman points out that he did not set his *hand* to his oath that the wolf should have his oxen (line 2277); the wolf's temporary amity with the fox as they set out together in search of the cheese is marked by their walking

---

[19] Caxton (*Reynard*, 70) uses the phrase 'he has stryked hem with his tayl' when he is describing the way in which, by the end, the fox has played false with every one of his allies. N. F. Blake offers as a translation 'he has deceived them in the end', and notes that the expression does not occur elsewhere in English, but it seems clear that the reference is to the fox's blinding trick, which is mentioned frequently enough in other contexts (such as the hunting manuals) to suggest that it was widely known about.

'hand in hand' (line 2371). However, hands may not be quite what they seem, for, although the wolf seems to be able to show a 'hand' whenever it suits him, it is not a *hand* but a *foot* that he brings forth to the pledge he and the husbandman make on the fox's tail. The tale works to problematize the distinction between animals and humans in so far as this is based on physical difference. In the 'hovering and equivocal relationship' which it proposes, bodies themselves appear to forgo both closure and continuance.[20]

Such a reading, which highlights shifting, unstabilized identities, can help us to appreciate Henryson's *moralitates*, which have always provoked debate among critics. J. A. Burrow, for instance, writes: 'most present-day readers . . . find his Moralitates at best unpleasing and at worst desperately confusing; and I think they are justified on the whole, despite the best efforts of Professor Fox and Professor MacQueen to prove the contrary.'[21] However, the *moralitates* start to make sense once one abandons the humanocentric perspective the text of the fables has been working to undermine. As C. David Benson explains:

The frequent gaps between story and moral are deliberate and serve to make the reader aware of other tensions and conflicts in the work. . . . By exploiting the dissonance between story and moral to lead the reader into the deeper complexities of his work, [Henryson] teaches us not what to think, but how to think.[22]

Elision of the boundary between human and animal characterizes the *moralitas* to 'The Fox, the Wolf, and the Cadger'. Here men, in their greed to cram their 'sacks' with worldly possessions, run into a death that corresponds to the one the fox of the fables inflicts upon his victims:

> Ʒit suddandlie men seie it oft disseuer
> With thame that trowis oft to fill the sek—
> Deith cummis behind and nippis thame be the nek.   (2221–3)

---

[20] The phrase is Douglas Gray's: *Robert Henryson* (Leiden, 1979), 74.

[21] J. A. Burrow, 'Henryson's *The Preaching of the Swallow*', *Essays in Criticism*, 25 (1975), 35.

[22] C. David Benson, 'O Moral Henryson', in Robert F. Yeager (ed.), *Fifteenth-Century Studies: Recent Essays* (Hamden, Conn., 1984), 217. Also Douglas Gray: 'The "dark" moralities . . . involve the reader in the difficult but pleasing search for significances under the enigmatic surface, and in the teasing out of moral implications' (*Robert Henryson*, 128).

The lightning assault of death is like the swift bite on the back of the neck with which the fox dispatches a hen or a goose. This 'meaning' coexists with the stated equivalences of the *moralitas*, in which the fox is the world and its temptations, the wolf is man, and the Cadger death. The effect is to make us rethink the whole structure of differences on which we had previously relied, as we realize that *we* are just as susceptible to the downrush of fate as any farmyard fowl.

The same provocative and unsettling play of 'bodies' can be observed in the *moralitas* to 'The Preaching of the Swallow' (which Burrow describes as 'no worse than unpleasing'). Fable and moral are held together by the biblical image of the chaff blowing in the wind—for the birds the 'calff' is the false corn the fowler scatters to deceive them; for humans it is the 'gudis vane', as airy and valueless as chaff, that they cling to in their sinful blindness. When the birds are killed in the fable, they are seen, for the moment, almost as human:

> Allace, it wes grit hart sair for to se
> That bludie bowcheour beit thay birdis doun,
> And for till heir, quhen thay wist weill to de,
> Thair cairfull sang and lamentatioun.
> Sum with ane staf he straik to eirth on swoun,
> Off sum the heid, off sum he brak the crag,
> Sum half on lyfe he stoppit in his bag.   (1874–80)

It is not only the grieving response of the narrator ('grit hart sair') that humanizes here, but such details as the vocalized lament of the birds, their apparent foreknowledge of their fate, and the disconcerting attention both to the individual parts of their tiny bodies (heads, necks) and to the time-span of their dying ('Sum half on lyfe he stoppit in his bag'). This passage finds its echo in the *moralitas*. Here it is the fate of the human soul that is being described:

> Quhat help is than this calf, thir gudis vane,
> Quhen thow art put in Luceferis bag,
> And brocht to hell, and hangit be the crag?   (1934–6)

Henryson constantly plays with these shifting perspectives, disturbing our expectations of closure to brilliant and unsettling effect.

The fox, therefore, has a unique role within medieval culture. In one sense it is an animal of the periphery, banished to the margins by its evil smell and its association with the devil. Yet it is also an intimate neighbour, lurking in the cottager's cabbage-patch in *The Nun's Priest's Tale*, and, in a comparable move, insinuating itself into the heart of texts, where it makes frequent bids for the role of narrator and generates fictions which cast doubt upon the whole system of inside and outside, human and far-from-human. In the end, even its most repellent qualities can be assimilated in a view of humanness, for in a primary sense it is not just the fox's body but *every* human body that is 'cursit carioun', earth-bound and unclean, the 'flesche crabbed' that has to be tamed and purified in the school of penance. In death, too, all bodies are alike: an early fifteenth-century will requests that 'My stynkynge carion . . . be Buried in þe chirchehawe of Bedford'.[23] Death has no room for fastidiousness, and none of our articulations of status or hierarchy can save us from finally being reduced to the same level as everything we had once despised.

Again it is Henryson who presents this most tellingly. His fable of 'The Fox and the Wolf' ended, as we saw, with the fox being shot by the goatherd whose kid he had eaten. 'The Trial of the Fox' opens where that tale left off, with the fox's son discovering his father's body by its putrefying smell:

> As nature will, seikand his meit be sent,
> Off cace he fand his fatheris carioun,
> Nakit, new slane . . .   (810–12)

The body is 'nakit' because the goatherd has skinned it, taking the pelt away in recompense for his slain kid. However, in a brilliant conflation of imagery, the body is also that of a dead knight on a battlefield where the 'pilours' have been at work[24]—and for a second, too, the son is caught and held in the same chivalric stasis:

> and till him is he went,
> Tuke vp his heid, and on his kne fell doun . . .   (812–13)

The tableau is posed only for an instant, of course, as the son, instead of lamenting, roundly thanks God for 'that conclusioun', which means he can at last come into his inheritance.

---

[23] F. A. Page-Turner, *The Bedfordshire Wills and Administrations Proved at Lambeth Palace etc.* (London, 1914), ii. 20. See *MED, careine* n., 1(a).

[24] Cf. *The Knight's Tale*, lines 1005–8: 'To ransake in the taas of bodyes dede, | Hem for to strepe of harneys and of wede, | The pilours diden bisynesse and cure | After the bataille and disconfiture.'

The medieval fox plays across the categories, a dangerous free radical. In the stories about him, everything and everyone becomes involved in a Bakhtinian process of endless change and revivification. Bodies freely metamorphose, bits of one pass to another—as food, as instrument, as clothing—but there is no sense of final destruction because all mingles together and is reanimated, much as the fox himself steps freshly out in each new Reynard story. (The fox in 'The Trial of the Fox' is supposed to be the son of the one in the previous fable, but he is essentially the same persona.) Bakhtin's description of the grotesque body—'It is never finished, never completed; it is continually built, created, and builds and creates another body'[25]—could certainly be applied to the bodily reapportionings of the Reynard cycle, and also to the accretive development of the stories themselves. The fox's 'history' is never closed— there is always more that might be said about him—and so it is perhaps appropriate that he will reappear in this book, in another guise, in the chapter on Hunting, below.[26]

[25] Mikhail Bakhtin, *Rabelais and his World*, trans. Hélène Iswolsky (Bloomington, Ind., 1984), 317.

[26] The fox's story also continues into Renaissance times: in Spenser's *Prosopopoia, or Mother Hubberd's Tale* (*Works*, ed. Edwin Greenlaw, Charles Grosvenor Osgood, Frederick Morgan Padelford, and Ray Heffner, *The Minor Poems*, vol. ii (Baltimore, 1947), 101–40), a fox accompanies an ape to court, where he dons various disguises in order to trick people out of their money. The pair progress to stealing the skin and crown of the lion, whom the ape impersonates as king of the beasts. When the lion is finally woken and alerted to the deception, 'The Foxe, first Author of that treacherie, | He did vncase, and then away let flie' (lines 1379–80); by contrast, the ape has his tail and half his ears cut off.

CHAPTER FOUR

The Heraldic Image

BIRDS AND FOXES—and other creatures too—are the subject of playful manipulation in medieval art and literature. Such play is founded on an awareness of bodily idiosyncrasy and takes its cue from the perceived contrast between particular animal bodies and those of humans. Animals, though, can be brought into a more intimate relationship with people, used to enhance an individual's, or a group's, sense of identity or to assert particular values. The modern urban Rottweiler, Sir Geoffrey Luttrell's powerful war-horse, or the svelte leopards attending the Magi in the *Très Riches Heures* of the duc de Berry are all examples. This chapter examines the partnering of man and signifying animal within the discourse of heraldry, 'that peculiar form of reification', as Lee Patterson describes it, 'whereby the names of the nobility were related totemically to the natural world, especially to animals'.[1] I explore some of the ways in which particular works of art and literature are informed by the dynamics of this relationship.

Heraldry, of course, is not just about animals. The total field of heraldic imagery included all kinds of devices—inanimate objects and geometrical divisions and patterns as well as those taken from the world of nature. However, images of animals—and birds—seem to have been accorded particular value: as John Blount puts it, in his translation of the heraldic writer Nicholas Upton's *De studio militari*, 'amonge all signes or markes of the worlde those be more worthy wiche be quicke and lyuyng'.[2] Certainly, living creatures as heraldic signs offered far richer possibilities for the sort of ironic play upon the theme of identity which, as I will show, engaged writers and artists at the time.

---

[1] Lee Patterson, *Chaucer and the Subject of History* (London, 1991), 192.
[2] Bodl. MS Eng. misc. d. 227, fo. 117^r.

Patterson's comment above is applied to Chaucer's milieu—the late fourteenth century in England. By this time, heraldry had developed far beyond its origins in the first half of the twelfth century, when knights started to bear motifs on their shields to identify themselves in tournaments, to become an intricately articulated set of rules and conventions.[3] The court of Richard II, in particular, seems to have immersed itself in heraldic culture. Richard's lavish distribution of his own badge of the white hart was famous—and, later, notorious—and the king also involved himself personally in decisions concerning the bearing of heraldic devices. Froissart records how, during his campaign in Ireland, he assumed the ancient arms of Edward the Confessor, at the expense of the English leopards and fleurs-de-lis:

> And therfore our soverayne lord kyng Richarde this yere past, whan he was in Irelande, in all his armories and devyses, he lefte the beryng of the armes of Englande, as the lybardes and flour delyces quarterly, and bare the armes of this saynt Edwarde that is a crosse patent, golde, and goules, with four white martenettes in the felde: whereof it was said the yrisshmen were well pleased, and the soner they enclyned to hym.[4]

Richard also made several rulings in heraldic disputes, including that in the well-known case of *Scrope* v. *Grosvenor* in 1386, when two individuals laid claim to the same coat of arms. Chaucer's involvement in this case is also on record, since he affirmed in a deposition that the Scropes had long borne the arms that the Grosvenors were making out to be their own.[5] Interest in heraldry also showed itself in the decoration of palaces and other noble buildings with heraldic motifs,[6] and in the patronage of painters of armorial bearings such as

---

[3] For concise accounts of medieval heraldry, see: Rodney Dennys, *The Heraldic Imagination* (London, 1975); Dennys, *Heraldry and the Heralds* (London, 1982); W. H. St John Hope, *A Grammar of English Heraldry*, 2nd edn., rev. Anthony Wagner (Cambridge, 1953); Anthony Wagner, *Heraldry in England* (Harmondsworth, 1946).

[4] *The Chronicle of Froissart*, trans. Sir John Bourchier, Lord Berners, introd. W. P. Ker, 6 vols. (London, 1901–3), vi. 155.

[5] Martin M. Crow and Clair C. Olson (eds.), *Chaucer Life-Records* (Oxford, 1966), 370–4; see also Patterson, *Chaucer*, 180–5, 194–6. For Richard's general interest in heraldic questions, see Dennys, *Heraldry and the Heralds*, 104–13.

[6] The 'King's House' at Richard's new (but never completed) palace at Windsor Manor had a chapel decorated with white harts with gilded horns (Gervase Mathew, *The Court of Richard II* (London, 1968), 34), while the Bywater Tower in the Tower of London had floor tiles showing leopards and the white hart (E. W. Tristram, *English Wall Painting of the Fourteenth Century* (London, 1955), 36–7).

Gilbert Prince.[7] Meanwhile, heraldic culture was codified in treatises such as the *Tractatus de armis* of John de Bado Aureo, written at
the request of Richard's queen, Anne of Bohemia,[8] Nicholas Upton's *De studio militari*,[9] the Anglo-Norman *De heraudie*,[10] or Bartolo
di Sassoferrato's *De insigniis et armis*,[11] all of which had widespread
currency. In addition, Rolls of Arms prepared by heralds, whose
role as guardians of the heraldic corpus was quickly developing,
listed the bearings of individual noblemen.[12]

For Patterson, heraldry is inseparable from the chivalric ethos,
and shares with it a vulnerability to competing discourses. By
Richard's reign, the heraldic sign, and its offspring, the *devise* or
badge, were not innocent markers but counters in political debate.
On the one hand, conservative writers complained that coats of
arms—previously the prerogative of the noble orders—were now
being assumed by merchants, craftsmen, and corporations, and
asked for regulations to be more strictly enforced.[13] On the other,
there was widespread resentment at the abuse of the 'badge', which
lords dispensed to hosts of followers who, in return for pay, wore
their patron's livery and worked to support his interests.[14] Richard

[7] Mathew, *Court of Richard II*, 13, 47; J. J. G. Alexander, 'Painting and Manuscript
Illumination for Royal Patrons in the Later Middle Ages', in V. J. Scattergood and J. W.
Sherborne (eds.), *English Court Culture in the Later Middle Ages* (London, 1983), 155.

[8] See Dennys, *Heraldic Imagination*, 67–70. Bodl. MS Laud misc. 733 contains a 15th-
cent. English translation of this work; an excerpt is in Douglas Gray (ed.), *The Oxford
Book of Late Medieval Verse and Prose* (Oxford, 1988), 143–4.

[9] See Dennys, *Heraldic Imagination*, 76–82. The treatise was written in 1446 or 1447
and extensively copied thereafter. An English translation made *c.*1500 by John Blount is
in Bodl. MS Eng. misc. d. 227.

[10] Probably compiled in the late 13th cent. Its inclusion in the Cambridge MS of the
St Albans Formulary (written after 1382) suggests that it continued to circulate. The text
is transcribed in Ruth J. Dean, 'An Early Treatise on Heraldry in Anglo-Norman',
in Urban Tigner Holmes (ed.), *Romance Studies in Memory of Edward Billings Ham*,
California State Publications, no. 2 (1967), 21–9. See also Dennys, *Heraldic Imagination*,
59–62.

[11] Written in 1354. Dennys (ibid. 62–4) lists its chapters, and the treatise is transcribed
in E. J. Jones, *Medieval Heraldry* (Cardiff, 1943). For a checklist of all the treatises
mentioned above, and a number of others, see Dennys, *Heraldic Imagination*, 212–17.

[12] For Rolls of Arms, see Hope, *Grammar of English Heraldry*, 54–61, and Wagner,
Heralds and Heraldry, 46–55.

[13] See Patterson, *Chaucer*, 182; Dennys, *Heraldic Imagination*, 63.

[14] Patterson, *Chaucer*, 191–2. The classic discussion of 'bastard feudalism' is K. B.
McFarlane, 'Bastard Feudalism', *Bulletin of the Institute of Historical Research*, 20 (1945),
161–80; repr. in *England in the Fifteenth Century: Collected Essays* (London, 1981), 23–43.
For the unpopularity of badges, see Patterson, *Chaucer*, 193 and n. 80.

co-opted a large number of such adherents, who wore his device of the white hart. The author of *Mum and the Sothsegger* accuses him of favouring these 'harts' at the expense of the poor and needy who, in a play upon the heraldic image, are pictured as 'rascaile', young deer perishing for lack of food:

> For litill on ȝoure lyfe   þe list for to rewe
> On rascaile þat rorid   with ribbis so lene.
> For fauȝte of her fode   þat flateris stelen.[15]

The poet extends his theme with the introduction of the 'good greehounde', Bolingbroke (whose badge it was), whom the king should have 'cherischid as a cheffeteyne'; in the next passus Bolingbroke re-enters as the eagle, natural righter of wrongs, and the sovereign bird in heralds' Rolls of Arms:

> For he was heed of hem all   and hieste of kynde
> To kepe þe croune   as cronecle tellith.[16]

The heraldic image was therefore the site of competing discourses. The noble orders of society worked to maintain it as a signifier in a restricted code, in use only among an élite group. In their terms, the heraldic device was the guarantor of uniqueness: no two persons were supposed to bear the same one, and when this happened, as it did in the case of Scrope and Grosvenor, the matter was the subject of lengthy process and debate.[17] A device would be transmitted to its bearer's descendants, often in a traditionally modified form, and was thus a sign of the continuance of one's family (and of its privileged status). The image was therefore both an identifying token and a valuable piece of property—the earnest of particular benefits. This confluence is nicely illustrated in the rich clothes worn by nobles at the royal court: such garments were often embroidered with the owner's personal badge, underlining his claim to be the member of

[15] *Mum and the Sothsegger*, ed. Mabel Day and Robert Steele, EETS os 199 (1936), 2. 119–21. 'Rascaile' could also refer to 'the common people, the lower orders' (*MED* 1b), so there is another layer of wordplay here.

[16] *Mum and the Sothsegger*, 3. 92–3.

[17] *The Siege of Caerlaverock* features a dispute between Brian Fitzalan and Hugh Poyntz because they carried the same banners (ed. N. Harris Nicolas (London, 1828), 36; quoted in Wagner, *Heralds and Heraldry*, app. A), and Gerald of Wales describes a remarkable occasion in Ireland in 1176 when thirty members of a family appeared bearing identical arms: *Expugnatio Hibernica*, ed. and trans. A. B. Scott and F. X. Martin (Dublin, 1978), 169.

an élite, but they also served as a form of portable capital, representing assets which, if the need arose, could be realized in other ways: the courtier Simon Burley, for example, was able to raise money on the security of his clothes and his beds.[18]

So, although the heraldic image might seem to be firmly established, buttressed with regulations that defined and underscored its meaning, it was in fact subject to various kinds of fracturing. Its contested position as the marker of a social group has already been mentioned. However, the very reliance on a sign to convey information about identity was in itself open to deconstruction. Patterson makes this point, widening the implications to chivalry in general, when he comments on the *Scrope* v. *Grosvenor* case:

Yet the very ritual aspect of the case, its insistence that legitimacy is located in the material sign, was an indication of chivalry's lack of confidence in itself, of a gap where the signified essence ought to be. Such ceremonies are necessary because noble identity depends upon a system of signification—in this case, coats of arms—that is always open to misuse. . . . Because of its visibility, its location in the contingency of the material sign, rather than in an intangible inner realm, [chivalric identity] is always vulnerable to depredation and decay.[19]

In other words, if the heraldic image was the signifier, where, or what, was the signified?

The nature of the signifier first needs to be defined with more precision. For although many heraldic images are derived from the natural world, they come by way of an already analysed and divided corpus, that 'system of differences' that the Bestiary represents.[20] The animals and birds that appear on coats of arms frequently carry with them the qualities that Bestiary tradition has assigned to them. Some of them—especially the more fanciful ones that start to appear in Tudor times—are taken directly from that source, such as the

---

[18] Mathew, *Court of Richard II*, 26.

[19] Patterson, *Chaucer*, 186.

[20] The phrase is from Claude Lévi-Strauss, *The Savage Mind* (London, 1966), 116: 'When nature and culture are thought of as two systems of differences between which there is a formal analogy, it is the systematic character of each domain which is brought to the fore.' The theories developed in Lévi-Strauss's earlier study, *Totemism* (trans. Rodney Needham, introd. Roger C. Poole (Harmondsworth, 1969)), are also of relevance to heraldry, e.g. (p. 13): 'Everything depends on where a sign is found, on whether or not it is inverted, on what has been excluded in order that it should be there at all, and its relation to all other signs in a given context.'

'panther incensed', which is clearly the sweet-breathed Bestiary panther.[21] At least one herald—Thomas Benolt, created Clarenceux King of Arms in 1511—possessed two Bestiaries in his library.[22] Like the Bestiary, heraldic texts make a primary division between animals and birds. Within both groups there is an implicit hierarchy, again mirroring the graded universe of the Bestiary. The lion heads the lists of animals, while the eagle introduces the birds. So, in a Roll of Arms compiled between 1337 and 1350, crosses and all their variants come first, in acknowledgement of a sovereignty that goes beyond temporal lordship, then lions, then eagles, and after that all the other members of the animal kingdom.[23] Lions figured on the Royal Arms of England, and they were also extremely popular as a charge for noble persons of a variety of ranks, appearing in several different poses, each with its own special name. 'Wherefore beware who so euyr bere lyons or a lyon in armys, that he do not ayen the nature & kynde of a lyon', John de Bado Aureo warns,[24] making reference, of course, not to the real animal but to the Bestiary's codifed set of attributes. Eagles, in turn, gained extra prestige from their association with the Holy Roman Emperor, who 'berith egle in token that he is hede and pryncypall of all men, as she is shefe and pryncypall of all byrdes'.[25] Birds in general, however, were thought to signify less 'stable' qualities in those who bore them: 'And first say for a generall rule that they that bere birdes or wyldefoule be not so sadde nor stable as they are that bere .iiii. feeted beestes.'[26]

The discourse of hunting, which is explored more fully in the next chapter, also contributed to the heraldic catalogue—appropriately, given its association with noble values and a noble way of life. Just as beasts of the chase were placed in a special class, neither truly wild nor truly tame but subject to ritualized incursions from the human world, so in heraldry they were distinguished by being given their own terminology:

---

[21] See Dennys, *Heraldic Imagination*, 143–4, which includes an illustration. Partridges in heraldry also clearly derive their attributes from the Bestiary: ibid. 50.

[22] Ibid. 56–7.

[23] *Rolls of Arms of the Reigns of Henry III and Edward III*, ed. N. Harris Nicolas (London, 1829), second Roll in volume.

[24] Bodl. MS Laud misc. 733, fos. 5ᵛ–6ʳ.

[25] Bodl. MS Eng. misc. d. 227, fo. 158ᵛ. Eagles appear upon Richard II's robes in the Wilton Diptych (see n. 84, below).

[26] Bodl. MS Laud misc. 733, fo. 8ʳ.

Stags and their kindred animals have several terms peculiarly their own. Their antlers are *Attires*, the branches being *Tynes*, when they stand, they are *at gaze*...when in easy motion, they are *tripping*...when in rapid motion they are *at speed*...and when at rest, they are *lodged*...

All the fierce animals are armed of their horns; but a stag is *attired* of his antlers.[27]

Therefore the animal world as presented through heraldry was a world thoroughly edited to fit an existing design.[28] And, as the animals themselves were ordered into ranks, so their physical features were analysed and manipulated according to ideas of hierarchy drawn from the template of the human body. Bartolo di Sassoferrato writes: 'When arms are depicted on shields, the nobler part should face towards the part of the shield which, when carried, is on the bearer's right side. When arms are depicted on the caparisons of horses, the nobler parts should face the horse's head.'[29] The forward-facing martlets that cover the shield and the horse's skirts in the portrait of Sir Geoffrey Luttrell in the Luttrell Psalter are a copybook example of this precept.[30] Bartolo di Sassoferrato also stresses that a heraldic presentation should enhance an animal's intrinsic vitality: 'The Lion, Bear and other similar creatures are painted erect, rampant, and with gnashing teeth and clawing feet ...animals, whenever represented, must be depicted in their most noble act, and furthermore must exhibit their greatest vigour.'[31] In the suggestion of some people that the heraldic lion and leopard could be distinguished according to whether or not they were shown full-face, Nicholas Upton detects an ignorant slight to the first animal:

howebeyt ther be some dremyng in this mater wiche put difference betwyne a leon and a leoparde in painting of theyr faces, sayeng that a leoparde ought to be painted wyth his hole face shewde abrode openly to

[27] C. Boutell, *Heraldry, Historical and Popular*, 3rd edn. (London, 1864), 62.

[28] I would therefore qualify Patterson's phrases 'natural world', 'natural order of things' in his statement that the 'totemic' relationship between the names of the nobility and 'the natural world, especially... animals' ensured that those names, and the political and economic dominance that their badges asserted, 'were ... seen to be ordained by the natural order of things' (*Chaucer*, 192, 193). However, I agree with his next comment, that Chaucer 'found this semiotics both intriguing and disturbing'.

[29] Dennys, *Heraldry and the Heralds*, 12.

[30] See Janet Backhouse, *The Luttrell Psalter* (London, 1989), fig. 1.

[31] Dennys, *Heraldry and the Heralds*, 92.

the lookers on, and the leon wyth halfe a face: wherin they do a great iniury to this noble beeste the leon, kinge of all beestes, willing nott he shulde shewe his face, wiche ys gretely ayenst the lawes ffor the lawes woll that beestes be paynted in theyr moste ferse acte and maner: and yf a leon maye not shewe his face, he can nott be painted and shewed to appere soo as he ys in dede.[32]

The passage betrays various forms of anxiety, and shows up some of the fractures which beset heraldic discourse. The first problem stems from the fact that, because of ambiguities in terminology, it was sometimes hard to know how to describe a particular representation.[33] Yet any kind of misreading would impugn the integrity of its bearer. However, editing the animals' bodies to produce an uncontestable reading creates new difficulties. The human face, with its range of expressions, is the guarantor of identity and purpose, so if the lion is seen only in profile it becomes impossible to accord him full human equivalence. Upton heaps praise upon 'this noble beeste . . . kinge of all beestes', as if to appease him for the implied insult, but his protestations in fact bring out the closed, self-reifying nature of the whole system. Lions are only 'noble' because a particular culture has decreed that they should be so, and in addition they, like other heraldic icons, can only be read as 'noble' if their bodies are manipulated to mirror those whose qualities they are supposed to be aggrandizing in the first place.

Nicholas Upton's lion is strongly gendered, and the 'body' that underlies heraldic constructions is very often the armoured male body, poised for confrontation.[34] As well as being placed in the proper stance (for example, the lion *rampant* rears to meet its attacker), heraldic animals are frequently shown 'armed', that is, equipped with the bodily weaponry of teeth, talons, horns, or claws.

---

[32] Bodl. MS Eng. misc. d. 227, fo. 139[r–v].

[33] The confusion stemmed from the adoption of French heraldic terms: the French heralds called lions *passant* (i.e. walking) 'léopards'. In England, some writers tried to clarify matters by insisting that a lion had to be depicted *rampant*: therefore, an animal shown *passant* had to be a leopard. However, as the quotation in the text shows, this did not resolve the problem. See A. C. Fox-Davies, *A Complete Guide to Heraldry*, rev. and annotated J. P. Brooke-Little (London, 1969), 133–5.

[34] For an intriguing reading of a 'feminine' heraldic construction, the seal of Margaret, Lady Hungerford and Botreaux, see Carol M. Meale, ' . . . alle the bokes that I haue of latyn, englisch, and frensch: Laywomen and their Books in Late Medieval England', in Meale (ed.), *Women and Literature in Britain, 1150–1500*, Cambridge Studies in Medieval Literature, 17 (Cambridge, 1993), 128–58.

These parts are sometimes picked out in a contrasting colour, like gold. For example, among a list of badges borne by Richard, duke of York, the father of Edward IV, are entries such as:

by Kyng Edwarde is a blewe Bore with his tuskis, and his cleis, and his membrys of Golde.
. . . by the Honor of Clare ys a blacke Bolle, rowgh, his Hornes and his cleys and membrys of Gold.[35]

The fierce antelope of the Bestiaries, borne by several noble families, is always shown with massive tusks and formidably serrated horns: it appears so, for example, on the badges of Humphrey de Bohun (d. 1372/3) and Henry Bolingbroke.[36] The process reaches its peak in the 'male griffin' of Tudor heraldry, borne by Anne Boleyn as one of the supporters of her arms: it was 'depicted like an ordinary griffin, but without wings and also differing by having tusks, and curious spikes in bunches of three sticking out haphazardly from different parts of its body'.[37] Clearly, the practice could only go so far before toppling over into parody. By a similar process, heraldic signs in general may shed their dialogic relationship with the human body and become independent carriers of meaning—as the knights in Ariosto and Spenser simply *are* the devices that they bear. In the Seven Penitential Psalms page of the Grey-Fitzpayn Hours, the marginal figures of the owners have been absorbed into the heraldic patterning:

Joan Fitzpayn forms part of the angular corner of the lower bar border, her body quartered like one of the family's heraldic shields in the opposite margin, her arms rigid in prayer compared to the curvilinear 'low life' all around her. Richard Fitzpayn is 'higher' in the marginal matrix, and even closer in form to the heraldic signs that legitimate his marriage, title, and lands.[38]

---

[35] Bodl. MS Digby 82, transcribed in Henry Ellis, 'Enumeration and Explanation of the Devices formerly borne as Badges of Cognizance by the House of York', *Archaeologia*, 17 (1814), 226–7.

[36] For de Bohun, see Dennys, *Heraldry and the Heralds*, 123 and fig. 68. For Bolingbroke, see Dennys, *Heraldic Imagination*, 147–9, and see also the plate facing p. 176, which shows the antelope badge of Sir John Beauchamp, taken from the Buccleuch MS of the Wrythe Garter Book, fo. 80.

[37] Dennys, *Heraldic Imagination*, 121.

[38] Michael Camille, *Image on the Edge: The Margins of Medieval Art* (London, 1992), 38 and illus. 17.

However, it is more interesting to explore those cases in which the heraldic image maintains its dialogic relationship with the human body. We can start by looking at the principles heralds were supposed to follow in selecting a charge for an individual. The aim was to match the device to a personal feature, which might be physical, temperamental, or circumstantial. John de Bado Aureo considers that 'grete Abbottes' should bear leopards and mules in their arms, since these beasts, born in 'avowterie', have the instruments of generation but are unable to perform the deed.[39] One might expect there to be a 'bodily' reference here, to the monk's vow of chastity, but this explanation is by-passed in favour of a more oblique one, as the corresponding passage in Nicholas Upton's work reveals:

And here ys to be notyd that you moste allwayes have a Respect to the natures and condiciones of the beestes, as I shewed affore. Wherfore as touching hereto hyt maye be saide that these great Abbottes and Abbases ought to bere Leopardes, mules, bornells, and suche other in theyr armes, bycause they use the instrumenttes of bysshoppes, that ys to saye myters and croses, and yet they haue not that act to minester abowte sacramentalls and other jurisdiccions as bysshopes haue, lykewyse as these mules and leopards bere the instrumentes of horsys and leons but yet they vse theym not naturally nor they haue the act and excercyse of generation by theym.[40]

In this passage, the body seems to claim attention by its very *absence*. In another example, the heraldic martlet, a sort of composite of the swallow and house-martin and traditionally shown without feet, is suggested as an appropriate charge for those who have acquired noble status through their own endeavours rather than through inheritance.[41] In the English translation of John de Bado Aureo's work, however, the bird for such self-made men is said to be the merlin, which the author says should be painted without feet 'as though he wanted the grounde and substaunce'. Those who bear a merlin live in the households of knights and other magnates and rely on them for sustenance since they have no great possessions of

---

[39] Bodl. MS Laud misc. 733, fo. 6ᵛ.

[40] Bodl. MS Eng. misc. d. 227, fo. 138ʳ; see also Bodl. MS Ashmole Rolls 4, fo. 6.

[41] John de Bado Aureo, *Tractatus de armis*, quoted in Dennys, *Heraldry and the Heralds*, 118. Sir Geoffrey Luttrell in the Luttrell Psalter bears martlets as his device.

their own.[42] Here the bodies of the signifying animals have been modified in order to deliver a particular social message.

According to John de Bado Aureo, the 'geldyng', or castrated man, should bear a capon in arms, but Nicholas Upton records an instance when a device of oxen was bestowed instead:

To bere therfore oxen or theyr heddes hyt betokeneth that the berer of theym fyrste was geldyd, or maymed so in his priui partes that he was onable for generacion. And yt was my chaunce on a tyme to geue to a certen gentilman and squyere of my lorde and maysters householde iii blacke oxe heddes to bere in his armes in a felde of siluer, bycause at the batell of vernols he was stryken wyth a spere through the priui partes and so thereby made vn able to generation.[43]

Upton describes another apparently uncomplimentary grant, this time of a charge of partridges:

to bere therfore partryches in armes hytt betokenyth the fyrst berer to be a gret lyar or a sodomyte. Ther was a certain gentylman whose name I woll not shew, which by the reason of hys manhode was made a noble man by my lorde and master and he gave iii partryches in hys armes in a redde fylde.[44]

Upton's reluctance to name the bearer of the partridges seems to sit oddly with the function of the device as a public proclamation of identity. But perhaps an answer is to be found in the very width of the field of meaning within which the heraldic image might operate. Since the device that was settled on an individual came out of a large group of alternative possibilities, ironic distance is always implicitly present between human and signifying animal. A man who bears a 'luce', the writers point out, is not necessarily greedy and ravenous like a real pike, 'for sumtyme hit falleth as peuenture a man that is called Luce of good condicions and gentil birthe berith in his armys a luce'.[45] The employment of real names, and their associations, in the heraldic corpus further heightens our sense of the genre as a site of play and paradox—for in what sense might a name reflect its owner's

---

[42] Bodl. MS Laud misc. 733, fo. 10ʳ. The apparent confusion of the two birds might be a scribal error, but it is more likely that each was considered an appropriate symbol since it is usually seen in flight, when its feet are not visible.

[43] Bodl. MS Eng. misc. d. 227, fos. 142ᵛ–143ʳ. For the capon in arms, see Bodl. MS Laud misc. 733, fo. 10ʳ.

[44] Bodl. MS Eng. misc. d. 227, fo. 175ᵛ.

[45] Bodl. MS Laud misc. 733, fo. 10ᵛ.

true identity? Devices that played upon proper names (sometimes called 'canting' devices) were very common: Mauleverer bore three greyhounds,[46] John Griffin a silver griffin,[47] while Peter Dodge was ingeniously granted a woman's breast (or *dugge*) distilling drops of milk ('by the Teates sometimes are meant the plentiful fields wherewith men are nourished').[48]

Sometimes a heraldic writer settles on too 'bodily' a reading. This happens when John de Bado Aureo describes the horse, and ends up comically confusing man and animal:

> To bere a hors in armys betokenyth a welwilling man to fight . . . hit betokenyth a well shapen man and a man hauyng iiii propretees the which been these Shappe ffairenesse rewardi and colour. Shappe that he haue a myghty body and hie with long sides small: his buttokkes rounde the brest well spredded and brode and all the body proporcioned sumwhat thik. Ffairenesse shuld be hadde that he haue a small hede with the skyn clevyng all oonly to the bonys. Erys shorte and sharpe and grete yes thykke mane and a shorte taill . . . [49]

The possibilities offered by heraldry's signifying code were taken up, and played upon, by writers of political poetry in the late fourteenth and the fifteenth centuries. Here, the devices borne by various nobles could be made to interact with one another—with varying results. Sometimes, where an animal's traditional ferocity matches the kind of action it is seen to be engaged in, the verse is moderately effective:

> The wolf cam fro Worcestre, ful sore he þouȝt to lyte;
> Þe dragon cam fro Glowcestre, he bent his tayle to smyte.[50]

Sometimes, however, the result is either bafflingly cryptic—as in the poem 'The Cock in the North', whose survival in a number of

[46] Calais Roll of Edward III (1347; surviving copy 1607), in *Nomina et Insignia gentilitia equitumque sub Edoardo primo rege militantium . . .* , ed. E. Rowe Mores (Oxford, 1749), 17: 'Sir William Mauleuerer de argent, a iii leuerers de goules.'

[47] *Rolls of Arms of the Reigns of Henry III and Edward III*, ed. Nicolas, 49: 'Monsire John Griffen, sable, a une griffin argent, beke et peds d'ore.'

[48] John Guillim, *A Display of Heraldrie*, 5th edn. (London, 1679), 188; quoted in Dennys, *Heraldic Imagination*, 131–2. For more examples of 'canting' heraldry, see Patterson, *Chaucer*, 192 and n. 79.

[49] Bodl. MS Laud misc. 733, fo. 7ᵛ.

[50] *Historical Poems of the XIVth and XVth Centuries*, ed. R. H. Robbins (New York, 1959), no. 90, lines 51–2.

variant versions suggests that it early forfeited any claim to a stable meaning[51]—or (to modern readers at least) engagingly surreal:

> The fisshe hoke cam into þe felde with ful egre mode,
> So did þe cornysshe chowghe & brou3t forthe all hir brode.[52]

In a poem about the battle of Northampton, preserved in the same manuscript as the one quoted above, there is an ingeniously extended treatment of the heraldic theme.[53] Here the motifs which identify the various noble participants, as well as the associations of their names, are set in a narrative which draws its continuity from a carefully developed metaphor of the hunt. The poem describes the encounter in 1460 in which the Yorkist forces defeated the Lancastrians, removed the king, Henry VI, from their custody, and returned with him to London. It first presents a 'bearward' (Edward, earl of March, later Edward IV), who leads his 'bear' (Richard Neville, earl of Warwick, whose arms were the well-known bear and ragged staff) in pursuit of some disloyal 'dogs', whom they chase and chastise. One of the dogs is called 'Talbot' (John Talbot, second earl of Shrewsbury), another 'Bauling bewmond' (John, viscount Beaumont). 'Talbots' were hunting dogs, and appear as representatives of their owner, the first earl, in the Devonshire tapestries (discussed below). The wordplay in 'Bauling bewmond' is a little more subtle. The name was a popular one for a hound, but, more specifically, for one with a 'sweet mouth' whose cry guided the pack and who was unerringly swift in following prey: 'and if eny of his houndes fynde and grete of þe hare where he haþ be, he shalle say to hem in þis wyse, Oiez a beamond la vailaunt, or what þe hounde highte.'[54] 'Bauling bewmond' is therefore a dog who deliberately betrays his noble name and nature, and acts to frustrate the proper activity of the chase (the hunt, as prosecuted by the nobility, was strongly associated with well-living and well-doing, as will be discussed in more detail in the next chapter). The epithet has point and force.

The bear and its keeper next find a 'buck' (Humphrey Stafford, first duke of Buckingham), which they kill. The 'hunter' (Henry VI)

---

[51] Ibid., no. 44 (and nn. on pp. 309–12).   [52] Ibid., no. 90, lines 36–7.

[53] Ibid., no. 89. The identifications of the various nobles are those made by Robbins.

[54] Edward, second Duke of York, *The Master of Game*, ed. W. A. and F. Baillie-Grohman (London, 1904), 103.

thanks them both for their good service, and complains that his dogs behaved like 'curre-dogges' since they conspired with the buck to foil his efforts at finding game. (The nature of this dereliction will, again, appear more fully in the next chapter.) Meanwhile, in London, the 'eagle' (Richard Neville, earl of Salisbury, one of whose badges it was) waits to fish. This eagle has to be one of the fishing kind, for its intended victim is Thomas, Lord Scales, one of the Lancastrian nobles left guarding the Tower of London. Scales tried to escape by water, but was recognized by the London boatmen, who killed him and afterwards 'leyde him naked in Saint Mary Overes chirche yerde':[55]

> All þei had scaped vpon a nyght,
> Saue þeire skales were plucked away:
> Þan had þe fisshe lost all here might,
> And litel ioy in watyr to play.[56]

The image is a powerful and effective one. Scales's dishonoured body is seen as the fish, landed and scraped clean, the scraping of its 'scales' correlating with the dead man's loss of status and identity.

The poem therefore makes effective use of the metaphor of the hunt to justify its partisanship. It relies on the fact that the discourse of the hunt was strongly identified with right relationships—both among the hunters themselves and between the hunters and their animals. Dogs, for example, occupied a pivotal position, since it was on their unquestioning loyalty that the hunter's success depended (the next chapter discusses the various devices and ploys by which men attempted to ensure that loyalty). These 'curre-dogges', who go over to the side of the deer, are therefore guilty of treachery of the worst possible kind. In a final *coup*, the poem actually draws attention to its own rhetorical strategy:

> Now god, þat madest both nyght & day,
> Bryng home þe mayster of þis game,
> Þe duke of yorke, for hym we pray,
> Þat noble prynce, Richard be name.[57]

---

[55] *Three Fifteenth-Century Chronicles*, ed. James Gairdner, Camden Soc., NS 28 (London, 1880), 73.
[56] Robbins, ed. cit., no. 89, 137–40.
[57] Ibid., lines 141–4.

Richard, duke of York is the subject of the poet's petition, but behind him stands the figure of the original 'master of game'—his uncle Edward, the second duke, who had written a well-known hunting manual with that title.[58]

Hunting also features in a slightly earlier poem, about the arrest of the unpopular William de la Pole, duke of Suffolk.[59] This time the hunted beast is the fox—Suffolk—who is first driven into his hole and later into 'the towre'. The metaphor then changes abruptly, and Suffolk becomes 'Iack napys', the tethered ape, after his badge of the clog and chain:

> Iack napys, with his clogge,
> Hath tied talbot, oure gentil dogge,
> Wherfore Beaumownt, þat gentil rache,
> Hath brought Iack napys in an evill cache.[60]

Here Talbot and Beaumont assume their proper 'noble' roles—one the victim of the ape's underhand trick, the other acting swiftly to avenge his companion. V. J. Scattergood thinks that the switch from Suffolk as fox to Suffolk as ape makes for 'a not very well integrated artistic whole';[61] perhaps a partial explanation can be found in the shifting, malleable nature of heraldic identity. The ironic distance between a person and their sign is always apt to generate play and paradox. Here, an additional influence might be the marginal illustrations to manuscripts, which often show interactions between different animals, and, like the poem, force the eye to travel quickly from one locus to the next.[62] A visual parallel is perhaps also relevant to the next poem in Robbins's collection, which deals with Suffolk's banishment to France, capture at sea, and murder.

> Iac Napes wolde on the see a maryner to ben,
> With his clog & his cheyn, to seke more tresour.[63]

Apes were favourite subjects for marginal illustrations,[64] and here their traditional curiosity and acquisitiveness are employed to poke

---

[58] See above, n. 54, and Ch. 5, *passim*.   [59] Robbins, ed. cit., no. 75.

[60] Ibid., lines 19–22.

[61] V. J. Scattergood, *Politics and Poetry in the Fifteenth Century* (London, 1971), 162–3.

[62] See e.g. the pages from the Ormesby Psalter and the Grey-Fitzpayn Hours reproduced in Camille, *Image on the Edge*, pls. 15 and 17 respectively.

[63] Robbins, ed. cit., no. 76, 3–4.

[64] See Lilian M. C. Randall, *Images in the Margins of Gothic Manuscripts* (Berkeley and Los Angeles, 1966), 48–65 (III–XIII).

fun at Suffolk's motivation. The deliberately playful tone of the poem—echoed in the frolicking creatures of the margins—forms a mocking counterpoint to the real outcome of the voyage.

Suffolk makes another appearance in the Devonshire tapestries, three of which, as Ann Claxton has shown, were commissioned by John Talbot, earl of Shrewsbury.[65] In the Otter and Swan tapestry, a dead otter hangs from a pole carried by a huntsman sounding his horn. John Talbot and his second wife, Margaret, point at the otter, although averting their gaze, while a pair of talbot hounds snap at the beast's tail. Below, John Talbot, the elder John's heir and son of his first wife, digs more otters out of their holts, aided by another pair of talbots. The play is upon Suffolk's family name, de la Pole, and the conflation of hunting imagery effectively reduces him to the level of an animal whom no one doubts it is right to track down and kill.[66]

'Talbot' hounds appear very frequently elsewhere in the tapestries, always enhancing their owner's potency and status. In the Boar and Bear tapestry, which Claxton cogently argues represents the family's male side (in contrast to the Falconry tapestry, which illustrates the female), one of the bearers of the crossed boar-spears in the left-hand foreground 'turns to look directly at . . . paired talbot hounds',[67] while holding up a horn. Claxton suggests that he is about 'to sound a fanfare of introduction' to his master, but the implicit allusion to the discourse of hunting may be equally—if not more—important. The horn was used as a signal to direct dogs on the hunting field, and here it could well be a call to action to the two talbots who are seen straining eagerly at their leash. Above the spearmen, another pair of talbots grip a boar by its ears, while John and Margaret point at them approvingly. In real life, John Talbot's identity seems to have been as thoroughly intertwined with his

---

[65] Ann Claxton, 'The Sign of the Dog: An Examination of the Devonshire Hunting Tapestries', *Journal of Medieval History*, 14 (1988), 127–79. The fourth tapestry, the Deer Hunt, is of later date and inferior quality, and was probably bought 'off-the-peg' (pp. 127–38). The tapestries are now in the Victoria and Albert Museum; see also George Wingfield Digby, *The Devonshire Hunting Tapestries*, HMSO (London, 1971).

[66] Otters are listed among the beasts of the chase in *The Boke of St Albans* (*English Hawking and Hunting in 'The Boke of St Albans'*, ed. Rachel Hands (Oxford, 1975), line 1850), which includes them under those of the 'swete fewte'; other texts class them as 'of the stynkynge fewte' (ibid. 148, n. to line 1850).

[67] Claxton, 'Sign of the Dog', 148.

heraldic familiars as it does in the tapestries he ordered to be made. Talbot hounds were his constant companions, both on the hunting field and as guards for his home, and he himself was known to his contemporaries as 'Good dog Talbot'. Consonantly, 'his rent to the crown for Sheffield Castle was two hounds yearly at the feast of St John the Baptist'.[68] In John Talbot's case, the heraldic signifier has become a part of his persona, and has been shaped to express his particular relationship—combative, dominant—to the world around him. The nature of the tapestries themselves contributes to this effect, for, as Claxton points out, they could be rolled up and carried with him from place to place, unfurled as eloquent signs wherever he set up his court. As a final touch, they were woven in *wool*, the commodity upon which Talbot's wealth was based, and so proclaimed his power in their very creation.[69]

The visual code of the Devonshire tapestries suggests that the meaning that heraldic devices embodied was well understood within medieval society. A literary example confirms this: Froissart's story of Math, the greyhound belonging to Richard II:

And it was enformed me, kynge Rycharde had a grayhounde called Mathe, who always wayted upon the kynge, and wolde knowe no man els; for whansoever the kynge dyde ryde, he that kept the grayhounde dyde lett hym lose, and he wolde streight rynne to the kynge and fawne upon hym, and leape with his fore fete upon the kynges shulders. And as the kyng and the erle of Derby talked togyder in the courte, the grayhounde, who was wont to lepe upon the kyng, left the kynge and came to the erle of Derby, duke of Lancastre, and made to hym the same frendly countinaunce and chere as he was wonte to do to the kyng. The duke, who knewe nat the grayhounde, demaunded of the kyng what the grayhounde wolde do. Cosyn, quod the kyng, it is a gret good token to you, and an yvell signe to me. Sir, howe know you that? quod the duke. I knowe it well, quod the kyng: the grayhounde maketh you chere this day as kynge of Englande, as ye shal be, and I shal be deposed: the grayhounde hath this knowledge naturally; therfore take hym to you, he wyll folowe you and forsake me. The duke understode well those wordes, and cherisshed the grayhounde, who wolde never after folowe kyng Rycharde, but folowed the duke of Lancastre.[70]

[68] Ibid.
[69] Ibid. 168–72. As Claxton also shows, certain scenes in the tapestries actually affirm John Talbot's title to particular lands, or inheritances.
[70] *Chronicle of Froissart*, vi. 369.

This story evidently had some currency, for the chronicler Adam of Usk tells an alternative version, in which the greyhound first belonged to the earl of Kent, after whose death it made its way, by instinct, to king Richard. It accompanied him devotedly until the king took flight from his army at midnight, when, supposedly disgusted by such cowardice, it travelled from Carmarthen to Shrewsbury, where it crouched before the duke of Lancaster 'with a look of the purest pleasure on its face'.[71] Henry, seeing the dog as a good portent, welcomed it enthusiastically, letting it sleep upon his bed. Later, when Richard had been overthrown, the dog was brought to him again, but 'it did not recognize him or treat him in any way differently from any ordinary person'—a snub which, not surprisingly, the deposed king 'took sorely to heart'.[72]

The interest of such a tale does not lie in its (dubious) truth to events but in its presentation of speaking images from the heraldic corpus. In Froissart's version, the greyhound shows its allegiance by standing upon its hind legs with its forepaws placed upon its master's shoulders. A real greyhound could, of course, have adopted such a position, but, within the story, this animal becomes the very pattern of a heraldic supporter. Its transference of loyalty from Richard to Henry is therefore not just a matter of a prescient beast's eye for the main chance, but a vivid enactment of the passing over of power and prestige, even of symbolic identity. In the same way, in the Falconry tapestry, John Talbot's first wife, Maud, delivers the Talbot hound into the safekeeping of her successor, Margaret.[73] In Adam of Usk's account, the hound constantly attended Richard 'with a stern and leonine expression fixed upon its face'[74]—a cast of feature that hardly fits a real greyhound but which serves to underscore its role here as heraldic guardian. The greyhound may well have been one of Richard's badges, along with the more familiar white hart: he is known, for instance, to have pledged five 'nouches' in the shape of white dogs studded with rubies to the City of London as security for

---

[71] 'humilimo et hilarissimo et gaudenti uultu inclinando': *The Chronicle of Adam Usk 1377–1421*, ed. and trans. C. Given-Wilson (Oxford, 1997), 86.

[72] 'et post depossicionem regis Ricardi, ad ipsum idem leporarius ductus, eum alio modo quam unum priuatum sibi incognitum respicere non curauit; quod idem tunc depositus dolenter ferebat' (ibid.).

[73] Claxton, 'Sign of the Dog', 161 and fig. 21. Maud also hands over a duck, which Claxton says is a symbol of love.

[74] 'rigido ac si leonino uultu': *Chronicle of Adam Usk*, 86.

loans in 1379 and 1380.[75] However, the heraldic greyhound was more securely identified with Bolingbroke, who, as we saw, appears in this role in *Mum and the Sothsegger*. Adam of Usk refers elsewhere to Henry as 'the dog', 'because of his livery of linked collars of greyhounds, and because he came in the dog-days, and because he drove utterly from the kingdom countless numbers of harts—the hart being the livery of King Richard'.[76]

More skilful writers than Adam of Usk make play with the themes and conventions of heraldry. In Chaucer's *Knight's Tale*, interest in the minutiae of courtly display and pageantry is very much to the fore, as is shown in the description of the arrival of Lygurge and Emetreus and in the preparations for the ensuing tournament. This makes it reasonable to detect a heraldic reference in the 'grifphon' to which Lygurge is compared: 'And lik a grifphon looked he aboute' (line 2133). Vincent J. DiMarco, in his notes to the *Tale* in the Riverside Chaucer, draws on Bartholomaeus Anglicanus for a description of this mythical creature, and then cites Sir Thomas Browne's *Pseudodoxia epidemica* for its particular affinity with generals and heroic commanders. However, in the immediate context, the narrator is not stressing Lygurge's qualities of leadership so much as his immense physical strength:

> His lymes grete, his brawnes harde and stronge,
> His shuldres brode, his armes rounde and longe;   (2135–6)

and this makes it more probable that a heraldic allusion is intended, since it was just this strength on the field of battle that the griffin was supposed to represent: 'To bere a gryffyn in armys is a tokyn of a grete man and a strong fighter and double of conditions and manere ffor that birde in the further partie is like an egle and in the hyndre partie is like a lyon.'[77]

There is perhaps gentle parody of heraldic conventions in Chaucer's description of the doughty warrior Sir Thopas, who bears the

---

[75] City of London Letter Book H, fos. cviii, cxxix; reference in H. Stanford London, 'The Greyhound as a Royal Beast', *Archaeologia*, 97 (1959), 152.

[76] 'merito canis, propter liberatam callariorum leporariis conueniencium; et quia diebus canicularibus uenit, et quia infinitos ceruos, liberatam scilicet regis Ricardi in ceruis excistentem, penitus a regno affugauit': *Chronicle of Adam Usk*, 52.

[77] Bodl. MS Laud misc. 733, fo. 10^r. Another bearer of the heraldic griffin is Lybeaus Desconus, whose notable (indeed, *only*) virtue is his prodigious strength as a fighter (*Lybeaus Desconus*, ed. Maldwyn Mills, EETS OS 261 (1969), Cotton MS: lines 81, 231).

head of a boar, next to a 'charbocle', on his shield. 'To bere a boore in armes', the writers say, 'hyt betokeneth the man to be enviouse and a sotell and stronge warrior, wiche will rather dye in batell than be fleing aways to saue his lyfe.'[78] It is just those qualities that Sir Thopas gives the lie to, when he beats a hasty retreat from the stone-throwing giant Sir Olifaunt:

> Sire Thopas drow abak ful faste;
> This geant at hym stones caste
> Out of a fel staf-slynge.
> But faire escapeth child Thopas,
> And al it was thurgh Goddes gras,
> And thurgh his fair berynge.   (827–32)

In *Troilus and Criseyde* Diomede's supplanting of Troilus in Criseyde's affections is imaged in the trophies he receives from her—trophies which he displays as badges of sexual conquest. First there is the 'pencel of hire sleve' (5. 1043)—inconclusive, perhaps, since she allegedly gives it to him to relieve his sorrow, but still highly suggestive of intimacy. All ambiguity vanishes, however, when Deiphebus brings home the 'cote-armure' he has that day taken from Diomede:

> And whan this Troilus
> It saugh, he gan to taken of it hede,
> Avysyng of the lengthe and of the brede,
> And al the werk; but as he gan byholde,
> Ful sodeynly his herte gan to colde,
>
> As he that on the coler fond withinne
> A broch that he Criseyde yaf that morwe
> That she from Troie moste nedes twynne,
> In remembraunce of hym and of his sorwe.
> And she hym leyde ayeyn hire feith to borwe
> To kepe it ay! But now ful wel he wiste,
> His lady nas no lenger on to triste.   (5. 1655–66)

Some of Troilus's shock here stems from the fact that signs that proclaim their owner's pride and potency—and therefore ought to deliver those qualities into the hands of the man who now possesses them—turn out to have a subversive, hidden meaning. Diomede

---

[78] Bodl. MS Eng. misc. d. 227, fos. 139ᵛ–140ʳ.

wears the brooch 'withinne'—closer to his body than the devices he
shows to the world. The heraldic image is fractured at root, for there
are kinds of truth it can never reflect: Diomede can lose his 'armour'
but still claim ultimate victory.

In between the two 'trophies'—'pencel' and 'cote-armure'—
comes Troilus's dream of the boar, which he sees asleep in a forest,
holding Criseyde in its arms:

> So on a day he leyde hym doun to slepe,
> And so byfel that yn his slep hym thoughte
> That in a forest faste he welk to wepe
> For love of here that hym these peynes wroughte;
> And up and doun as he the forest soughte,
> He mette he saugh a bor with tuskes grete,
> That slepte ayeyn the bryghte sonnes hete.
>
> And by this bor, faste in his armes folde,
> Lay, kyssyng ay, his lady bryght, Criseyde.   (5. 1233–41)

At this stage there appears to be nothing, beyond Troilus's fevered
imaginings, to link the boar explicitly with Diomede: indeed,
Pandarus adeptly produces an alternative reading in which the
creature is Criseyde's aged father Calchas, lying stretched out in
the sun 'o poynt to dye' (5. 1285). However, there are hints that a
heraldic identification may be relevant. In true heraldic style, the
aggressive 'tuskes' of the boar are its most prominent feature, while
in its disconcerting shifting between animal and human (it has
'armes', in which it enfolds Criseyde) it offers exactly that play of
bodily ambiguity which typifies the heraldic image. Diomede 'is'
the boar, Cassandra later reveals, since he inherited the emblem
from his ancestor Meleager, slayer of the monstrous Calydonian
boar. But does that also mean that he is 'like' a boar in lust and
degraded appetite? Not necessarily so, for a man whose badge is a
pike may still be 'of good condicions and gentil birthe'. We are
forced to keep judgement in abeyance—as, perhaps, we are with
Criseyde herself.

Therefore, in the discourse of heraldry, there is constant play
between the image and its referent, between beast and man. There
are also readings which depend upon the sign's *absence*. Members of
the Burgundian Order of the Golden Fleece (the Toison d'Or) who
had offended against its strict rules of conduct had plain black

shields, or shields reversed, displayed in their former station.[79] A relinquishing might signify an individual's absorption into a greater, collective whole, as in the case of the crusading knights, the *cruce signati*, who wore only the device of the cross on their armour. Again, characters in literary texts are allowed to sample different forms of experience by stepping free of the accoutrements that designate their status or identity. The Man in Black in Chaucer's *Book of the Duchess* appears as a plainly suited Everyman, who has laid aside with his visible signs of rank his demeanour as a person who would naturally command respect. 'Loo, how goodly spak thys knyght, | As hit had be another wyght; | He made hyt nouther towgh ne queynte', the narrator marvels (lines 529–31). Within the discursive space the Man in Black has created, he and the narrator are able to talk to one another about an emotion—grief—which both understand simply by virtue of being human. Yet the episode moves towards closure: the ending of the hunt (typically associated with the end of the day, as I explain in the next chapter) marks the ending of the relationship between the two characters. With the mention of the king's return home, the world of dignities and distinctions re-enters the poem, and the chiming bell in the white-walled castle returns the narrator to his own milieu, outside its bounds. Status laid aside has to be resumed, for the social fabric to remain in place. In the same way, the knights who enter tournaments in disguise—often bearing plainly coloured arms instead of their usual devices—are always eventually recognized (or reveal themselves), and are restored to their former position.[80]

In *Sir Gawain and the Green Knight*, the Green Knight signals his self-exclusion from the orders, and ordering, of Arthurian chivalry by refusing to wear those devices which might give clues—even oblique ones—to his identity. Riding into Arthur's court, he brandishes a holly branch in one hand and an axe in the other. Yet he insists that he has all the conventional signifiers of knighthood safely stowed at home: it is simply that he has chosen a different, 'softer' guise for this occasion:

---

[79] Otto Cartellieri, *The Court of Burgundy*, trans. Malcolm Letts (London, 1929), 56–9.

[80] Chrétien's Lancelot bears plain red arms: *Le Chevalier de la charrete*, ed. Mario Roques (Paris, 1960), lines 5575–6058; and his Cligés carries plain black, green, and red arms on successive days at the tournament at Oxford: *Cligés*, ed. Stewart Gregory and Claude Luttrell (Cambridge, 1993), lines 4609–5094.

> For had I founded in fere in fe3tyng wyse,
> I haue a hauberghe at home and a helme boþe,
> A schelde and a scharp spere, schinande bry3t,
> Ande oþer weppenes to welde, I wene wel, als;
> Bot for I wolde no were, my wedez ar softer.   (267–71)

Gawain, by contrast, carries his device, the pentangle, displayed for all to see. The narrator is at pains to point out how shining and new it is (the pigments on the shield are 'schyr goulez' and 'pure golde hwez', lines 619, 620) and how well it looks upon him ('Þat bisemed þe segge semlyly fayre', line 622). The virtues that the pentangle represents are also said to 'fit' Gawain: just as the device gleams gold, so his nature is 'as golde pured' (line 633). Perhaps that is where the trouble lies: the description, as it stands, leaves no room for conceptual play between emblem and bearer—one is simply superimposed on the other. The poet avoids that ironizing perspective so commonly associated elsewhere with the heraldic theme. The 'endeles knot' allows no point of entry, at which its principles may be interrogated and weighed against other systems of value; so Gawain's self-esteem totally evaporates when a cut is made at one small link—his failure to keep a playful bargain word for word. So, when the narrator tells us that 'alle þese fyue syþez, for soþe, were fetled on þis kny3t' (line 656), it is perhaps not over-fanciful to point out that the verb *fetlen* is related to *feter*, 'fetter',[81] and to view the pentangle as a device which, in its refusal of irony, restricts its bearer as much as it enables him.

There is a final ironic aspect to the heraldic image, and that is the fact that, no matter how stocked with weaponry—as rampant lion, clawed bear, spiked griffin, or horned and tusked antelope—it could, in the end, offer its bearer no protection against fortune's slings and arrows. This truth occurs to the knights who watch Chrétien's Tournament of Noauz from the sidelines:

> 'Et cil autres si est de l'uevre
> D'Engleterre, et fu fez a Londres,
> Ou vos veez ces deus arondres
> Qui sanblent que voler s'an doivent.
> Mes ne se muevent, ainz recoivent
> Mainz cos de aciers poitevins:
> Sel porte Thoas li meschins.'[82]

---

[81] MED, *fetlen* v.   [82] *Le Chevalier de la charrete*, lines 5816–22.

And that other one is English work, and was made in London. You see those two swallows on it who look as though they are about to fly off. But they do not move: instead they receive many blows from Poitiers steel. That one is carried by young Thoas.

The *arondres* (probably martlets) look as though they are about to fly away, yet of course they cannot. They—and, by extension, their bearer, Thoas—have to suffer the blows of enemy lances. The birds cannot be injured, but the knight whose symbol and intended protection they are certainly can. Similarly, John Talbot's inseparable hounds could not prevent his death and mutilation on a battlefield in France.[83] And though, in the Wilton Diptych, Richard equips each member of the company of heaven with his badge of the white hart, there is nothing they can do to save him from his eventual fate.[84]

The Wilton Diptych directs us once more towards art, and it is in art, perhaps, that this sense of the fragility of the image—its vulnerability to time and fate—can be conveyed most effectively. At the foot of the effigy of Margaret Courtenay (d. 1391) in Exeter Cathedral, two swans stand with their long necks interwreathed. Margaret inherited the swan as a device from her father, Humphrey de Bohun, and in the twining of the necks of the mourning birds (a gesture Chaucer in the *Parliament of Fowls* associates with springtime love and the choice of a mate) human and animal worlds, counterposed to ironical effect throughout the heraldic corpus, come together in a singularly eloquent and moving image.[85]

[83] Claxton, 'Sign of the Dog', 167.

[84] See Joan Evans, *English Art 1307–1461* (Oxford, 1949), 102–4, pls. 50, 51; Dillian Gordon, *The Wilton Diptych*, National Gallery: Making and Meaning (London, 1993).

[85] For a reproduction of the swans, and a discussion of the swan device generally, see Anthony Wagner, 'The Swan Badge and the Swan Knight', *Archaeologia*, 97 (1959), 127–8 and pl. XXXIX(b).

CHAPTER FIVE

Bodies in the Hunt

IN HERALDRY, HUMAN and animal bodies stand side by side, fixed in postures which express chivalric aspiration. There are, of course, narratives constructed around heraldic premisses, and I discussed some of these in the previous chapter. Essentially, though, heraldry is the art of the static image. By contrast, hunting sets images in motion: its bodies act and are acted upon. Like heraldry, it is a discourse concerned with the meeting of bodies—man and animal—in a socially charged context, and, again like heraldry, a series of texts codified approved practice.[1] In this chapter I do not discuss all the ways in which hunting figured in medieval culture. My aim is a more limited one: to locate hunting within the debate concerning animal bodies and their role in social imaging and social discourse which is the theme of this book. Consequently, I refer only in passing to themes like the erotic hunt or the hunt as religious quest. Fortunately, there are other studies which treat these topics in a full and interesting way, as there are also books which explain the actual routines and customs of the classic hunt in much more detail than I have space for here.[2]

---

[1] There is a good review of the various hunting manuals current in England in Anne Rooney, *Hunting in Middle English Literature* (Woodbridge, 1993), 7–20. The two I shall mainly refer to are: (1) the *Boke of Huntyng* in *The Boke of St Albans* (1486), edited by (i) Gunnar Tilander, *Julians Barnes Boke of Huntyng*, Cynegetica, xi (Karlshamn, 1964), and (ii) *English Hawking and Hunting in 'The Boke of St Albans'*, ed. Rachel Hands (Oxford, 1975), henceforth *BH*; (2) Edward, second Duke of York, *The Master of Game* (c.1406–13), ed. W. A. and F. Baillie-Grohman (London, 1904), henceforth *MG*. The latter is largely a translation of the *Livre de chasse* by Gaston Phoebus, count of Foix, and the edition cited reproduces illustrations from a luxury copy (c.1410) of that text, Paris BN MS fr. 616.

[2] For descriptions of the classic hunt, see: John Cummins, *The Hound and the Hawk: The Art of Medieval Hunting* (London, 1988); Marcelle Thiébaux, 'The Medieval Chase', *Speculum*, 42 (1967), 260–74, and *The Stag of Love: The Chase in Medieval Literature* (Ithaca, NY, 1974), 28–40. The theme of the love-hunt is discussed in Thiébaux, *Stag of Love*, 89–143, and in Rooney, *Hunting*, 45–52. For the holy hunt and the holy hunter, see ibid. 42–4.

Like heraldry, hunting was especially identified with the élite orders in society, and was closely related to their other primary concerns, courtship (in the theme of the love-hunt) and war.[3] The classic hunt *par force* (with horses and hounds) was an activity accorded unique value by its participants, shaping and regulating their lives in an exemplary fashion and contributing directly to both physical and spiritual well-being. The author of the well-known hunting manual *The Master of Game* sets out to prove in his Prologue

þat þer nys no mannys lif that vseth gentil game and disport lasse displesable vnto God than is the lyff of a perfit and skylful huntere nor þat more good cometh of. The first resoun is for the game causeth ofte a man to eschewe the vij deedly synnes. Secoundly men byn bettir rydyng, and more just and more vndyrstondyng, and more appert, and more esye and more vndirtakyng, and bettir knowyng of all contrees and of alle passages and short and long alle good gustumes and maners commethe thereof and helthe of man and of his sowle . . .[4]

Hunting offers a better view and understanding of the world and its ways (the rider ranges more widely, and *sees* more, by virtue of his elevated position) and at the same time it promotes the agency and capability implicit in that view. Because hunters *see* more, they are more active participants in the social sphere, more skilful controllers of other men. But there is also more than a hint of that closed, self-reifying circle encountered in heraldic discourse—for what, after all, is '*gentil* game', and who has decided that it should be so?

'Game', as Edmund Leach explains, is a term used to denote a class of animals with which humans conduct a particular relationship.[5] Game animals may only be killed during certain seasons and under certain conditions, and set forms of behaviour must be adhered to during their pursuit. Leach suggests that our assigning the label 'game' to some—but not other—animals derives from the

---

[3] Hunting was seen as useful training for war since it kept men fit and also acquainted a prince with the lie of his land. See Thiébaux, 'Medieval Chase', 261; Niccolò Machiavelli, *The Prince*, introd. Peter Bondanella, trans. Peter Bondanella and Mark Musa (Oxford, 1984), ch. 14.

[4] *MG* 4.

[5] Edmund Leach, 'Anthropological Aspects of Language: Animal Categories of Verbal Abuse', in Pierre Maranda (ed.), *Mythology* (Harmondsworth, 1972), 39–67. (My diagram is based on the diagram on p. 48.) See also Harriet Ritvo, *The Platypus and the Mermaid, and Other Figments of the Classifying Imagination* (Cambridge, Mass., 1997), 189–94.

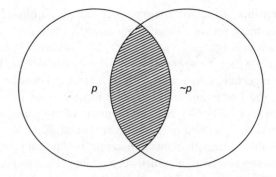

basic, binary distinctions we make between classes of phenomena in the natural world. Although—or, more accurately, because—our perception of the integrity of each class rests on the difference between it and its neighbour, there is also an area of overlap, where ritual value, or taboo, inheres. This is shown as the shaded area on the Venn diagram, in which *p* represents a particular verbal category and ~*p* 'the "environment" of *p*, from which it is desired to distinguish *p*'. Leach goes on to draw up a table, summarizing the relationship between humans and various sorts of animals:

p	both *p* and ~*p*	~*p*
man	'man–animal'	not man
(not animal)	('pets')	(animal)
TAME	GAME	WILD
(friendly)	(friendly–hostile)	(hostile)

Ritual value, he argues, attaches to the intermediate categories 'pets' and 'game', since these correspond to the shaded area on the Venn diagram, the region we must suppress if we are to maintain our binary vision of the world. But an even more intense taboo is associated with animals who inhabit *the gaps within the gaps*: with rabbits, for instance, who are not quite 'game' although they may be hunted under certain circumstances,[6] or with foxes, who are wild

---

[6] When dogs broke off from hunting proper game to chase after rabbits, the cry of 'riot' was raised: 'for non oþer wilde best in Engelond is callid ryott sauf þe Conynge alonly' (*MG* 41). Rabbits, introduced by the Normans, were much rarer in medieval Britain than they are today, and the right to hunt them (conferred in a charter of free-warren) was a jealously guarded seigneurial privilege. See Mark Bailey, *A Marginal Economy: East Anglian Breckland in the Later Middle Ages*, Cambridge Studies in Medieval Life and Thought, 4th ser. 12 (Cambridge, 1989), 128–35.

but who are like 'game' in certain respects. Leach's interest is in how these ambivalent feelings about some animals are reflected in particular kinds of language—verbal abuse, for instance. However, his schema has a wider relevance, since it helps to establish hunting as a discourse especially concerned with maintaining boundaries, with patrolling the borderline between one territory and the next. In such an enterprise, bodies become counters in the game, claimed, manipulated, and marked over by the dominant side.

Historically, hunting has always had this 'bodily' subtext, and has dealt in human as well as in animal corporeality. The 'forest', within which hunting took place, was not so much a geographical feature as a demarcated game preserve within which special laws applied. The Norman kings had declared large areas of England, not all of them wooded, to be 'forest', and had appointed a small army of officials to protect them against encroachment and poaching.[7] Certain animals that lived within the forest—the red, roe, and fallow deer, and the wild boar[8]—were protected by law, and unauthorized attempts to kill them were punished very severely.

The creation of the royal forests had a serious effect upon the people who relied upon the resources of these areas for their livelihood. The author of the *Peterborough Chronicle*, for instance, places William the Conqueror's establishment of forest law high on the list of that king's oppressive actions:

> He wæs on gitsunge befeallan,
> 7 grædinæsse he lufode mid ealle
> He sætte mycel deorfrið,
> 7 he lægde lage þærwið
> þet swa hwa swa sloge heort oððe hinde,
> þet hine man sceolde blendian.
> He forbead þa heortas,
> swylce eac þa baras.
> Swa swiðe he lufode þa headeor

<hr />

[7] For the creation of the royal forests, see Charles R. Young, *The Royal Forests of Medieval England* (Leicester, 1979), 7–32; and for the establishment and enforcement of forest law, Barbara Hanawalt, 'Men's Games, King's Deer: Poaching in Medieval England', *Journal of Medieval and Renaissance Studies*, 19 (1988), 175–93. The visual rendering of forest law in some Bestiary illustrations is discussed in Debra Hassig, *Medieval Bestiaries: Text, Image, Ideology* (Cambridge, 1995), 46–51.

[8] The roe deer was removed from the list in 1339: *Select Pleas of the Forest*, ed. G. J. Turner, Selden Soc. 13 (London, 1901), pp. x–xiv.

swilce he wære heora fæder.
Eac he sætte be þam haran
þet hi mosten freo faran.

His rice men hit mændon,
7 þa earme men hit beceorodan;
ac he [wæs] swa stið
þet he ne rohte heora eallra nið.

Ac hi moston mid ealle
þes cynges wille folgian,
gif hi woldon libban,
oððe land habban,
land oððe eahta,
oððe wel his sehta.[9]

He fell into covetousness, and he loved greediness very much. He set up many deer preserves and also enacted laws that whoever killed a hart or hind should be blinded. He placed a ban on harts, and also on boars. He loved the stags as much as if he were their father. He also made laws concerning hares, that they should run free. His great men complained about it and poor men bewailed it, but he was so stern that he cared nothing for all their hatred. But they had to follow the king's will if they wanted to live or hold land—land or property, or especially his favour.

The passage foregrounds bodies in the struggle for the control of the forest and its resources. The king punishes those who kill his deer by blinding them, but his opponents counter with the gibe that he loved those deer 'as if he were their father'. The same note appears in a case related by Eadmer concerning some Saxons who had been put to the ordeal of hot iron after being accused of poaching the king's deer. An English jury affirmed that their hands were actually healthier afterwards than they had been before—to the disgust of the king, William Rufus, who cried out, 'Is God a just judge?'[10] As one side tried to reserve the good things of the forest for its own use, inscribing marks of control on the bodies of those who offended, so the other side fought back, recycling the same terms in parody or in plain denial of their power.[11]

---

[9] *The Peterborough Chronicle 1070–1154*, ed. Cecily Clark, 2nd edn. (Oxford, 1970), 13.

[10] The incident is recorded in Eadmer, *Historia novorum*, ed. Martin Rule, Rolls Series, 81 (London, 1884), 101–2; see also R. I. Moore, *The Formation of a Persecuting Society* (Oxford, 1987), 128.

[11] The battle between poachers and enforcers is discussed (somewhat tendentiously) by Barbara Hanawalt as 'a game that reinforces male gender identity' ('Men's Games,

The battle for the forest continued throughout the Middle Ages: the king's appropriation of its benefits was among the grievances presented by the barons in Magna Charta, whilst, according to one chronicler, one of the demands made by the rebels in the uprising of 1381 was that all private game reserves in water, park, or woods should be made common.[12] Again, bodies figured prominently in the debate. The Assize of the Forest in 1198 increased the penalty for killing the king's deer laid down in the earlier Assize of Woodstock: offenders were now to have their eyes and testicles removed.[13] Dogs—the accomplices of poachers—were also subject to reprisals: the Assize of Woodstock (1184) decreed that all dogs within the boundaries of the forest should have three toes or the ball of the forefoot cut off to prevent them running after deer. Such crippling was called 'lawing'.[14] The violence inflicted, or threatened, on those who infringed forest law was no doubt often reciprocated. In the ballad of 'Robin Hood and Guy of Gisborne' (which, according to its editors, probably 'preserves the substance of a late medieval ballad'[15]) Robin, the champion of poachers everywhere, after killing his enemy, Guy, cuts his head off, sticks it on his spear, and slashes it with his 'Irish kniffe' until it is unrecognizable.

Such mutilations are, in a sense, tropes for the treatment of the bodies of the animals on which the hunt focused. Those bodies too were subject to divisions and inscriptions, as the hunting élite remodelled them to make them express their particular view of the world. In the following sections I discuss the activity of the

King's Deer', 175). A fascinating study of attempts to suppress poaching in a later period is E. P. Thompson, *Whigs and Hunters: The Origins of the Black Act* (London, 1975).

[12] See Young, *Royal Forests*, 60–73; Henry Knighton, *Chronicon*, ed. J. R. Lumby, 2 vols., Rolls Series, 92 (London, 1889–95), ii. 137.

[13] Roger of Howden, *Chronica*, ed. William Stubbs, 4 vols., Rolls Series, 51 (London, 1868–71), iv. 62–6. Young (*Royal Forests*, 30) points out, though, that this was the maximum penalty and was probably not often exacted.

[14] See *English Historical Documents 1042–1189*, ed. David C. Douglas and George W. Greenaway, 2nd edn. (London, 1981), 453. The provision for 'lawing' is in one of three clauses which are appended to the original text of the Assize and which Young suggests 'probably represent authentic forest custom' (*Royal Forests*, 29). For 'lawing' as codified by Sir John Manwood at the end of the 16th cent., see Simon Schama, *Landscape and Memory* (London, 1995), 146 and refs. in nn.

[15] R. B. Dobson and J. Taylor, *Rymes of Robin Hood: An Introduction to the English Outlaw* (London, 1976), 140.

hunt, with especial reference to two of its quarries, the deer and the fox; then the dogs who, as the hunter's invaluable helpers, occupied a unique and peculiarly privileged role; finally I apply some of the ideas I have developed to the hunting scenes in *Sir Gawain and the Green Knight*.

THE HUNT *PAR FORCE*

As I explained above, hunting, properly conducted, was seen as a wholly admirable pursuit. The classic hunt *par force* started at sunrise and ended at sundown, completely filling the participant's waking hours with purposeful, all-absorbing activity. In fact, the hunt's good influence extended back over the previous night too, since the hunter, lying down in his bed, would be so busy rehearsing to himself his forthcoming role that he would be proof against any temptation to think about 'Synnes or... evil dedis'.[16]

Early in the morning of the hunt, a small number of huntsmen would set out separately, each with his 'lymer' (a specially trained hound), to look for signs of the deer. Each would try to find the place where one had rested during the night, the grass still warm from its body, and would note any tracks or broken branches showing the way the deer had gone. By placing his hand in the deer's prints, and by noting the height of branches marked by its passage, the hunter would be able to estimate its size, likely age, and general suitability for the chase. Effectively, he was engaged in reconstructing a body from its *absences*—a body which, none the less, he was required to *know* in intimate detail, since he would be closely questioned about it when he returned. The only physical objects he could bring back with him were the deer's droppings, or 'fewmets', which he would collect and carefully place inside his hunting horn, stopping it up with grass.

The hunters would then return to the 'gathering' in the forest to make their report. This was where all the participants assembled prior to the pursuit—a place specially chosen for its pleasant aspect and amenities, ideally 'a faire mede wel grene where faire trees welex alle about þe on for from þat oþer and a clere wel or some

---

[16] MG 5.

rennyng breke besides'.[17] Here tables would be set out, laden with food and drink, and a festive atmosphere would prevail: 'some shuld drynk and some laugh, some jangle, some borde, som play and shortly do alle manere disportis of gladnesse'.[18] The gathering proclaimed the hunters' ideological victory over the creatures they were about to subdue by physical means—tables and altars, fine towels and abundant food, all set within a cameo 'garden', hymned man's ability to shape and redefine the 'wild' according to his own terms.

At the gathering, the returning hunters would inform the lord of the hunt of what they had seen and noticed, so that he could make the final decision on which individual deer to pursue. They would also show him their one actual trophy, the fewmets. If the lord was sitting at table, the fewmets might be spread before him on the tablecloth, in rival piles, so that he could make his choice. An illustration in a sumptuous copy of Gaston Phoebus's *Livre de chasse* shows this happening, with two hunters displaying their wares,[19] while in a woodcut in an early edition of *Turbervile's Booke of Hunting* no less a person than Elizabeth I receives the fewmets on a sort of platter of leaves from her kneeling Master of Game.[20] In the Phoebus illustration, the proximity of the droppings to the knives which the lord is using to cut up his food says a great deal about the forthcoming assimilation of the deer—its planned ingestion, almost—into the hunters' society.

First, though, a deer had to be approved as a proper object of pursuit, and for this to happen it had to fulfil various conditions. Special attention was paid to the spread of its antlers (which the hunter might be able to describe directly, if he had actually caught sight of the deer). There were special terms for the number of tines borne by an animal, with the added convention that the number

---

[17] *MG* 93. In the 'gathering' described in the romance of Ipomadon, the Lady's tent is set 'Vppon a lavnde fayre and wyde' (line 578), and there are also 'Logys and pavelons' (line 578) for other noble guests (*Ipomadon A*, ed. Eugen Kölbing, Breslau, 1889). For pictures of the 'gathering', see: *MG*, pl. XXXIV; *Turbervile's Booke of Hunting 1576* (Oxford, 1908), 90.

[18] *MG* 93.

[19] *MG*, pl. XXXIV.

[20] *Turbervile's Booke of Hunting*, 95. The author (now known to be George Gascoigne) provides a verse which the huntsman may recite when he makes his presentation (pp. 96–7).

given always had to be an even one. The tines of a buck (a male fallow deer) were reckoned 'as sone as a man may hang a baudrike or a lessh þerupon, and non oþer wise'.[21] The greater the number of tines, the more highly prized the deer—but there was the added requirement that the arrangement of the tines must be pleasingly balanced and attractive to look at. Lop-sided deer lost out (that is, from the hunter's point of view):

> And ȝif he se an hart þᵗ haþ a diuers hede, or þᵗ he hauntelers ben behynde or þᵗ he had double beemes or oþer aduersitees þan oþer hertis comonly ben wonned to bere, and men axen what hede he berethe, he may answere a diuerse hed, or a countirfethed, for he is counterfeted so.[22]

The ideal was a head that was well 'affeted'—fashioned or trimmed —a word that is used elsewhere in connection with the training of hawks or the disciplining of dogs.[23] The wild, unruly bodies of the deer had to be tamed, made neat and acceptable to the human gaze.

The hunters' assertion of control over their prey was also shown in the plethora of terms with which they categorized it: a net of linguistic entrapment to parallel the physical capture. First, the range of animals that might be hunted was divided into three categories: beasts of venery, beasts of the chase, and vermin (although the classification of individual species is not entirely consistent across different texts).[24] The beasts of venery—the hare, the hart, the wolf, and the boar—were the rightful objects of noble pursuit. Associated with each animal was a whole vocabulary of specialized terms: for example, in the *Boke of Huntyng* the listener or reader is catechized about the right words to use to describe a hart:

> Ye shall hym a calfe call at the fyrst yere,
> The secunde yere a broket, so shall he hym call,
> The therde yere a spayad, lerneth thus all,
> The fowrith yere a stagge call hym by any way,
> The fithe yere a grete stagge, youre dame bide yow say.
>   The VI yere ye call hym an hert.[25]

---

[21] *MG* 78.   [22] *MG* 79.

[23] See *MG* 79, and 115 (appendix); *MED*, *afaiten* v., 2.

[24] See Rooney, *Hunting*, 16–17. A further term, 'rascal' (*BH*, lines 13–16) or 'folly' (*MG* 18), covered deer too immature to be hunted.

[25] *BH*, lines 18–23.

Even adjectives had to be correctly assigned: the same text goes on to declare that a large stag should never be called a 'fair hart' but a 'great hart', although it would be proper to speak of a 'fair doe'.[26] The language of the hunt dissected its subjects according to age, sex, behaviour[27]—even the different sorts of excrement they dropped.[28] The rather surprising inclusion of the hare among the noble 'beasts of venery' is perhaps explained by the semantic challenges it posed: it seemed to zigzag across the categories with as much energy as it twisted and bounded aside during the chase. Hares were thought to chew the cud, to bear both sorts of fat, 'tallow' and 'grease' (other animals had only one kind), to give birth to offspring in two different stages of development, and to switch from being male to female and back again.[29] The medieval hare, in fact, rivals the anthropologists' favourite, the pangolin of the Lele tribe, as a challenge to binary categorization.[30] No wonder, therefore, that the author of the *Boke of Huntyng* praises it as 'kyng . . . of all venery',[31] or that Chaucer's high-living Monk considers it worth all his time and money to pursue:

> Of prikyng and of huntyng for the hare
> Was al his lust, for no cost wolde he spare.
> (*General Prologue*, 191–2)

As language marked the hunters' primary ability to anatomize their prey, so it continued to resonate in the pursuit, as a leitmotiv of human ascendancy. Many different calls were made during the chase—sometimes words shouted to the dogs, sometimes notes blown on a hunting horn. As might be expected, the elusive and anomalous hare inspired a particularly sophisticated deployment of terms:

[26] *BH*, lines 59–64. See also Rooney, *Hunting*, 15.

[27] Ibid. 15–18.

[28] *MG* 78.

[29] *BH*, lines 117–32; *MG* 103. On hares and hare-lore in general, see George Ewart Evans and David Thomas, *The Leaping Hare* (London, 1972).

[30] The pangolin, or scaly anteater, 'the benign monster to which Lele pay formal cult', 'contradicts all the most obvious animal categories. It is scaly like a fish, but it climbs trees. It is more like an egg-laying lizard than a mammal, yet it suckles its young. And most significant of all, unlike other small mammals its young are born singly' (Mary Douglas, *Purity and Danger: An Analysis of the Concepts of Pollution and Taboo* (London and New York, 1966), 168).

[31] *BH*, line 118.

And he [i.e. the hunter] se þat she be goon in to þe playn or in þe feld or in areable lond or in to þe woode if his houndes fynde wel of hire þan he shal say, la douce amy il ad est illeoqs, and þerwiþ he shal say, Sohow illeoqs cy douce cy vaillaunt, and twies Sohowe, and whan he is commen þere as he supposeth þe hare wil dwell þan he shal say þus, la douce la est il venuz. And þerwiþ thries, Sohow, and no more . . . [32]

Each hunting call had its proper context and might only be made within that context—such as the 'forloyn', blown by a hunter who had become separated from the main body of the chase,[33] or the 'death', which could only be blown when the animal was lying dead on the ground.[34] As Anne Rooney points out, this emphasis upon words, and upon correspondingly ritualized actions, is a particular feature of the hunting manuals that circulated in England, as opposed to Continental examples, which tend to concentrate more on practical instruction.[35] She also comments that the language of the hunt, considered in its entirety, 'performed a socially divisive function and rendered the hunt élitist, a closed book to the uninitiated'.[36] This is surely true, for the horde of esoteric terms performed a dual role, both elevating their users as members of a human élite and proclaiming their conceptual mastery over the bodies of the creatures they pursued. I would argue, though, that Rooney's description of such 'social details' as 'peripheral' misses the point: in their concern with boundaries, with the encoding and verifying of the components of a discontinuous universe, they are the essence of what the medieval hunt was about.

The actual dissection of the body of the deer, once it had been hunted down and killed, mirrors the prior dissection of the corpus of 'game' animals through language. The 'breaking' of the deer involved special skills, and is always described in detail in the hunting manuals. Its importance, and currency, is shown by its appearance in literary texts, such as *The Parlement of the Thre Ages*, whose narrator, although a poacher, shows that he knows how the task should

---

[32] *MG* 104.

[33] The blowing of the 'forloyn' is mentioned by Chaucer in the *Book of the Duchess* (line 386). See David Scott-Macnab, 'A Re-examination of Octovyen's Hunt in *The Book of the Duchess*', *MÆ* 56 (1987), 192–5.

[34] *MG* 98–9.

[35] Rooney, *Hunting*, 7.

[36] Ibid. 13.

be done;[37] the version of the Tristram romance preserved in the Auchinleck manuscript;[38] and *Sir Gawain and the Green Knight*. Skill in breaking up the deer was highly esteemed: the hero Ipomadon impresses his lady in this way, while Tristrem acts as instructor in the art to an admiring group of King Mark's followers.[39]

The way the deer was dismembered was very different from the treatment of any animal that was not 'game'. For instance, the recipe for preparing pork with sage in a fifteenth-century cookery book is beguilingly basic: 'Take a pigge, Draw him, smyte off his hede, kutte him into .iiij. quarters, boyle him til he be ynow, take him vppe, and lete cole, smyte him in peces...'.[40] The contrast between these two types of bodies also features in the Auchinleck *Sir Tristrem*, as the hero watches the ignorant huntsmen break up the deer as though they were 'martirs'—cattle slaughtered at Martinmas for winter provisions:

> Bestes þai brac *and* bare,
> In quarters þai hem wrouȝt,
> Martirs as it ware
> þat husbond men had bouȝt.
> Tristrem þo spac þare
> *And* seyd wonder him þouȝt:-
> 'Ne seiȝe y neuer are
> So wilde best y wrouȝt
> At wille.
> Oþer,' he seyed, 'y can nouȝt,
> Or folily ȝe hem spille.'[41]

Whereas the pig had been crudely 'smitten' into pieces, the Master of Game is instructed to 'undo' the deer, while the huntsmen in

---

[37] *The Parlement of the Thre Ages*, ed. M. Y. Offord, EETS OS 246 (1959), lines 65–99.

[38] *Sir Tristrem*, ed. George P. McNeill, STS (Edinburgh, 1886). The romance hero Tristram was usually credited with introducing both good hunting practice and, importantly, the correct terminology. See e.g. Sir Thomas Malory, *Works*, ed. Eugène Vinaver (Oxford, 1954), 279–80: 'And as the booke seyth, he began good mesures of blowynge of beestes of venery and beestes of chaace and all maner of vermaynes, and all the tearmys we have yet of hawkynge and huntynge.'

[39] *Ipomadon A*, lines 657–68; *Sir Tristrem*, lines 463–518.

[40] *Two Fifteenth-Century Cookery Books*, ed. Thomas Austin, EETS OS 91 (1888), 72. An illustration in the Luttrell Psalter shows a man preparing small animals (possibly suckling pigs) for the table by chopping them in half with a cleaver: Janet Backhouse, *The Luttrell Psalter* (London, 1989), pl. 47 (fo. 207ᵛ).

[41] *Sir Tristrem*, lines 452–62.

Gawain carefully 'unbind' their backbones'.[42] It is almost as though the deer had been specially assembled in the first place in order to provide this test of deconstructive skill.

In the dismembering of the animal, each part had a name and was to be treated in a certain way. The fat was measured in finger breadths—again, a juxtaposition of animal and human bodies and the assaying of one by the standards of the other.[43] Even after the deer was decisively dead, and in pieces, a fiction preserved the integrity of its body: before the hounds received their reward of blood and offal mixed with bread and served on the hide, 'þe lord shuld take vp þe hertis hede bitwene þe susreal and þe fourche or troche, whedir it be þat he bere, and þe maister of þe game þe lift side in þe same wise, and holde þe hede vp right and þat þe nose touch þe erth'.[44] As humans could unmake the bodies of the deer, so—this ritual asserted—they could reconstitute them at will.

The division of the parts of the deer's body also reinscribed divisions of status in the human society of the hunters. The head was reserved as a trophy for the lord of the hunt,[45] but there were also special rewards for other participants, such as the man whose dog had first raised the deer, and for the lymer itself. In *Sir Tristrem* Tristrem gives the 'forster' the left shoulder 'for his riȝtes', while some of the hide is cut up to make shoes for the huntsmen.[46] The 'heart bone'—actually cartilage—was traditionally given to a pregnant woman or to a child, to wear as an amulet.[47] However, before the treats were shared out, the ravens' portion—the 'corbeles fee'— would be thrown into the bushes. This small piece of gristle at the end of the breastbone was offered to creatures who seem to have been associated with a sinister, suspect kind of femaleness, at odds

---

[42] *MG* 100: 'he þat he biddeþ . . . shuld vndo hym þe moost wodmanly and clenly þat he can'; *Gawain*, line 1352. Later in *Gawain* the body of the fierce boar is 'unlaced' (line 1606). In *Sir Tristrem* the words 'atire' (line 469) and 'graiþed' (line 483) are used to describe the cutting up of the deer.

[43] e.g. *Parlement of the Thre Ages*, line 71: 'And he was floreschede full faire of two fyngere brede'; *Gawain*, line 1329.

[44] *MG* 100.

[45] See Cummins, *Hound and Hawk*, 43–4.

[46] *Sir Tristrem*, lines 496–7, 476–7. See also *BH*, lines 627–32; Cummins, *Hound and Hawk*, 45. *MG*, pl. XXXVII shows the lymer being fed separately from the other hounds, with the hart's head held ceremonially in front of it.

[47] *BH*, lines 607–8; *La Chace dou cerf*, ed. Gunnar Tilander, Cynegetica, vii (Stockholm, 1960), lines 393 ff.; *Les Livres du Roy Modus et de la Royne Ratio*, ed. Gunnar Tilander, 2 vols., SATF (Paris, 1932), i. 69, 117.

with the assurance of the pregnant wife.[48] Such powers needed to be propitiated, as the hunters silently acknowledged that beyond their avidly partitioned world lay another kind of reality, in no way amenable to human control.

The finale of the hunt was when the deer was borne triumphantly home, its head often carried in front of its conqueror. In a similar way, in *Gawain*, the head of the boar, which has proved to be the most fearsome of Bertilak's adversaries in the hunting field, precedes him back to the castle:

> Þe bores hed watz borne bifore þe burnes seluen
> Þat him forferde in þe forþe þurȝ forse of his honde
>   so stronge.   (1616–18)

The body of the dead animal thus becomes a way of acclaiming the prowess of its human conqueror: certainly, Bertilak's urging of Gawain to view and comment on the tails of the deer and the mighty head of the boar he has killed is presented as an important summation of the whole hunting experience.

So, in the hunting of the deer, the 'wild' was declared to be beneficent, and its products, having been thoroughly plumbed by human hands, ingested into human society. The Devonshire tapestries, previously discussed in the light of the heraldic references they incorporate, show this in pictorial form.[49] A courtly society has shifted itself into the wild, the forest, and continues to deploy all its gestures there, confident that they will retain their full meaning. Ladies marvel at the bravery shown by men and dogs, and lovers plight their troths, against a backcloth of grass strewn with the same flowers that appear upon their embroidered garments. The hunted animals themselves—boar, bear, otter, swan, or deer—have been absorbed into the pattern and are there to be pointed to or gazed at as they succumb to ritualized assault. In the Boar and Bear Hunt, there

---

[48] *BH*, lines 571–2: 'That is corbyns fee | At the deeth he wil be'; *Sir Tristrem*, lines 502–3; *Parlement of the Thre Ages*, line 80; *Gawain*, line 1355. In *Turbervile's Booke of Hunting* the raven is 'she' (p. 137: 'And I haue seene in some places, a Rauen so wont and accustomed to it [i.e. the bone], that she would neuer fayle to croake and crye for it'), while in Ben Jonson's *Sad Shepherd* she is later seen in human form, as a witch, boiling the bone that was thrown to her (*Works*, ed. C. H. Herford and P. and E. Simpson, vol. vii (Oxford, 1941), I. vi. 42–66 (p. 23)).

[49] See Ch. 4, above. George Wingfield Digby, *The Devonshire Hunting Tapestries*, HMSO (London, 1971), includes reproductions of both the whole tapestries and selected details.

is literally no space between the boar being mauled by dogs and the rich gowns of the noble characters who stand and observe the scene. The presence in the same tapestry of turbaned 'Saracens' riding camels shows that in this case the human 'wild' too has been rendered decorative and tame.

The bodies of the hunted deer were appropriated without hindrance, but the fox, also a frequent object of the hunt, especially during the closed season, was treated very differently. The fox, as I mentioned earlier, was an animal of the gaps, of taboo, hovering between legitimate prey and common vermin. In the hunting manuals the fox's depravity and cunning are emphasized: the vixen, we are told in *The Master of Game*, 'is a fals beest and a malicious as a wolf'.[50] The same book tells of foxes eating many disgusting things, such as 'fowle wormes' (the French of Gaston Phoebus, of which the English text is largely a translation, has 'ordures'), and of deliberately defecating while being chased so that the dogs are discouraged by the smell. The fox is thus associated with the body's outgoings, those products which transgress the boundary between the self and the not-self and, liminal between two categories, are themselves objects of taboo. Foxes were also accused of resorting to underhand methods of hunting: for example, of causing havoc in warrens of rabbits, 'þe whiche þei ete and take hem so gynnously and withe grete malice, and not with rennyng'.[51] (Only a low type of human used nets and traps to take his prey.[52])

The body of the dead fox was not handled in the same way as the body of the deer. Instead of being carefully flayed, the skin was stripped off from nose to tail. Foxes, of course, were not eaten, but their fur—well tanned to get rid of the stink—could be used to make cuffs. The husbandman in Henryson's fable thinks of the warm mittens he can make from his fox, and *The Master of Game* recommends their marrow and 'grease' for 'the hardyng of þe synowes'.[53]

This peremptory treatment of the fox's body is linked to its alleged smell and the repugnance this is said to arouse in humans.

---

[50] MG 36.   [51] MG 37.

[52] MG 14: 'Trewly I trowe that a good hunter wold sle hem [i.e. hares] so for no good.'

[53] *The Poems of Robert Henryson*, ed. Denton Fox (Oxford, 1987), lines 2072–3; MG 37.

When the fox is finally pulled out of its hole, Henry of Lancaster writes, in his *Livre de seyntz medicines*, the first thing men say is: 'Fy! Au diable! Q'il put!' ('Fie! To the devil! How he stinks!')[54] The characteristic gesture seems to be that of Bertilak in *Gawain*, who hoists Reynard out of the worrying pack of dogs and holds him 'heʒe ouer his hede' (line 1908), literally at arm's length.

In the *Livre de seyntz medicines*, a book which uses the hunting of the fox to construct a spiritual allegory, there is an extended comparison between foxes and the sins that lurk in the human heart. The author alludes to the tradition associating the fox with the devil, which was discussed in Chapter 3, above, and which emerges here in the captors' cry of 'Au diable!'. The dog fox, the vixen, and five cubs together make up the number of the deadly sins. The narrator says his heart is like a foxes' hole, for the sins hide there by day and come out at night—that is, when nobody can see them. The orifices from which the sins issue are the gates of the senses (eyes, ears, etc.), but the comparison with the fox adds a further resonance, since that animal is typically linked with discharged matter that is vile, excremental—the products of the body rather than of the spirit. Henry of Lancaster therefore employs the signifying potential of the body of the hunted fox to reinforce his moral lesson. He goes on to describe how the skins of killed foxes are hung up in the hall for everyone to see—so, the interpretation runs, we must first root sins out of our hearts and then keep them freshly displayed in our memory.[55]

The status of the fox in medieval culture as a creature of the gaps, neither one thing nor the other, gives rise to a particular sort of play within texts. Such play typically re-sites him within human society, and then, doubling back in a truly foxlike manœuvre, abruptly rescinds his rights and throws him back into the outer darkness to which he belongs. The complaint quoted above, that foxes take rabbits from warrens 'gynnously and withe grete malice', is an example of this—for why should it matter *how* foxes catch their prey? It only matters if the fox is being treated momentarily as an honorary human. Henry of Lancaster engages in the same kind of play when he comments ruefully that, although the hunting of men's sins stops at Easter (with the end of the period of Lent), the

---

[54] Henry of Lancaster, *Le Livre de seyntz medicines*, ed. E. J. Arnould, Anglo-Norman Text Society, no. 2 (Oxford, 1940), 105. Cf. also *MG* 36: 'he stinkeþ euermore.'

[55] *Le Livre de seyntz medicines*, 115.

open season for real-life foxes goes on a good deal longer (in fact, foxes could be hunted all the year round).[56]

As Edmund Leach reminds us, the word 'game' implies a playful, joking relationship with the category of animals it describes.[57] This is certainly true in the cases of the hunted foxes quoted above, and will prove so again in *Gawain*. Yet it is a game that only one side can win, since that side has written the rule-book. The fox is presented as a cheat because he catches rabbits unsportingly, without giving them a chance to run—yet foxes themselves were often killed by similarly devious means: trapped within their earths, for instance, and suffocated there by the infusion of sulphurous smoke. Henry of Lancaster includes a realistic description of such a practice.[58] Hunters who placed crossed wands in front of the earths they were blocking up were also toying with this idea of the fox as human (more than human, even—diabolical), yet at the same time their mastery over his wiles and wickedness, their power to reduce him instantly to 'beast' level, is never seriously in question.[59] Occasionally, though, the fox did fight back: Alexander Neckam tells the story of one who tried to escape his pursuers by hanging *himself* up among a number of foxskins on a wall.[60] We can be sorry—but hardly surprised—that his ruse proved unsuccessful.

DOGS AND THEIR OWNERS

If foxes operated within a particularly shady area, dogs too were creatures of the gaps, of taboo. Their status as pets, or as helpers to humans, placed them ambiguously between animals on one side and men on the other. However, dogs were treated very differently from foxes, both in texts and in reality. The narratives and practices associated with them centre around their willed assimilation into the world of human relationships and, particularly, into that of language.

---

[56] Ibid. 106–7.
[57] Leach, 'Anthropological Aspects', 59.
[58] *Le Livre de seyntz medicines*, 104.
[59] See Cummins, *Hound and Hawk*, 143 and fig. 27.
[60] Alexander Neckam, *De naturis rerum*, ed. Thomas Wright, Rolls Series, 34 (London, 1863), 204.

Hunting—especially the chase *par force*—could not take place without the assistance of dogs. Yet there was a paradox here: dogs are beyond doubt animals, and might therefore be expected to give their allegiance to other animals rather than to humans. Somehow they had to be coaxed over the borderline, inveigled with all the resources of human society and the gifts of status it could bestow. There is a great deal of evidence to show that medieval hunting dogs were indeed both highly prized and lovingly tended. They were often given as noble gifts.[61] Elaborately jewelled collars were wrought for them, while some wore ornate body armour as an additional protection.[62] The kennels the hounds lived in were constructed with regard for both their comfort and hygiene, and one of the hunt attendants slept with them at night to make sure their rest was undisturbed.[63] The manuals go into great detail when describing the various ailments of hounds and the proper treatment for each: a wonderful illustration in a copy of Gaston Phoebus's *Livre de chasse* shows a selection of sick hounds each with his human servant assiduously tending him.[64] If the prescribed remedies failed to work, the hounds might be sent on a pilgrimage to a shrine and have masses said for them to speed their recovery: details of such a journey appear in the accounts prepared in 1388 by the master huntsman of the French king Charles VI.[65]

Language—the pre-eminent human attribute—played a vital part in the training and treatment of hounds. First, each dog had its own name, and it was the task of the apprentice huntsman to learn these by heart: 'and first I shal teche hym for to take hym by writt as þe names of þe houndes and of þe hewis of þe houndes, in to þe tyme þat þe childe knowith hem both by hewe and by name.'[66] Once in the hunting field, the hounds would be guided, scolded, or encouraged by a whole repertoire of calls:

[61]   *MG* 143–4 (appendix); Cummins, *Hound and Hawk*, 20.

[62]   *MG* 144 (appendix); Cummins, *Hound and Hawk*, 14 and pl. 47.

[63]   *MG* 70 and pl. XXII.

[64]   *MG*, pl. XV (also reproduced in Derek Pearsall, 'Hunting Scenes in Medieval Illuminated Manuscripts', *Connoisseur*, 196/789 (Nov. 1977), pl. C).

[65]   *MG* 188 (appendix); Cummins, *Hound and Hawk*, 30. Not only dogs were treated in this way: Edward I 'sent wax images of sick falcons to shrines and even sent sick birds themselves on pilgrimage': Robin S. Oggins, 'Falconry and Medieval Views of Nature', in Joyce E. Salisbury (ed.), *The Medieval World of Nature: A Book of Essays* (New York, 1993), 50.

[66]   *MG* 69.

And when he has of[f] cast his cowples at will,
Then shall he speke and say his howndes till:
'Hors de couple! Avaunt, ay, avaunt!', twis so,
And then 'So ho, so ho [so ho]!' thries and no mo,
And þen 'sa, sa, cy avaunt', hie and noȝt lowe,
And then 'sa, cy, avaunt, sa, cy, avaunt, so howe'.[67]

The hounds, of course, had to be *taught* how to respond, and the manuals offer advice on this stage too:

and also as towchyng greyhoundes men may wel helpe to make hem good techyng as to lede hem to wode and to feeldes and to be ay nye hem, in makyng of many good guyrreis, whan þai han wel idon and astyng ['ascrying', calling to them] and biteng hem whan þai done amys for þei ben beestis and þerfore þei have nede to be lernyd to þat men wil þat þei shuld do.[68]

Apart from the rather touching concession that 'þei ben beestis', the writer could be describing the education of a young child.[69] In the encomium on hounds which opens the twelfth chapter of *The Master of Game*, the quality which is most emphasized—through repetition—is, indeed, the hound's *knowingness*, its ability to distinguish accurately the subtle shadings of human intercourse: 'an hounde is of greet vndirstondynge and of greet knowynge... An hounde is a wise beeste and a kynde... an hounde is of good obeysaunce, for he wil lerne *as a man* al that a man wil teche hym.'[70] Here the hound is presented as a vessel with sufficient capacity for all that his master chooses to pour into him: there appears to be no qualitative difference between their respective learning potentials.

As dogs were enticed towards humans, through their initiation in the magic world of language, so a distance had to be opened up between them and other animals. The result is the sort of Janus-faced creature depicted by *The Master of Game*: the good greyhound, who should be 'curtaise and nouȝt to felle... wel willyng and goodly to all maner folkes, saue to wilde beestis vpon whom he

[67] *BH*, lines 245–50.   [68] *MG* 58.

[69] 'Good teaching', for example, is also mentioned by the Knight of La Tour-Landry in his advice on 'How men oughte to sette and put theyr children to scole' (William Caxton, *The Book of the Knight of the Tower*, ed. M. Y. Offord, EETS ss 2 (1971), 122, lines 13–14).

[70] *MG* 44 (my italics).

shuld be felle spitous and egre'.[71] Hounds, in fact, were encouraged
to take upon themselves the power of language, accusing and
insulting their quarry: running hounds 'must hunt all the day ques-
teyng and making great melody in their language and saying great
villainy and chiding the beasts that they chase'.[72] Such speech, of
course, had to be meaningful and not mere noise—the *Master of
Game* has harsh words for those disobedient dogs who 'jangle'
instead of talking properly.[73] In the next section, on *Gawain*, I shall
have more to say about this intriguing mixture of animal and human
voices in the hunting field.

As a reward for their understanding, and their loyal and purposeful activity, the hounds were allowed within that charmed circle of
human reciprocity, of gift-giving and gift-receiving, which marked
the climax of the hunt. At the death of the deer, they were encouraged to bay loudly while the huntsmen blew their horns. They then
took part in the precise ritual of the 'quarry'. According to *The
Master of Game*, the quarry, or 'curée'—the offal of the deer soaked
in its blood and mixed with bread—should be prepared on the hide
of the deer, which should remain intact until the hounds had fed
from it.[74] The lord of the hunt and the Master of Game himself
should lift up the deer's head between them, standing at the neck
end of the hide, where the head would have been in life, and
holding it by its antlers so that its nose touched the earth. Attendants
should bring the hounds on leashes to within 'a smal cotes cast' and
make them stand still until the Master of Game gave the cry
'Dedow!' ('Devour!'). Then 'halow euery wight, and euery hunter
blowe þe deeþ'. The voices of the dogs, as they joined whole-
heartedly in the deafening chorus, was confirmation that they had
given their allegiance to the human side.

The close relationship between men and dogs prescribed, and
described, in the hunting manuals finds echoes in other texts too.
When Malory's Sir Dynas finds that his lady has fled his castle, taking
his two hunting dogs with her on her assignation with a secret lover,
he is 'the more wrother for hys brachettis, more than for his lady'.[75]

---

[71] *MG* 63.   [72] *MG* 60.

[73] *MG* 61: 'Oþer maner houndes þer byn which openeþ a jengeleþ whan þei be
vncouplid.'

[74] *MG* 100–1; also *BH*, lines 620–6.

[75] *Works*, 409. In the story about the killing of a wild man illustrated in a series of *bas-
de-page* drawings in both the Smithfield Decretals (BL MS Roy. 10 E IV, fos. 72^r–74^v)

In the version of the 'Gelert' story included in *The Seven Sages of Rome*, the lord who has mistakenly killed his loyal greyhound is so overcome with remorse when he realizes his mistake that he rushes out into the wild forest, without even saying goodbye to his wife or child, to suffer penance there for the wrong he has done his hound.[76] Most charmingly of all, Neckam tells the story of an old dog ('canem nobilem qui vulgo leporarius dicitur'—a noble greyhound, naturally) rejected by the knight who was its master, and supplanted in his favour by two puppies. The dog first killed the puppies and then fled into the forest, from where it launched attacks upon the knight's livestock. It finally succeeded in capturing his infant son, forcing the knight to send his steward (whom the dog was extremely fond of) to parley with it.

Quid moror? Canem tanquam animal rationale dulcibus verbis convenit, spondens et paciscens quod ipsum domino suo reconciliaret, si puerulum ei redderet. Canis conquiniscens, visus est annuere quod senescallus petebat.[77]

What more is there to say? He addressed the dog with sweet words, as a rational beast, making a solemn and binding promise that he would reunite him with his master if he would give the little boy back to him. The dog, squatting down, was seen to nod its agreement to what the steward was requesting.

This dog is not only a reasoning creature capable of understanding human speech, and cognizant of the bargaining involved in diplomatic negotiations—it can also tellingly mimic human body language, sitting down to show its peaceful intent and nodding to convey its acceptance of the terms offered. At the conference table, it is quite the equal partner. However, once it had agreed to the treaty, and been restored to its former position in the household, the greyhound seems to have reverted to being just a dog again, for we

and the Taymouth Hours (BL MS Yates-Thompson 13, fos. 60ᵛ–67ᵛ), the loyalty of the old knight Enyas's greyhound is contrasted with the fickleness of the lady who deserts him after he has rescued her. The Taymouth Hours (first half 14th cent.) contains the fuller version of the story, summarized in an accompanying sequence of Anglo-Norman inscriptions. See R. S. Loomis, 'A Phantom Tale of Feminine Ingratitude', *Modern Philology*, 14 (1917), 751–5.

[76] *The Seven Sages of Rome*, ed. Karl Brunner, EETS os 191 (1933), 27–32. Escape into the wild forest is a common knightly motif in the romances, but, as I show below in Ch. 8, it is always prompted by disappointment or transgression in a *human* relationship.

[77] Neckam, *De naturis rerum*, 253–5.

are told that it would allow the knight to beat and chastise it without complaining. Presumably, it felt it had made its point.

In spiritual terms, undue attachment to one's dogs could well prove problematic—in the *General Prologue to the Canterbury Tales*, for instance, the Prioress's 'smale houndes', fed on 'rosted flessh, or milk and wastel-breed' (line 147), absorb the pity and charity that should properly be directed towards the poor. The preacher John Bromyard warns against the grave consequences of such attachments in his exemplum of the hunter who was unable to make his deathbed confession because he was so preoccupied with talking about his hounds,[78] while a fifteenth-century nun has a vision of one of her fellow-religious, Margaret, tormented in purgatory by a cat and a dog, who gnaw her arms and legs, because 'thay wer hir mawmettes the whil sho was on lyve, and sho sett hyr hert to mych on such foul wormes'.[79] In God's eyes, treating dogs as surrogate humans was plainly a sin, since it lifted them above their proper, subordinate place in creation.

In romances, dogs are often part of the story's erotic currency, functioning as go-betweens or stand-ins for the lovers. In *Partonope of Blois*, the lady Melior persuades the hero to hunt on her land, sending her own, exquisite lymers (hounds hunting by scent) to assist him:

> Lemers to hym thenne come lepynge,
> They where as soffte as eny selke,
> And ther-to whyte as eny mylke.[80]

The lymers who come bounding eagerly to Partonope afterwards help him to slay a boar. With their enticingly sensuous appeal, they provide the code through which Melior's desire for the hero can be acknowledged—and indeed, the same night finds her in bed with Partonope.

In *Sir Tristrem*, the hound Hodain licks the cup containing the love-potion which Brengwain is offering to Tristrem and Ysonde, and consequently is united with them in the intensity of their passion:

---

[78] BL Add. MS 11284, fo. 31ʳ; quoted in Rooney, *Hunting*, 131 n. 65.
[79] *A Revelation of Purgatory by an Unknown, Fifteenth-Century Woman Visionary*, ed. Marta Powell Harley (Lewiston, NY, 1985), lines 628–30.
[80] *Partonope of Blois*, ed. A. Trampe Bödtker, EETS ES 109 (1912), lines 2236–8.

> Þai loued wiþ al her miȝt,
> *And* hodain dede al so.[81]

The other dog in the story, Peti Crewe, is given to Tristrem by a grateful king after he has killed a giant in Wales:

> Þe king, a welp he brouȝt
> Bifor tristrem þe trewe;
> What colour he was wrouȝt
> Now ichil ȝou schewe.
> Silke nas non so soft,
> He was rede, grene *and* blewe.
> Þai þat hi*m* seiȝen oft
> Of hi*m* hadde gamen *and* glewe,
> Y wis
> His name was peti crewe,
> Of him was michel priis.[82]

Peti Crewe's variously coloured body and silky fur emblematize the sensual delights of Tristrem and Ysonde's relationship. In the statement that the little dog gives pleasure to everyone who sees him, there is also the suggestion that their love, too, may bring joy to all who witness—or read about—it. Towards the end of the story, Tristrem, returning from Brittany, sees Ysonde and Brengwain riding together with the two dogs running by their side. He sends his companion Ganhardin to greet them, telling him to show Ysonde his ring, and especially to praise the dogs. Ganhardin's fondling of Peti Crewe is intimately linked to the queen's recognition of her lover:

> Þe kniȝt him self bi dene
> Stroked þe hounde pencru;
> Þe quen þe ring haþ sene
> *And* knewe it wele ynouȝ,
> Þat fre.[83]

Earlier, when the lovers fled into the forest, the two dogs went with them. Hodain accompanied Tristrem on his hunting expeditions,

---

[81] *Sir Tristrem*, lines 1693–4.

[82] Ibid., lines 2399–2409. Another many-coloured dog is the one captured by Lybeaus Desconus, who subsequently presents it to the maiden Elene: 'He was of all colours I Þat man may se of flours I Be-twene Mydsomer and May' (*Lybeaus Desconus*, ed. Maldwyn Mills, EETS os 261 (1969), Cotton MS: lines 1021–3).

[83] *Sir Tristrem*, lines 3107–11; 'pencru' is the scribe's error over an unfamiliar name.

and was instructed by him in the skills of the chase, and both he and
Peti Crewe lay beside the lovers, sharing their earthen shelter:

> Hodain, soþ to say
> *And* peti crowe wiþ hem ȝede.
> In on erþe hous þai lay,
> Þo raches wiþ hem þai lede.[84]

Such intimacy is well reflected in the commemorative tableau of
lifelike figures that the giant Beliagog constructs for Tristrem, for in
it Peti Crewe and Hodain both appear, with as much *gravitas* as the
human actors in the story.[85]

The long version of the Ipomadon romance provides another
example of a hunting dog in an erotic context. Its plot turns on the
fact that the hero chooses to present himself as a skilled huntsman
but not as a warrior—to the chagrin of the Lady who has fallen in
love with him, since she has vowed to marry no one but the bravest
knight in arms in the whole world.[86] Ipomadon's prowess in hunting is demonstrated by his slaying of seven enormous harts, and by
his skilful breaking up of one of them in plain sight of his beloved. In
this enterprise the hero's dog performs a vital role, tracking the deer
closely, and standing guard over its body while its master is away. In
the final stage of the pursuit, the 'lytill rache' and the hart both
collapse exhausted in front of the Lady, who is highly amused and
remarks that the dog's owner cannot be far behind:

> Att the brachet lowde she lowȝe:
> 'Now ser*tes*, he can of fete inowȝe,
> That þus his hounde gan lere:
> Hym selffe comys sone, he is not ferre!'[87]

In a romance that seems to depend for its appeal on the ingenious
postponement of the union of the lovers (there are several disguises
and many tribulations to be gone through before they are finally
brought together), the little hunting dog may be seen as a sort of
erotic surrogate, collapsing almost (but not quite) in swooning
surrender, announcing in one sense (but not in another) Ipomadon's
arrival at his goal. The playful, teasing way in which hunting
motifs are treated here is shown in the description of the Lady

---

[84] *Sir Tristrem*, lines 2467–70.   [85] Ibid., line 2841.
[86] *Ipomadon A*, lines 109–20.   [87] Ibid., lines 651–4.

admiring the seven mighty harts' heads when they are displayed before her:

> In a stody full stylle she stode:
> I hope, here lokynge dud here goode.
> Be god and my lewte!
> The righte, I trowe, who vndertoke,
> She had more luste, on hym to loke,
> Then any hert*es* hedde to see.[88]

The showing of the trophies of the hunt was the traditional assertion of masculine strength and prowess, but the text nicely undercuts this motif with its comment that the Lady would much rather see the hero himself than the spoils he has brought her. Harts' heads may do very well as symbols of virility, but they are no substitute for the real thing!

Dogs, therefore, are given an interestingly extended role in various medieval texts. As participants in the hunt, they become the focus of language, which both confirms their identity and edges them over the line dividing them from their human partners. This peculiarly intimate relationship is taken up and developed in the romances, and in romantic iconography too—for example, in the many little lapdogs who lie cradled in their mistresses' arms.[89] In *Sir Gawain and the Green Knight*, dogs appear again, and the hunting scenes in that romance bring together several of the themes which have so far been explored.

HUNTING AND *SIR GAWAIN AND THE GREEN KNIGHT*

In *Sir Gawain and the Green Knight*, the three separate hunts that Bertilak undertakes are treated at length by the poet, and interlaced with the visits of the Lady to Gawain's bedroom. Their function within the story has puzzled generations of readers—at one level, as

[88] Ibid., lines 749–54.
[89] Several 14th-cent. French ivory mirror-cases show ladies, accompanied by their lovers, carrying small dogs in the crook of the arm. See e.g. O. M. Dalton, *Catalogue of the Ivory Carvings of the Christian Era of the British Museum* (London, 1909), nos. 374, 375. An ivory casket (also French, 14th cent.) illustrates the story of the Châtelaine de Vergi, who kept her meetings with her lover secret by training her pet dog to run ahead to him (ibid., pp. 123–4, pls. LXXXIII–LXXXIV).

Anne Rooney says, they 'may appear to be a distraction',[90] yet once they are probed for a meaning beyond the literal they yield a proliferation of possible contrasts and correspondences that then have to be integrated into one's reading of the poem as a whole. That 'yielding', of course, isn't innocent—because the hunts are so fecund in signifying features, it is all too easy to pick out those that will buttress the reading one already has in mind. For example, if one wants to emphasize Gawain's courage in rejecting the advice of his guide and pressing on to meet the Green Knight at the Green Chapel, one might argue that there is a parallel between the knight and the boar, whose heraldic counterpart prefers a brave death on the battlefield to ignominious flight. However, if one thinks that Gawain's essential virtue is his *mesure*, his guarded control in the face of provocation, one might point up a *contrast* between boar and knight, adducing the boar's brutish aggressiveness, and its traditional connection with the vice of *luxuria*. On this reading, Gawain's polite declining of the Lady's favours is hardly 'boarlike', while his *patientia* beneath the Green Knight's fearsome axe is the complete opposite of the snorting, thrashing frenzy with which the cornered boar fights for its life.[91]

In addition, a reading of the hunts—or, indeed, of any one of the hunts—once settled on, tends to produce its own dynamic, compelling further patternings. For instance, if one is convinced that the boar represents sins—lust, wrath, or whatever—that Gawain is tempted to commit, one is then predisposed to look for the further sins that the deer and the fox represent.[92] In turn, an emphasis on sins, and on the moral testing of the hero, may impel one towards exhibiting Bertilak as a more uncompromising God (or Devil)

---

[90] Anne Rooney, 'The Hunts in *Sir Gawain and the Green Knight*', in Derek Brewer and Jonathan Gibson (eds.), *A Companion to the 'Gawain'-Poet* (Woodbridge, 1997), 158. Rooney provides a useful summary of various recent critical treatments of the hunts, updating the references she gives in *Hunting* (nn. to pp. 159–65: 'The Hunts and the Critics').

[91] Contrast, for instance, the view of Muriel Ingham and Lawrence Barkley ('Further Animal Parallels in *Sir Gawain and the Green Knight*', *Chaucer Review*, 13 (1979), 384–6) with those of Peter McClure ('Gawain's *Mesure* and the Significance of the Three Hunts in *Sir Gawain and the Green Knight*', *Neophilologus*, 57 (1973), 375–87) and John Speirs ('Sir Gawain and the Green Knight', *Scrutiny*, 16 (1949), 290).

[92] See e.g. G. Morgan, 'The Action of the Hunting and Bedroom Scenes in *Sir Gawain and the Green Knight*', *MÆ* 56 (1987), 212: 'If one of the hunts is symbolically significant, all three are likely to be symbolically significant.'

figure than the text really warrants. Or, to take another example, pointing up the sly skill with which the Lady tries to entrap Gawain may lead one to over-emphasize the degree to which these qualities are deployed in each of the hunts.[93] Pinning down any strand of the web with one's finger seems to set up tensions and reverberations everywhere else!

I am certainly not saying that the action of the hunts bears no relation to Gawain's situation. However, I propose to alter the angle of approach, and—leaving Gawain aside for the moment—consider instead the way the hunts themselves are described, before returning to wider questions.

A basic point to make about the first of the hunts, the deer hunt, is that it conforms closely to the practice laid down in the hunting manuals. It is not a hunt *par force* but a 'bow and stable' hunt, in which herds of deer are driven towards waiting dogs and bowmen.[94] The description of the breaking of the deer is particularly detailed, and, again, corresponds to the written texts. Correctly, too, the animals hunted are hinds and does, not harts and bucks, for it is winter, the close season for the male deer:

> For þe fre lorde hade defende in fermysoun tyme
> Þat þer schulde no mon meue to þe male dere.　　(1156–7)

We are reminded of winter once again when Gawain comments admiringly on the fatness of the deer (measured, as was traditional, in finger breadths):

> 'Ȝe iwysse,' quoþ þat oþer wyȝe, 'here is wayth fayrest
> Þat I seȝ þis seuen ȝere in sesoun of wynter.'　　(1381–2)

His gladness at the appearance of fresh meat matches his earlier relief when, on first entering Bertilak's castle, he was led to the fireside and wrapped warmly in furs—recognition that he had come in from the bitter cold. Whatever other function the deer may fulfil, they are real deer, providing real sustenance, fully related to the basic human needs that the poem acknowledges so positively.

---

[93] Ibid. 202: 'the lady reveals the cunning that is necessary for one in pursuit of a deer, for the deer is a wise animal.' In fact, this deer hunt, in which (as I point out below) the deer are not stalked but driven pellmell towards posted dogs and hunters, does not involve great stealth or cunning on the hunters' part—or any wisdom on the deers'.

[94] The 'bow and stable' hunt is described in Cummins, *Hound and Hawk*, 47–67, and in *MG* 107–12.

Beyond this, the bodies of the deer offer a contrast to the bodies present in the other two hunts. The terrified herds of hinds and does are absorbed smoothly, resistlessly, into the human world, their efforts to escape no match for the circumscribing foresight of the hunters and their hounds:

> Þe hindez were halden in with hay! and war!
> Þe does dryuen with gret dyn to þe depe sladez;
> Þer my3t mon se, as þay slypte, slentyng of arwes—
> At vche wende vnder wande wapped a flone—
> .   .   .   .
> What wylde so atwaped wy3es þat schotten
> Watz al toraced and rent at þe resayt,
> Bi þay were tened at þe hy3e and taysed to þe wattrez;
> Þe ledez were so lerned at þe lo3e trysteres,
> And þe grehoundez so grete, þat geten hem bylyue
> And hem tofylched, as fast as frekez my3t loke,
>   þer-ry3t.
>   Þe lorde for blys abloy
>   Ful ofte con launce and ly3t,
>   And drof þat day wyth joy
>   Thus to þe derk ny3t.   (1158–61, 1167–77)

The emphasis is upon the perfect compassing of the animal world by the human. The sheer numbers of deer killed show how complete man's ascendancy is—so that there is never an obstacle to Bertilak's jubilant progress, from break of day through to nightfall.

The boar, however, is a very different proposition. His fierceness and enmity are strongly stressed:

> Þen, braynwod for bate, on burnez he rasez,
> Hurtez hem ful heterly þer he forth hy3ez...   (1461–2)

Even the country where he lives has the same hostile aspect as the cliffs and crags Gawain toiled over on his journey north:

> In a knot bi a clyffe, at þe kerre syde.
> Þer as þe rogh rocher vnrydely watz fallen,
> Þay ferden to þe fyndyng, and frekez hem after...   (1431–3)

The alienation of the boar from the world of humans is constantly emphasized. He is a solitary animal, who left the herd a long time ago because of his age, and as such he bears a note of particular estrangement in a poem that celebrates the joys of human society.

The hunting manuals treat boars with great respect.[95] The dangers of the boar hunt are pointed out, and the boar himself is given many of the accoutrements of a human adversary: the hard, impervious skin on his shoulders is called the 'shield' (in *Gawain* it protects so well that arrows merely bounce off it), and constant reference is made to the fearsome tusks which he sharpens against each other, like a warrior whetting his sword. As Gaston Phoebus puts it, the boar trusts only 'en sa défense et en ses armes'.[96] That he meets his human enemies as an equal is shown in the illustration to the *Livre de chasse* in which a small 'army' of wild boars, tusks at the ready, confronts an advancing line of dogs and huntsmen. Certainly the boar in *Gawain* is able to inflict a frightening amount of damage on both men and dogs, and to daunt them so that they all hold back warily from the final encounter. All, that is, except Bertilak. His approach to the boar on foot, armed with a sword and not a boar-spear—although it would hardly have been endorsed by the hunting manuals, since it involves such great personal risk—links him with heroes such as Arthur and Guy of Warwick, both of whom fight boars in this way.[97] His victory is celebrated in a triumphant cacophony of sounds from men and dogs together:

> There watz blawyng of prys in mony breme horne,
> Heȝe halowing on hiȝe with haþelez þat myȝt;
> Brachetes bayed þat best, as bidden þe maysterez
> Of þat chargeaunt chace þat were chef huntes.   (1601–4)

In the last hunt, for the fox, it is not the men but the hunting pack of hounds who are the prime movers. This pursuit—of an animal which is not that different from them in biological terms—may be seen as a test case for the dogs: have they really learned their lesson and traversed the boundary, turned their back on their animal kin and thrown in their lot with humans? The answer is a *yes, fortissimo*.

For, if the mood of the boar hunt was in some sense dark, with real risks encountered and real injuries sustained, this, by contrast, is

---

[95] See e.g. *MG* 27–30: 'It is þe beest of þis world þat is strongest armed and rathest shul slee a man of eny other.' The boar-hunt is discussed in Rooney, *Hunting*, 78–85; Cummins, *Hound and Hawk*, 96–109.

[96] *MG* 28 n. 6.

[97] See e.g. *The Avowing of King Arthur*, ed. Roger Dahood (New York, 1984), lines 69–272; *The Romance of Guy of Warwick*, ed. J. Zupitza, EETS ES 25, 26 (1875, 1876; repr. 1966), lines 6417–60.

both a decidedly festive occasion and a highly verbal one. The hound who first sights the fox calls out, and is answered by the pack: 'A kenet kryes þerof, þe hunt on hym calles...' (line 1701). Once in pursuit, the hounds loudly voice their scorn, 'Wreȝande hym ful weterly with a wroth noyse...' (line 1706). Later, as Reynard is assailed with insults as thickly as the deer in the first hunt were showered with arrows, it becomes impossible to distinguish human from animal speech in the excited, challenging words flying hither and thither:

> Thenne watz hit list vpon lif to lyþen þe houndez,
> When alle þe mute hade hym met, menged togeder:
> Suche a sorȝe at þat syȝt þay sette on his hede
> As alle þe clamberande clyffes hade clatered on hepes;
> Here he watz halawed, when haþelez hym metten,
> Loude he watz ȝayned with ȝarande speche;
> Þer he watz þreted and ofte þef called...   (1719–25)

Language is playfully tossed back and forth between the hounds and their masters, as they greet and berate, threaten and hail, their intended victim.

The fox is finally killed, not in solitary combat as the boar was, but in the midst of a gathering that is already shaping itself for even more festivity. Hounds bay, and hunters blow their horns:

> Alle þat euer ber bugle blowed at ones,
> And alle þise oþer halowed þat hade no hornes;
> Hit watz þe myriest mute þat euer men herde,
> Þe rich rurd þat þer watz raysed for Renaude saule
>   with lote.   (1913–17)

The phrase 'myriest mute' means 'the merriest hunting-pack' or 'the merriest baying of hounds'—in other words it refers to the noise made by dogs, not by men.[98] But here it is juxtaposed to the *human* sounds of horn-blowing and hallowing. Animals and humans are united in an explosion of the same exultant language.

Afterwards, the hunters reward and pet their dogs, stroking and fondling their heads. In the trial, they have been proved true. Reynard's body, however, receives a very different treatment:

---

[98] See *MED, mute* n., 1.

> And syþen þay tan Reynarde,
> And tyruen of his cote.   (1920–1)

In his role as adversary, the fox had been construed as a *person*, who could 'listen' to the 'speech' of the hounds and hunters and who could devise strategies to counter theirs. Now his human dress—his 'coat'—has to be roughly pulled from him and revealed for what it truly is, a 'foule fox felle'. In the same way, the mention of his 'soul'—for which the din of men and hounds supplies a mock requiem—only serves to emphasize that he really has *none*, that he is finally beast and not human, a creature outside the pale.

These three episodes, therefore, illustrate several of the themes which have already been discussed in this chapter. In their depiction of the deer as bodies to be absorbed fully into the human milieu, of the fox as a shifty adversary, a mock-human who must finally be unmasked, and of the dogs as allies whose pledge of loyalty is a shared language, they reflect patterns that are intrinsic to the discourse of the hunt. At the same time, the length of the hunting passages, and their vivid elaboration of detail, remind us of the vital importance of the hunt in the ethic of nobility—they are of a piece with the arming of Gawain *à point devis* in one court and his sumptuous entertainment in another, and the poem's first audience were surely meant to enjoy them for their own sake, quite apart from any symbolic meaning that they might find in them.

However, that question of meaning will not go away. It will be clear by now that I am reluctant to claim that there are specific symbolic connections between Gawain and the hunted animals. Yet in our experience of reading the poem, hunts and temptation scenes are intimately interlinked. We move from one setting to the other usually within the span of a single sentence: conjunctions such as *And*, *Whyle*, and *Bot* emphasize the parallelism. 'While *this* is going on here, *that* is going on there,' the poet insists. In the third hunt, the enchainment itself becomes a part of the fiction—for we leave the fox leading Bertilak and his men a merry dance ('And 3e he lad hem bi lagmon, þe lorde and his meyny', line 1729), and then spend so long in Gawain's bedchamber, where the green girdle is being argued over, that our eventual return to the pursuit, besides reflecting the fox's own long-drawn-out wiles, appears to close a hiatus in the narrative through which he just *might* have slipped.

Danger and death are common to all three hunts: each ends in a killing (a mass killing, in the case of the deer), and in the breaking and division of flesh. But the hunters, too, are flesh and blood, just like the animals they slaughter. As Felicity Riddy writes:

The person in *Sir Gawain and the Green Knight* is insistently material. . . . Through their physical selves, the humans are connected to the palpably and luxuriantly material world of courtly display, to the food, clothing, and armor on which the poet constantly dilates. But their bodies also link them with the natural world which plays so large a part in this poem.[99]

The death that Gawain faces is unsparingly 'bodily'—and, although he survives, the Green Knight's axe slices through actual flesh and makes blood spurt on to the ground. While on one level Gawain is not at all like a deer, boar, or fox, on another he is exactly like them—a body that can be cut, sheared through, dismembered. And for Gawain, just as for any animal, that would mean final extinction: 'þaȝ my hede falle on þe stonez, | I con not hit restore' (lines 2282–3).

In this way the hunts in the poem provide a 'bodily' subtext to the narrative of Gawain's stay at Bertilak's castle and his subsequent journey to the Green Chapel. Hunting was a celebration of man's ability to order and re-shape the natural world, to ordain boundaries, to inscribe human sovereignty upon the bodies of the not-human, but its discourse rested upon a forgetting of the fact that humans are bodies too. Of the characters in the poem, the only one who is not a 'body' in this sense is the Green Knight—even though he appears to have the most outrageously material body of all. His flaunting of the normal rules that apply to bodies points up their iron hold upon everyone else, and pens humans and animals together in a common mortality—for Gawain is much more like a deer or a fox than he is like a being that can put its own head back on its shoulders. The hunts raise the stakes—they remind us, graphically, of what is lying in wait for the hero.

This interpretation of the hunts involves a shift of emphasis away from the individual animals and towards their common fate. It also—perhaps—entails finding fewer responsive images in Gawain's

---

[99] Felicity Riddy, 'The Speaking Knight: Sir Gawain and Other Animals', in Martin B. Schichtman and James P. Carley (eds.), *Culture and the King: The Social Implications of the Arthurian Legend: Essays in Honor of Valerie M. Lagorio* (Albany, NY, 1994), 150.

bedchamber and more at the Green Chapel, where it seems that the *mort* is finally going to be blown. I suggest (for example) that when we hear about Gawain's final stand, on rocky ground next to a running stream, and how he flinches from the glinting blade of the axe, we do think back to the cornered boar and the fox—which, too, shrank from the hunter's bright sword. Gawain, of course, saves himself by acting in a way no animal ever would—by standing quite still and readying himself for death. He is nobler than any animal— nobler, too, than most of us, the pearl among the white peas—but he is also, as he himself admits, 'þe flesche crabbed', defined, and betrayed, by that bodiliness he shares with every other mortal creature. The poet has devised a subtle and intriguing play between these two poles, and, within that play, the hunting episodes, with their emphasis upon bodies threatened and divided, perform an important role.

CHAPTER SIX

A Reading of *The Knight's Tale*

HERALDRY AND HUNTING, the subjects of the last two chapters, are both allied to privileged groups in society. In both, man's relationship to the world of the non-human is expressed. That relationship is one of control: animals are used to say things about the identity of humans, and to this end their bodies are remade to answer human needs—metaphorically in the case of the heraldic bestiary, literally in the case of hunted animals like the deer, plumbed in every part before being ingested as both food and trophy. It is part of this discourse that man should be seen as totally distinct from the animals he either pursues or enlists as emblems of his prowess. Man dictates the terms of the relationship, extending to some creatures—such as dogs—the magic password of language, which gives them access to his privileged sphere, while construing others—such as boars or foxes—as enemies, to be vanquished in ritualized combat. This chapter presents a reading of Chaucer's *Knight's Tale* which takes up, and expands upon, the theme of human–animal relations as an enterprise of control. I argue that the degree to which the human characters attain mastery over events is partly expressed through the way they are linked with different animals, and that the tale ends by problematizing a relationship which, at its outset, had seemed to be straightforward. The underlying question is, what happens when the bodies of men and the bodies of animals can no longer be kept entirely separate? Such a mingling is treated playfully in the heraldic corpus. It is explored in a different way in the figure of the wild man, the subject of the next two chapters, and therefore this chapter extends a link to what is to come, as well as offering an application of this book's argument to a particular literary text.

The Knight's Tale is a complex and challenging poem, which has probably inspired more critical debate than any other of the *Tales*.

The roles of all its characters—including the narrator—have been variously appraised, and even its overall tone has been brought into question.[1] One or two very basic observations may be made, however: *The Knight's Tale* is a highly wrought work of art, in which elements of patterning and artifice immediately strike the eye, and ear.[2] It embodies many contrasts: between the spheres of influence allotted to the gods; between the order Theseus in particular seeks to impose and the dreadful *dis*order that plagues the lives of the characters; and, at the level of language, between the formal rhetoric of the lovers' Boethian complaints against fortune and the brisk demotic of Theseus's comments on their behaviour:

> Ye woot yourself she may nat wedden two
> Atones, though ye fighten everemo,
> That oon of you, al be hym looth or lief,
> He moot go pipen in an yvy leef...   (1835–8)

One of the most vivid contrasts is that between men at the top of Fortune's wheel and those at the bottom. An individual may fall, dramatically, from the highest point to the lowest in a short space of time—as happens to king Cappaneus, who is stripped of his splendour by Creon and left a mere corpse to be eaten by dogs. This motif receives particular realization in the fates of Arcite and Palamon, who start off in almost the same state as Cappaneus, distinguished from him only by being not quite 'fully dede'. When Arcite is freed from prison but Palamon is not, each sees his own fate as sublimely cruel. Arcite complains:

> But I, that am exiled and bareyne
> Of alle grace, and in so greet dispeir

[1] Richard Neuse, for example, finds a comic vision in the tale as a whole, even extending to Arcite's fatal accident ('The Knight: The First Mover in Chaucer's Human Comedy', *University of Toronto Quarterly*, 31 (1962), 299–315); by contrast, Elizabeth Salter sees Chaucer choosing to stress the cruelty of the fates his characters suffer (*Chaucer: The Knight's Tale and The Clerk's Tale* (London, 1962), 7–36). The range of critical opinion is well summed up in Lee Patterson, *Chaucer and the Subject of History* (London, 1991), 165–7 and n.

[2] See e.g. the schematic analysis of the tale's events in Helen Cooper, *The Canterbury Tales*, Oxford Guides to Chaucer (Oxford, 1989), 74. The first critic to present the *Tale* as a verbal artefact, expressing, through balanced contrasts, 'the struggle between noble designs and chaos', was Charles Muscatine: 'Form, Texture, and Meaning in Chaucer's *Knight's Tale*', *PMLA* 65 (1950), 911–29—still a cogent study, although it will become clear that I question his foregrounding of Theseus's role at the expense of those of Palamon and Arcite.

> That ther nys erthe, water, fir, ne eir,
> Ne creature that of hem maked is,
> That may me helpe or doon confort in this,
> Wel oughte I sterve in wanhope and distresse.   (1244–9)

Later, when Arcite returns secretly to Athens and becomes a servant in Theseus's household, he sharpens his sense of evil fortune by contrasting his present lowly position with his noble descent from Cadmus, founder of Thebes:

> Of his lynage am I and his ofspryng
> By verray ligne, as of the stok roial,
> And now I am so caytyf and so thral,
> That he that is my mortal enemy,
> I serve hym as his squier povrely.   (1550–4)

In a similar vein, Palamon had earlier begged Venus that, even if it should be his own destiny to die in prison, she should, nevertheless,

> Of oure lynage have som compassioun,
> That is so lowe ybroght by tirannye.   (1110–11)

Both the young knights lament the loss of status, and exclusion from effective action, which their change in fortunes has brought.

Set against the misery and debasement of Arcite and Palamon is the triumphant bliss of Theseus, who reigns untroubled at the top of the wheel throughout the course of the *Tale*. He is often referred to in terms which stress his dominance over events: 'in his tyme swich a conquerour | That gretter was ther noon under the sonne' (lines 862–3), or, later, 'Arrayed right as he were a god in trone' (line 2529). To emphasize Theseus's absolute security, the narrator makes it clear to us that he is not a whit threatened by the element that threatened real-life rulers in Chaucer's day—popular discontent. Unlike Walter in *The Clerk's Tale*, he hears no mutinous 'murmur': instead his subjects practically queue up to give their assent to his sovereignty:

> The peple preesseth thiderward ful soone
> Hym for to seen, and doon heigh reverence,
> And eek to herkne his heste and his sentence.   (2530–2)

The poem therefore embodies ideas about hierarchy, and about how men may be either elevated or depressed by the caprices of fortune. It also contains a large number of references to animals—as critics have pointed out, Chaucer has developed, and added to, the 'scattered bestial images' in Boccaccio's *Teseida*.[3] The animals are related directly to the humans, most usually in the form of a comparison, as when we are told that Arcite and Palamon are fiercer than, respectively, a tiger and a lion when they fight each other in the tournament (lines 2626–33). The animals also stand for a range of values on the hierarchical scale: 'high' animals such as the eagle or the lion, with their privileged association with heraldry, appear in different contexts and with different significations from 'low' beasts such as the cuckoo, the hare, or the drunken mouse.[4]

One important locus for animal imagery—and for the presence of real animals too—is the description of Lygurge and Emetreus, the two mighty kings who come to support Palamon and Arcite in the tournament. Seated in a chariot drawn by four white bulls, Lygurge looks around him 'like a grifphon' (line 2133), while more than twenty 'white alauntz', 'as grete as any steer' (line 2149), run alongside him. His adversary, Emetreus, bears a white eagle upon his wrist, and is accompanied by 'Ful many a tame leon and leopart' (line 2186); he himself has the gaze of a lion. Critics writing about the two kings have most commonly seen them as images of ferocity, representatives of the savage forces which are always threatening to break through the veneer of civilization. Jeffrey Helterman, for example, thinks that Lygurge 'seems almost a bear since he wears a "beres skyn" instead of "cote-armure"',[5] while A. C. Spearing characterizes the champions as 'terrifyingly like wild animals in appearance and trappings. . . . Emetreus particularly is totally meta-morphosed into a wild beast, or rather into a composite symbol of the savage, and the two together make up a magnificent and terrify-ing image of the animal in man.'[6] 'When the human statutes of kinship break down,' Frederick Turner declares, 'mere animal an-archy is loosed upon the world.'[7]

However, what we are presented with in the portraits of the two kings is not the crude 'anarchy' of the animal world but that world

[3] See e.g. Jeffrey Helterman, 'The Dehumanizing Metamorphoses of the *Knight's Tale*', *Journal of English Literary History*, 38 (1971), 497.

[4] See Cooper, *Canterbury Tales*, 8.

[5] Helterman, 'Dehumanizing Metamorphoses', 498.

[6] *The Knight's Tale*, ed. A. C. Spearing (Cambridge, 1966), 69.

[7] Frederick Turner, 'A Structuralist Analysis of the *Knight's Tale*', *Chaucer Review*, 8 (1974), 289.

already tamed and ceremonialized, viewed through the prism of heraldic discourse. Emetreus' eagle is a case in point. Critics have found it hard to accept that this bird really is an eagle—because it is white and white eagles are not found in nature.[8] However, eagles of many different colours, including white, are certainly to be found in heraldry, and in all kinds of applied art—carvings, embroideries, jewellery, etc.—of a heraldic inspiration. White eagles were among the heraldic motifs on a richly ornamented belt ('un seinture d'or et de perles ove neof barres d'or ovesque eegles blancz') which Edward III in 1376 restored to Joan Holand, the second wife of John de Montfort, duke of Brittany and earl of Richmond, after she had pledged it to another man.[9]

I have already argued for a heraldic source for the description of Lygurge as a 'grifphon' (see above, Chapter 4); the bear's skin which he wears as 'cote-armure', and which critics have seen as a symbol of raw animality, provides a further example. Its yellow nails were explained long ago by Skeat as a recollection by Chaucer of the tiger's skin with gilded claws in the *Thebaid*.[10] Later commentators have followed along the same track, adding the observation that both Agamemnon and Evander in the *Teseida* wear cloaks of animal skins adorned in this way. So, for F. N. Robinson, the reference is clearly to 'the ancient practice of gilding an animal's claws when its hide was worn as a cloak'.[11] However, it was not only 'ancient practice' which decorated the claws and other 'aggressive' parts of an animal to make them stand out from the body colour: as I showed in Chapter 4, such highlighting was common in heraldic ornamentation. Bears were certainly popular as devices, the best-known being the bear and ragged staff of the earls of Warwick. Bears' heads and

---

[8] F. N. Robinson thinks that 'probably a falcon is meant' (*The Complete Works of Geoffrey Chaucer*, 2nd edn. (Oxford, 1974), 679, n. to line 2178). A. C. Spearing, too, suggests that the bird is 'perhaps a falcon' (ed. cit. 179, n. to line 1320), and so does Charles Moseley (*The Knight's Tale*, Penguin Masterstudies (Harmondsworth, 1987), 157, n. to line 1320). The editors of the Riverside Chaucer point out that Marco Polo saw white eagles in India (p. 837, n. to line 2178).

[9] Patent Roll 50 Ed. III, part 1, membrane 7, 2 July (1376), quoted in H. Stanford London, 'The Greyhound as a Royal Beast', *Archaeologia*, 97 (1959), 152 n. 3.

[10] *Thebaid*, 6. 722–4; *The Complete Works of Geoffrey Chaucer*, ed. W. W. Skeat, 6 vols., vol. v (Oxford, 1894), *Notes to the Canterbury Tales*, 84–5, n. to line 2141.

[11] Robinson, ed. cit. 678, n. to line 2141. See also the Riverside edn., p. 837, n. to lines 2140–2.

bears' paws also occasionally appear.[12] My argument is not that Lygurge's garment is derived *exclusively* from a heraldic model: on the contrary, the animal-hide cloaks worn by the princes in the *Teseida* probably provided Chaucer with his initial inspiration. Rather, heraldic references are present as distinguishable elements in a deliberately eclectic whole.

Such mixing of features is in fact characteristic of the portraits of the kings, and can be seen again in the tame lions and leopards that run alongside Emetreus. Both animals are extremely common in heraldry,[13] but they are also traditionally to be found among the exotic beasts in the trains of visiting monarchs, such as the beautiful leopards who accompany the Magi in the *Très Riches Heures* of the duc de Berry. Emetreus, as king of India, is naturally the lord of such wonderful and fearsome creatures. Again, the alaunts, who follow Emetreus, recall the world of hunting as well as having definite heraldic associations.[14] In other words, various discourses contribute to the portrayal of the kings, and their cumulative effect is to enhance our sense of Lygurge and Emetreus as *rulers*, as wielders of effective power through their ascendancy over the animal kingdom. All the power embodied in bulls and bears, eagles and giant hunting dogs, is under human control and made to redound to human glory. The pattern is epitomized in the description of the alaunts, in which praise of their power and magnificence modulates into acknowledgement of their subservience to their master: muzzled for safety, and adorned with golden collars with *tourettes* through which leashes could be threaded, they follow obediently in their lord's train as if they were human retainers wearing his 'badge':

> Aboute his chaar ther wenten white alauntz,
> Twenty and mo, as grete as any steer,

---

[12] For the badge of Warwick ('The rampant bear chain'd to the ragged staff', *2 Henry VI*, v. i. 204), see *Boutell's Heraldry*, rev. J. P. Brooke-Little (London, 1950), 167–8, and for bears' heads and paws, ibid. 71. A 17th-cent. banner of the Swiss town of St Gallen shows a rampant bear with a golden collar and claws: see Ottfried Neubecker, *Heraldry: Sources, Symbols, and Meaning* (London, 1976), 118, 119.

[13] For the use of lions and leopards in heraldry, see Rodney Dennys, *The Heraldic Imagination* (London, 1975), 133–44; *Boutell's Heraldry*, ed. cit. 63–9. A ruling by Richard II on the right to bear a leopard in arms is recorded in *Calendar of Patent Rolls*, Richard II, vol. v, p. 350.

[14] See London, 'Greyhound', and my article: Dorothy Yamamoto, 'Heraldry and the *Knight's Tale*', *Neuphilologische Mitteilungen*, 93 (1992), 210–11.

> To hunten at the leoun or the deer,
> And folwed hym with mosel faste ybounde,
> Colered of gold, and tourettes fyled rounde.   (2148–52)

In the treatment of Theseus, prime mover of most of the poem's events, animals are again used to reinforce ideas of human dominance and prestige. Like the kings, Theseus asserts his lordship over brute creation through his involvement in the worlds of hunting and heraldry. One of his greatest pleasures is to hunt the hart *par force*, attended by a dutiful company of 'houndes swiche as that hym list comaunde' (line 1695), while his golden pennant displays the Minotaur, the monster he killed in the Cretan labyrinth.[15] Almost alone among the characters in the *Tale* (even Emily is momentarily seen as a cuckoo or a hare, line 1810), Theseus is not likened to any animal. The one animal comparison that does involve him does so in a decidedly *negative* way: in resolving to spare Arcite and Palamon, to temper his rage against them with reason and compassion, Theseus chooses *not* to behave like a lion, as another, more impetuous lord might do:

> And in his gentil herte he thoughte anon,
> And softe unto hymself he seyde, 'Fy
> Upon a lord that wol have no mercy,
> But been a leon, bothe in word and dede . . .'   (1772–5)

The interesting point is that the *positive* comparison would have been equally, or even more, appropriate here: the Bestiary lion was not known for pitiless ire, but rather for sparing its victims out of lordly magnanimity.[16] It is as though Chaucer wished to divorce Theseus completely from any hint of animal complicity and thus highlight his role as the supreme exemplar of rightly constructed humanity, of man as he *should* stand, at the furthest end of the scale from the brute creation. Theseus disposes of, and dominates, the

---

[15] For the associations of the Minotaur, see R. H. Green, 'Classical Fable and English Poetry in the 14th Century', in Dorothy Bethurum (ed.), *Critical Approaches to Medieval Literature* (New York, 1960), 128–33.

[16] 'The nature of the lion is such that he is not enraged by men if he is not harmed by them . . . The merciful nature of lions is confirmed by numerous examples: they will spare men lying on the ground, and will lead captives whom they meet to their home' (*Bestiary*, trans. and ed. Richard Barber (London, 1992), 25). The lion in Henryson's 'Taill of the Lyoun and the Mous' is another magnanimous beast.

beasts and their bodies, but he can never, even for an instant, be seen as one of them.

If Theseus stands free of any admixture of animal traits, Arcite and Palamon occupy far more shifting and ambiguous ground. As Stephen Knight puts it, they are 'worst-case examples of the knight who has hit bottom',[17] and their chronic and desperate searching for new status is mirrored in the violent turns of their language and equally violent outbursts of emotion. They are frequently compared to animals—very often in a reductive way, or to animals that occupy a lowly place in the hierarchy, without the dignity of enrolment in the heraldic corpus. Arcite compares the two of them in their dispute over Emily to two hounds fighting over a bone (line 1177)—hardly in the same league as the stately alaunts. Later he says that in our wavering, uncertain pursuit of 'felicitee' we resemble 'he that dronke is as a mous' (line 1261), and Palamon memorably accuses the gods of having no more regard for man than 'the sheep that rouketh in the folde' (line 1308). Receiving what he thinks is good news from the statue of Mars, Arcite returns to his lodgings 'As fayn as fowel is of the brighte sonne' (line 2437); after the tournament he will lie, fatally injured, 'As blak . . . as any cole or crowe' (line 2692).

In keeping with their socially marginal status, and with their association with 'lowly' animals whose fate is to be victims rather than agents, acted upon rather than actors themselves, Arcite and Palamon are the focus within the *Tale* for questions about human freedom and identity. The language they use about themselves often locates them at the extreme limit of social functioning, as, for example, in the passage previously cited, where Arcite describes himself as 'exiled and bareyne | Of alle grace, and in so greet dispeir | That ther nys erthe, water, fir, ne eir, | Ne creature that of them maked is, | That may me helpe or doon confort in this'. (When he says these words he is, of course, 'In derknesse and horrible and strong prisoun' (line 1451), quite literally barred from any participation in society.[18]) Later, as we have seen, Palamon complains against the cruel gods, who seem to place no more value on his life than on a

[17] Stephen Knight, *Geoffrey Chaucer* (Oxford, 1986), 84.
[18] Chaucer has made the conditions of the knights' imprisonment much grimmer than they are in the *Teseida* (bk. II, st. 98–9), where Palamon and Arcite have comfortable rooms befitting their status.

sheep's. Worse than this, man, unlike the beasts, is expected to live by certain moral standards and is therefore prevented from fulfilling 'al his lust' while he is alive; and after death he continues to suffer whereas animals simply pass into oblivion. Such questions challenge man's exalted place in the hierarchy, and therefore the ontologically normative view that Theseus represents. At the end of the *Tale*, with Arcite dead, Theseus will show himself particularly concerned to assert and celebrate Arcite's *human* identity and achievements, dressing him carefully in cloth of gold, having his bier carried by 'The nobleste of the Grekes' (line 2899), and (as various critics have pointed out[19]) vigorously expelling whole populations of non-human creatures so that a mighty funeral pyre may be built for him in the forest. In the long speech with which he brings the *Tale* to a close, Theseus again refuses to see events from any other perspective than the orthodox one:

> 'Of man and womman seen we wel also
> That nedes, in oon of thise termes two—
> This is to seyn, in youthe or elles age—
> He moot be deed, the kyng as shal a page . . .'   (3027–30)

Against this, we can place Arcite's anguished questions, 'What is this world? What asketh men to have?' (line 2777)—and we might also remember that, for the two young knights, the 'foule prisoun' that Theseus takes in purely abstract terms as an image of life once had a distressingly literal meaning.

My argument, therefore, is that Arcite and Palamon, within the *Tale*, act, and speak, to problematize the normative view of man's status, as a 'divyne beest' qualitatively distinct from animal creation, that Theseus consistently espouses. The various animal references contribute directly to this end. A close look at a particular episode— the fight between the two knights in the grove and its interruption by Theseus—will bring out the function of these allusions in more detail.

The reason why Theseus breaks in on the knights' bloody combat is that he is out hunting and hears from his men that there is a hart in that particular grove. Theseus's participation in the hunt is a symbol of his human supremacy, his ability to dominate animal bodies—but

---

[19] e.g. Knight, *Geoffrey Chaucer*, 89: 'the funeral arrangements [are] massively destructive of the natural world'.

the hunt also works as a symbol, in a rich way, for Palamon and Arcite.

First, there is the fact that Palamon, by lurking in the grove all day, mimics the behaviour of the hart—and may even have been mistaken for one by Theseus's prospecting huntsmen.[20] He should, of course, be the pursuer, not the pursued, but his status as an escaped prisoner, a man of the margins, has reduced his self-assurance to the tremulous stepping of a hunted deer: 'With dredeful foot thanne stalketh Palamon' (line 1479). The ambiguity already hinted at—is this a man, or has he become, in some ways, an animal?—is brilliantly maintained in the passage that precedes the knights' actual battle:

> To chaungen gan the colour of hir face;
> Right as the hunters in the regne of Trace,
> That stondeth at the gappe with a spere,
> Whan hunted is the leon or the bere,
> And hereth hym come russhyng in the greves,
> And breketh bothe bowes and the leves,
> And thynketh, 'Heere cometh my mortal enemy!
> Withoute faille, he moot be deed, or I,
> For outher I moot sleen hym at the gappe,
> Or he moot sleen me, if that me myshappe.'
> So ferden they in chaungyng of hir hewe,
> As fer as everich of hem oother knewe.   (1637–48)

The passage postpones the moment of engagement: the huntsman waits, not knowing exactly who, or what, will come crashing out of the undergrowth. His identity—his survival, even—rides upon the outcome of the conflict. This is not Theseus's effortless triumphing over animal bodies but a far more momentous enterprise. Arcite and Palamon are *both* the hunter *and* the hunted: each stands, metaphorically, at 'the gappe'—that space where human and non-human confront one another and where final mastery is set at hazard. That these lines signal a crucial transition for them is emphasized by the fact (repeated) that their faces change colour: having followed the

---

[20] For harts hiding in groves, see Edward, second Duke of York, *The Master of Game*, ed. W. A. and F. Baillie-Grohman (London, 1904), 89: 'it befalleþ somtyme þat hertis byn so malicious of hem self and of her nature þat þei pasture within hem self, þat is to say wiþ inne her Couerte, and goon not out ne to þe feeldis ne to þe copoys ne to yong wode ...'

rules of knightly honour in making sure they are properly equipped for battle, they are now to step beyond the bounds of knighthood— in fact beyond any social order—and mark out their arena for combat on the borderline between animal and human. As they arm one another, they do not speak a word. Once the fight has started,

> Thou myghtest wene that this Palamon
> In his fightyng were a wood leon,
> And as a crueel tigre was Arcite;
> As wilde bores gonne they to smyte,
> That frothen whit as foom for ire wood.
> Up to the ancle foghte they in hir blood.   (1655–60)

Critics have read these lines as a straightforward rendering of the ferocity of the fight, but in fact the perspective is a finely shifting one.[21] By prefacing the comparison with 'Thou myghtest wene...', the narrator tells us that he is offering only one possible, not the definitive, point of view. 'Perhaps you would think of them like that...but perhaps not.' The ambiguity extends to the combatants' bodies—only wild boars froth at the mouth with rage, but only humans have 'ancles'. Yet even those assuredly human features seem to lack confirmation, for it is hardly believable that the blood that has been shed reaches up to them. Resolution is deliberately deferred, and the two battling knights remain 'in the gap', their identities deeply complicit with the animals to which they have previously been compared.

The arrival of Theseus puts a stop to all this—to the fight itself and to its attendant ambiguity. As the human hunter in search of a quarry, he first of all sees the knights as 'bores two', engaged in just the sort of combat that was typical of the ferocious wild boar. However, he is quick to realize his mistake, and to impose a proper reading of the situation:

> 'But telleth me what myster men ye been,
> That been so hardy for to fighten heere
> Withouten juge or oother officere,
> As it were in a lystes roially.'   (1710–13)

---

[21] e.g. Helterman, 'Dehumanizing Metamorphoses', 497; P. M. Kean, *Chaucer and the Making of English Poetry*, vol. ii: *The Art of Narrative* (London, 1972), 34; Turner, 'Structuralist Analysis', 289.

Theseus invites Palamon and Arcite to reassume their human roles by *telling* him what has happened—that is, they must break their previous, animal-like silence—and he looks ahead to the future formalization and civilization of their unruly contest, 'in a lystes roially'.

So, in *The Knight's Tale*, animal references and allusions are used to point up questions about the uniqueness of human identity *vis-à-vis* the non-human world. Such questions cluster around Palamon and Arcite, whose role in the story involves chronic instability, triggered by a shattering fall from fortune. The two young knights are opposed, thematically, by Theseus, who is unambiguously aligned with human lordship and governance. Theseus does not resolve or cancel out the questions raised by Palamon and Arcite. Although in his final speech he tries to attain to a philosophical understanding of events, his measured declamation is heard against the throwaway comment by the narrator about Arcite's death,

> His spirit chaunged hous and wente ther,
> As I cam nevere, I kan nat tellen wher... (2809–10)

—which is not so much an example of bathos as a genuine admission of the limits of knowledge, even knowledge about who we, as humans, really are. Theseus, who holds the high seat as 'conquerour' throughout the *Tale*, may yet find even *his* basic certainties thrown into hazard by the irresistible turning of Fortune's wheel.

CHAPTER SEVEN

The Wild Man 1:
Figuring Identity

IN THE PREVIOUS chapter I suggested that the possible permeability of the boundary between animals and humans is one of the themes of *The Knight's Tale*, underlying the portrayal both of Palamon and Arcite and of Theseus, whose unchallenged ascendancy as the governor of humans requires him to be sited at the furthest remove from animal kind. Theseus is seen performing actions which emphasize that the young knights, too, are unequivocally members of the human community—for example, he organizes an elaborate funeral for Arcite which celebrates a life lived as both lover and warrior:

> And after this, Theseus hath ysent
> After a beere, and it al overspradde
> With clooth of gold, the richeste that he hadde.
> And of the same suyte he cladde Arcite;
> Upon his hondes hadde he gloves white,
> Eek on his heed a coroune of laurer grene,
> And in his hond a swerd ful bright and kene.   (2870–6)

Questions about humanness are vital ones in a number of other medieval texts, and in many cases they are posed through a figure whose possession of full humanity is far more dubious than Arcite's—that of the wild man. Poised between two worlds, the wild man brings to a head questions about the dividing line between animals and humans, and the distinctiveness of human identity. He is the subject of the next two chapters: in the present chapter I explore the ways in which his body and selfhood are constructed and the kinds of questions which are focused upon him, and in the following chapter I look at a particularly telling and frequently occurring contrast, that between wild man and knight.

Wild men are certainly familiar denizens of medieval culture, for their images appear countless times: in marginal decorations in manuscripts and in illustrations to—for example—the Alexander romances; on ivory caskets and mirror-backs; on spoons, bed-hangings, and tapestries; and, in church art, in misericords, roof-bosses, and carvings upon porches and around fonts.[1] The wild man also features in numerous literary texts, either as the traditional opponent of the knight, like the *wodwos* who assail Gawain on his winter journey, or as the knight himself, temporarily gone wild and living in the wilderness. So frequent are his appearances that it is understandable that Richard Bernheimer, the author of the best-known and most thorough study of wild men in art and literature, treats him as a substantive phenomenon, inviting the same degree of biological definition as an elephant or a giraffe:

[the wild man] is a hairy man curiously compounded of human and animal traits, without, however, sinking to the level of the ape. It exhibits upon its naked human anatomy a growth of fur, leaving bare only its face, feet, and hands, at times its knees and elbows, or the breasts of the female of the species. Frequently the creature is shown wielding a heavy club or mace, or the trunk of a tree; and, since its body is usually naked except for a shaggy covering, it may hide its nudity under a strand of twisted foliage worn around its loins.[2]

The body Bernheimer describes is basically a human body which has been overwritten with animal characteristics—specifically, exces-sive hairiness. But what kind of identity lurks behind this shaggy

---

[1] Timothy Husband's catalogue of an exhibition at the Metropolitan Museum of Art in New York, *The Wild Man: Medieval Myth and Symbolism* (New York, 1980), provides a wealth of artistic examples. See also: O. M. Dalton, *Catalogue of the Ivory Carvings of the Christian Era of the British Museum* (London, 1909), nos. 364 (pl. LXXXI), 369 (pl. LXXXVII); Felicity Dracopoli, 'Wild Men in Suffolk', programme book of the 25th Aldeburgh Festival of Music and the Arts (1972), 12–15; H. D. Ellis, 'The Wodwose in East Anglian Church Decoration', *Proceedings of the Suffolk Institute of Archaeology and Natural History*, 14/3 (1912), 287–93; Lilian M. C. Randall, *Images in the Margins of Gothic Manuscripts* (Berkeley and Los Angeles, 1966), under 'Wildman'; and Raimond van Marle, *Iconographie de l'art profane au Moyen-âge*, 2 vols. (The Hague, 1931–2), i. 183–7.

[2] Richard Bernheimer, *Wild Men in the Middle Ages: A Study in Art, Sentiment and Demonology* (Cambridge, Mass., 1952), 1. Penelope Doob's 'portrait' of the wild man (in *Nebuchadnezzar's Children: Conventions of Madness in Middle English Literature* (New Haven, 1974), 134) is very similar in kind, although not identical in its details since Doob includes 'unusually great or small size' among her list of identifying characteristics, while Bernheimer excludes very large ('giants') and very small ('dwarves') specimens from the true genus of wild man.

exterior? Bernheimer's text encapsulates the problem, in the way its perspective shifts and wavers. Sometimes the wild man's aberrant physicality is regarded with the degree of detachment and depersonalization appropriate to an anatomical specimen ('It exhibits upon its naked human anatomy a growth of fur . . . '), elsewhere the subject is allowed volition, and a socially developed sense of propriety ('since its body is usually naked . . . it may hide its nudity'). And the question that is never conclusively grounded is, in what sense can this creature be said to *exist* at all?

There were, of course, real people—hermits, outlaws, outcasts from society—leading a more or less 'wild' life in the forests of the Middle Ages.[3] However, their verifiable experiences are not what Bernheimer is writing about, nor will they be the subject of this chapter. Instead, I propose to treat the wild man as an imaginative construction within medieval culture, used in various ways for varying purposes. If we read him as a symbol, it must be one with a negotiable meaning and focus, for symbolic knowledge, Dan Sperber reminds us, 'is neither about words nor about things, but about the meaning of words and things. It is a knowledge about knowledge, a meta-encyclopedia in the encyclopedia and not— contrary to the semiological view—a meta-language in language.'[4] In other words, a statement such as 'the wild man symbolizes wildness' requires us to jettison our assumption that we know, in essence, what 'wildness' is, and to explore instead the meaning it is accorded within particular contexts.

A basic schema for a symbolic reading of the wild man is proposed by Timothy Husband in his Introduction to the catalogue of an exhibition at the Metropolitan Museum of Art in New York. 'As the dialectical antithesis of all men should strive for,' Husband writes, 'the wild man was the abstract concept of "noncivilization" rendered as a fearful physical reality.'[5] Hayden White echoes this theory in his comment that the wild man was 'everything [men] hoped they were not'.[6] White sees the wild man's identity burgeon-

[3] See e.g. Maurice Keen, *The Outlaws of Medieval Legend* (London, 1961).

[4] Dan Sperber, *Rethinking Symbolism*, trans. Alice L. Morton, Cambridge Studies and Papers in Social Anthropology (Cambridge, 1975), 108–9.

[5] Husband, *Wild Man*, 5.

[6] Hayden White, 'The Forms of Wildness: Archaeology of an Idea', in Edward Dudley and Maximillian E. Novak (eds.), *The Wild Man Within: An Image in Western Thought from the Renaissance to Romanticism* (Pittsburgh, 1972), 5.

ing from the attempts made by a society to define itself in positive terms:

In times of socio-cultural stress, when the need for positive self-definition asserts itself but no compelling criterion of self-identification appears, it is always possible to say something like: 'I may not know the precise content of my own felt humanity, but I am most certainly *not* like that,' and simply point to something in the landscape that is manifestly different from oneself.[7]

White goes on to remark that the wild man, unlike the barbarian or member of the 'monstrous' races, 'is conventionally represented as being always present, inhabiting the immediate confines of the community':

He is just out of sight, over the horizon, in the nearby forest, desert, mountains, or hills. He sleeps in crevices, under great trees, or in the caves of wild animals, to which he carries off helpless children, or women, there to do unspeakable things to them. And he is also sly: he steals the sheep from the fold, the chicken from the coop, tricks the shepherd, and befuddles the gamekeeper.[8]

The observation that the wild man is always on the periphery of community, liminal between the known and the unknown, is an interesting and suggestive one, but White does not follow it through. His wild man lapses into a folkloric compound of ogre and trickster, and finally loses distinctive identity by becoming a symbol, internalized with the passage of history, for all of our wayward and forbidden desires.

Wildness and barbarism are regarded, in general, as potentialities lurking in the heart of every individual, whether primitive or civilized, as his possible incapacity to come to terms with his socially provided world. They are not viewed as essences or substances peculiar to a particular portion of human-ity *out there* in space or *back there* in time. At least, they ought not to be so regarded.[9]

Freud arose, and the wild men scampered back into the darkness of the Id, which is where, in White's view, they properly belonged all along.

However, although White finally has recourse to an ahistorical explanation for the existence of the wild man, he does at one point place him within a specific social context:

In the Christian Middle Ages, then, the Wild Man is the distillation of the specific anxieties underlying the three securities supposedly provided by

---

[7] Ibid. 4–5.   [8] Ibid. 20–1.   [9] Ibid. 35.

the specifically Christian institutions of civilized life: the securities of *sex* (as organized by the institution of the family), *sustenance* (as provided by the political, social, and economic institutions), and *salvation* (as provided by the Church).[10]

Timothy Husband takes up the same theme, although he chooses a different triad: 'Sublimated in the wild man were the preeminent phobias of medieval society—chaos, insanity, and ungodliness.'[11] Both Husband and Richard Bernheimer relate changes in the portrayal of the wild man to changing conditions in his environing society. They argue that, as more and more of the population moved away from the country to live in towns, so the wild man came to represent the lost pleasures of an earlier, supposedly 'simpler' way of life:

The wild man's disassociation from the collapsed institutions from which he had been barred and from which he had derived no benefit suddenly placed him in a positive light. As he was without knowledge of God he could not commit sin against Him. He indulged his impulses at will and without guilt. Unburdened with man's stagnant values he enjoyed a free existence. Once viewed with repugnance, the wild man now elicited envy.... Where his habitat was once vilified, the woodlands were now celebrated for their freedom from the trammels of convention and the corruption of man's society.[12]

Husband and Bernheimer locate this change in the later fourteenth and fifteenth centuries, and link it with the growing economic complexity of life in towns. In support of their thesis, they describe pictures and tapestries that show communities of wild people— women and children as well as men—fruitfully working the land or leading harmonious family lives in an idyllic natural setting.[13] In Germany, as Simon Schama has shown, the change in the image of the wild man from a brute to a noble savage, complete with family, coincides with the rediscovery of Tacitus' *Germania*, and the desire to assert native German culture, rooted in the solid virtues of the *Hochwald*, against its effete Italian counterpart.[14]

Wild men, therefore, are not unresponsive to social and economic forces. And such changes play out their dialectic in the body

---

[10] White, 'Forms of Wildness', 21.   [11] Husband, *Wild Man*, 5.   [12] Ibid. 15.
[13] Bernheimer, *Wild Men in the Middle Ages*, 112–20 and pls. 41–5; Husband, *Wild Man*, nos. 31 (colorplate IX), 32 (fig. 83), 33 (figs. 84, 85).
[14] Simon Schama, *Landscape and Memory* (London, 1995), 96–9.

of the wild man as it is realized in art and literature. Schama acutely observes that there is something 'oxymoronic' in the 'spectacle of wild-but-willing men diligently tending to flocks or even tilling fields'.[15] In a painting of 'L'État sauvage' by Jean Bourdichon (*c.*1500), a family group poses in front of the cave that is its home. The man grasps a branch broken from a tree—the typical wild man's club, but this time carefully stripped of twigs and leaves and planed to a smooth surface, only the tiny fork at the tip reminding us of its origin. Although he is hairy, his beard has been trimmed, and the hair on the head of his wife (for so we read her) has been neatly plaited. Their baby, while furry, is human in shape, and suckles exactly like a human infant. The entrance to the cave is squared with blocks of cut masonry, and its supply of spring water issues into a pond whose perfect circularity suggests labour and even artifice. David Sprunger, who reproduces the illustration, suggests an allusion to the Holy Family in the group's composition;[16] certainly these wild people have absorbed several aspects of the culture of the city that appears in the background, replicating its practices upon their own bodies. But some traces of wildness remain: besides the hair, the bare patches on the hands and elbows of the adults are the signs of animal-like crawling along the ground rather than a fully human, upright stance.

In other portrayals of the wild man, his physical aberrancy reflects divisions and countercurrents within the society which has devised him. For example, when Chrétien de Troyes, in his romance of *Yvain*, describes the phantasmagorically ugly Giant Herdsman who is the lord of the beasts of the forest, he links the creature's misshapen features to the putative 'ugliness' of peasants and other members of the lower orders—from whom his sophisticated audience might be expected to recoil with as much alacrity as they would from an actual wild man. Yvain declares himself eager to see this Herdsman,

> qui tant par est lez
> Granz et hideus et contrefez
> Et noirs a guise de ferron.[17]

[15] Ibid. 97.

[16] David A. Sprunger, 'Wild Folk and Lunatics in Medieval Romance', in Joyce E. Salisbury (ed.), *The Medieval World of Nature: A Book of Essays* (New York, 1993), 145. See also the illustration reproduced by Schama, *Landscape and Memory*, 97, and his accompanying commentary.

[17] *Yvain: Le Chevalier au lion*, text W. Foerster, introd. T. B. W. Reid (Manchester, 1942), lines 711–13.

who is so ugly, huge and hideous and deformed and black like a smith.

The Herdsman's blackness is likened to the blackness of a smith at his anvil, the one kind as disfiguring as the other to Chrétien's fastidious listeners. The equivalence becomes even clearer when Yvain actually meets the creature and marvels exceedingly

> Coment Nature faire sot
> Oevre si leide et si *vilainne*.[18]

how Nature was able to make something so ugly and base.

If the wild man himself needs to be contextualized, related to movements of ideas in his environing society, the same applies to his habitat, the forest. 'From biblical times to the present,' Hayden White writes, 'the notion of the Wild Man was associated with the idea of the wilderness—the desert, forest, jungle, and mountains—those parts of the physical world that had not yet been domesticated or marked out for domestication in any significant way.'[19] *As* wild man to civilized human being, the argument runs, *so* forest to cultivated land. However, an 'idea of the wilderness' can only be derived, dialectically, from its counterpart—what is *not* wilderness: neither term has an essential referent but stands, or shifts, according to the other's construction. In fact, the medieval forest, as Jacques Le Goff has demonstrated, bears the same marks of imaginative, and practical, colonization, as does the body of its legendary occupant.

'The "wild"', Le Goff argues, 'is not what is beyond the reach of man but what is on the fringes of human activity. The forest (*silva*) is wild (*silvatica*) not only because it is the place where one hunts for animals but also because it is the haunt of charcoal burners and swineherds.'[20] So the forest of the Middle Ages is by no means an unexplored, mysterious tract totally lacking any human imprint: it is, at least in part, inhabited, and its inhabitants are characteristically

---

[18]   Ibid., lines 798–9 (my italics).
[19]   White, 'Forms of Wildness', 7.
[20]   Jacques Le Goff, *The Medieval Imagination* (Chicago and London, 1988; trans. of *L'Imaginaire médiéval: Essais*, Paris, 1985), 115.

those on the margins of human society—hermits, outlaws—or those taking part in some kind of liminal activity—caring for animals, such as swine, or pursuing them in a hunt.

> The *bellatores* or warriors . . . attempted . . . to appropriate the forest and make it their private hunting ground. But they were obliged to share it with the *oratores* . . . whose mission was prayer and who turned the forest into a 'desert' for eremites, as well as with the *laboratores* . . . who gathered food, fuel, and honey and fed their hogs there, making it a region of supplemental economic activity.[21]

Just as the real forest was sporadically peopled, so the forest in the works of the romance-writers undergoes imaginative invasion, bowing and shifting to the narrative's demands. For example, Le Goff draws attention to the odd spatial qualities of the landscape through which, in Chrétien's *Yvain*, first Calogrenant and then Yvain himself travel. The forest of Broceliande, the 'wilderness par excellence', suddenly gives way to the other-worldly castle set in a moor where the questing knight is welcomed by a *vavasor* who tells him he is on the right path. Next, we are back in the forest, where the knight watches the battling wild bulls and meets their master, the Giant Herdsman. The Herdsman bestows a meaning on the forest by guiding the knight through it to the magic fountain that guards the castle whose lady is Laudine. After Yvain, untrue to Laudine, has run mad, the forest assumes a new role, becoming complicit in the penitential suffering he has to undergo. 'In terms of structural analysis,' Le Goff suggests, 'there is no forest as such. Even within the context of a single work the forest exists only in relation to what is not forest. Oppositions come into play even within what appeared to be simple.'[22]

Something similar happens in Geoffrey of Monmouth's *Vita Merlini*. Here forest and royal court alternate as settings in response to Merlin's varying apprehension of the real nature of human society. Merlin's first bout of madness is caused by his overwhelming grief at the death of his three brothers in battle. He flees to the woods, and lives there through the seasons until he is soothed by music from one of king Rodarch's retainers and allows himself to

---

[21] Ibid. 52.   [22] Ibid. 122.

be led back to the court. However, once within the court he is driven mad a second time by the sight of the great crowds of people there:

> At postquam tantas hominum Merlinus adesse
> inspexit turmas, nec eas perferre valeret.
> Cepit enim furias iterumque furore repletus
> ad nemus ire cupit furtimque recedere querit.[23]

But when Merlin saw such crowds of people there, he could not bear them. He went mad; and once more his derangement filled him with a desire to go off to the forest, and he longed to slip away.

The 'woods' are the term Merlin opposes to the unbearable tumult of the crowds. They are places in his mind. At the end of the story he has succeeded in completely re-forming them to his own demands, since he persuades his sister Ganieda to build him a forest home, complete with servants to wait upon him and prepare his meals. He also specifies a more remote building with several doors and windows, through which he can observe the heavenly bodies and predict what is going to happen in the kingdom. During the summer he plans to wander freely through the woods, but in the cold of winter he will return to his settlement, and his sister will see that he is supplied with food and drink. Merlin imposes upon the forest his own eclectic vision of the ideal life, and refashions it to his desires.

The forest's proximity—both literal and metaphorical—and its implication in many different areas of human activity, is reflected in the lives of those who inhabit it. The wild men of the romances are not generally to be found in remote or isolated places—instead, their ground is typically criss-crossed by the trackways of encroaching civilization and consequently generates many personal encounters. Their behaviour is continually being observed and commented on by the scouts of civilization, as Merlin's lament on his sufferings is overheard by a traveller, who reports it to one of king Rodarch's retainers. Orson, the knight Valentine's savage brother (in the romance discussed in more detail in the last section of the next chapter), crosses human pathways repeatedly and disastrously. A poor man complains to king Pepin:

---

[23]   *Life of Merlin*, ed. and trans. Basil Clarke (Cardiff, 1973), lines 221–4.

For euen so as I and my wyfe passed throughe the forest berynge breed, wyne, and other vytaylles, the wilde man came and toke al frome vs and ete it, and more ouer he toke my wyfe and dyde twyes his wyl with her.[24]

The wild man's nearness to humans, even in his so-called 'wilderness' home, is an index of his intimate dialectical relationship with the cultures that give him expression. Le Goff writes:

Societies . . . define their relations to alien beings by way of their representation of wild men. Indeed, historical societies were not interested in the wild man as such. In both written documents and images and even with respect to institutions the whole interest is in the relations between the wild man and his 'cultivated' brother.[25]

Some aspects of these relations will be explored in the following sections of this chapter.

IS HE A MAN?

There was no dodging the question: either a wild man was human, possessed of reason, descended from the first man, Adam, and therefore capable of receiving the benefits of Christ's work of salvation; or he was animal, lacking in reason, not responsible for his actions, and liable to be treated in the way that other animals were treated. As Hayden White explains:

It was because animals possessed such a soul [i.e. one devoid of reason] that they had been consigned to the service of man and to his governance. And because they possessed such a soul, man could do with animals what he would: domesticate them and use them, or, if necessary, destroy them without sin.[26]

And so there is nothing abnormal, or morally reprehensible, in the *bas-de-page* scene in Queen Mary's Psalter which shows a wild man being tormented by dogs. The correct 'reading' of this scene is supplied on the facing page, in which a courtly hunting party watch the sport. The wild man has simply taken the place of a stag or boar

---

[24] *Valentine and Orson*, trans. Henry Watson, ed. Arthur Dickson, EETS OS 204 (1937), 64.

[25] Le Goff, *Medieval Imagination*, 117.

[26] White, 'Forms of Wildness', 19.

or other quarry—a more unusual beast of the chase, perhaps, but a beast none the less.[27]

'Are you a man?' It was vital to find an answer to the question, but actually doing so was not straightforward. The wild man in the Psalter *looks* fairly human—apart from being covered with hair— but he is obviously not being presented as such. St Augustine, in his *De civitate dei*, had pondered the problem with regard to the 'monstrous races'. Were hermaphrodites, men without mouths, or dog-headed men human? Augustine was careful not to assert his unqualified belief in the existence of such creatures ('The accounts of some of these races may be completely worthless . . .'[28]), but if they *did* exist he saw no reason why they should not be included in God's providential scheme for mankind. If human, they had certainly descended from Adam, like all other people.[29] Augustine argued that human beings may be born with more or less serious abnormalities—with extra fingers or toes or with both male and female sexual organs. No one doubts that such 'monstrous births' are human, nor should anyone imagine that God had made a mistake in creating them that way:

For God is the creator of all, and he himself knows where and when any creature should be created or should have been created. He has the wisdom to weave the beauty of the whole design out of the constituent parts, in their likeness and diversity. The observer who cannot view the whole is offended by what seems the deformity of a part, since he does not know how it fits in, or how it is related to the rest.[30]

What is true of deformed human births is equally true of the 'monstrous races'—any of their members *may be* human, no matter

---

[27] BL MS Roy. 2 B VII, fo. 173[r], reprod. in *Queen Mary's Psalter*, introd. Sir George Warner (London, 1912), pl. 201. Raimond van Marle describes a painting in Granada, *c*.1400, which shows a wild man being killed 'de la façon que d'autres cavaliers appliquent pour le gibier [game]' (*Iconographie*, i. 187). Another wild man whose setting imposes an 'animal' reading appears on a roof-boss in St Edmund's chapel, Tewkesbury Abbey, where he is one among various animals who cluster round the Bestiary panther so that they can smell its sweet breath (see C. J. P. Cave, *Roof Bosses in Medieval Churches* (Cambridge, 1948), pl. 219 and p. 72).

[28] *City of God*, trans. Henry Bettenson, introd. John O'Meara (Harmondsworth, 1972), 664.

[29] Ibid. 662: 'But no faithful Christian should doubt that anyone who is born anywhere as a man—that is, a rational and mortal being—derives from that one first-created being.'

[30] Ibid.

how 'extraordinary such a creature may appear to our senses in bodily shape, in colour, or motion, or utterance, or in any natural endowment, or part, or quality'. God, in his capacious providence, knows the true nature of each individual component of his creation. The problem is that humans lack God's sublimely analytic vision. How are *they* to decide whether a being—a wild man—is human or not?

As we have seen, the wild man's status cannot be deduced from his physical appearance. Therefore, narratives involving him are often deliberately structured to elicit an answer in some other way—either through dialogue or through action. An example of the former method at work is Mandeville's tale of the meeting between a monster and a Christian hermit in the Egyptian desert:

Nota of a Merueyle. At the deserte of Egypte was a worthi man that was an holy heremyte, and there mette with him a monstre; that is to seyne, a monstre is a thing disformed ayen kynde bothe of man or of best or of ony thing elles, and that is cleped a monstre. And this monstre that mette with this holy heremyte was as it hadde ben a man that hadde ii. hornes trenchant on his forhede, and he hadde a body lyk a man vnto the navele, and benethe he hadde the body lych a goot. And the heremyte asked him what he was, and the monstre answerde him and sayde he was a dedly creature such as God hadde formed and duelled in the desertes in purcha-cynge his sustynance; and besoughte the heremyte that he wolde preye God for him, the whiche that cam from Heuene for to sauen alle man-kynde, and was born of a mayden, and suffred passioun and deth, as wee wel knowen, be whom wee kyuen and ben. And yit is the hede with the ii. hornes of that monstre at Alisaunder for a merueyle.[31]

This 'monstre', who to our eyes has elements of the classical satyr, starts off by appearing completely alien to the hermit, neither man nor beast. His assimilation to the narrator's culture takes place in stages: first he speaks, and asserts his creatureliness and mortality ('a dedly creature such as God hadde formed'); next, he claims to engage in purposeful activity ('purchacynge his sustynance'). His final step towards full humanity is taken when he beseeches the hermit to pray for him, and reveals his knowledge of Christ's birth,

[31] *Mandeville's Travels*, ed. M. C. Seymour (Oxford, 1967), 33. The original version of the story is in Jerome's *Vita S. Pauli primi eremitate*, in J.-P. Migne, *Patrologia Latina*, vol. 23, col. 23.

passion, and death. The narrator's voice joins approvingly in this catechism ('as wee wel knowen . . .'). Odd the monster may be—and he is certainly odder than the wild man in Queen Mary's Psalter—but human, and deserving of human sympathy and intercession, he undoubtedly is.

In the English prose life of Alexander in the Thornton manuscript, the all-important question is answered not through dialogue but through a practical test. Alexander and his army encounter a huge wild man beside a river:

And as it ware abowte none, þare come apon þam a wilde man, als mekill als a geaunte. And he was rughe of hare all ouer, and his hede was lyke till a swyne, And his voyce also. And when Alexander saw hym, he bad his knyghtis tak hym & bryng hym bi-for hym. And when þay come abowte hym, he was na thynge fered, ne fledd noȝte, bot stodd baldly bi-fore þam. And when Alexander saw that, he comanded þat þay sulde take a ȝonge damesell & nakken hir & sett hir bi-fore hym. And þay did soo. And onane, he ranne apon hir romyandd as he hadd bene wodd. Bot þe knyghtes with grete deficcultee refte hyr fra hym. And ay he romyed & made grete mane.[32]

This wild man has a head like a swine and cannot speak, only bellow. His fearlessness when surrounded by the knights, and his lack of deference towards Alexander also suggest that he exists outside the human commonalty. But the conclusive proof of this is his behaviour towards the young girl—by showing that he is unable to control his animal lusts, he demonstrates to the onlookers that he lacks reason and is therefore not a man at all but a beast.[33] Once this has been established, the knights have no further interest in him (although Alexander, we are told, 'wonderd gretly of his figure'), and he is summarily disposed of. 'And þan he [i.e. Alexander] gerte bynd hym till a tree & make a fyre aboute hym & brynne hym. And so þay didd.'

The version of this incident in the alliterative *Wars of Alexander* is different in several interesting respects:

---

[32] *The Prose Life of Alexander*, from the Thornton MS, ed. J. S. Westlake, EETS OS 143 (1913), 89–90.

[33] According to Trevisa, fauns and satyrs revealed their bestial identity by their lust towards women: *On the Properties of Things*, 3 vols. (Oxford, 1975–88), ii. 1199–1200.

Þan ferd he [i.e. Alexander] furth to a flumme & [ficchid] þare his tentis,
And newly eftir þe none or nere þareaboute
Þare coms a bonde of a brenke & breed þaim vnfaire.
A burly best & a bigge was as a [berne] shapen;
Vmquile he groned as a galt with grysely latis,
Vmquile he noys as a nowte, as an ox quen he lawes,
Ȝarmand & ȝerand, a ȝoten him semed,
And was as bristil[e] as a bare all þe body ouire.
Dom as a dore-nayle & defe was he bathe,
With laith leggis & lange & twa laue eres.
A heuy hede & a hoge as it a hors ware,
And large was his odd lome þe lenthe of a ȝerde.
With þat comands oure kyng his kniȝtis him to take,
And þai asaillid him sone, bot he na segge dredis,
For nouthire fondis he to flee ne na fens made,
Bot stude & stared as a stott & stirred he na forthire.
Þan callis to him þe conquirour a comly mayden,
Bad hire be broȝt before þe best & bare to be nakid.
And he beheld on þat hend & hissis as a neddire;
He wald haue strangild hire streȝt ne had stiffe men bene.
He wald haue schowid on þat schene had noȝt [schalkis] halden,
And to þe prince pauelion prestly him lede.
Quen he had ferlied his fill on his foule schapp,
He gers þaim bynde him at a braid & brent him to poudire.[34]

The author has considerably expanded the lines about the wild man in his primary source, the *Historia de preliis Alexandri Magni*, taking in several traditional elements of the creature's portrait, and building them into that composite of oppositional features which, as I show below, was also characteristic.[35] This wild man, though, occupies uneasy ground. He starts off as the kind of uncouth challenger at the river's brink that other romance heroes meet in the course of their quests: 'Þare coms a bonde of a brenke & breed þaim vnfaire'. In the next line, however, he has shifted to the animal ('A burly best & a bigge'), although still perceived as human in shape. The incoherent,

---

[34] *The Wars of Alexander*, ed. H. N. Duggan and T. Turville-Petre, EETS ss 10 (1989), lines 4866–89. For the likely date of this version (*c.*1400), and its place within the medieval Alexander tradition, see ibid., pp. xlii–xliii, and Peter Dronke, 'Poetic Originality in *The Wars of Alexander*', in Helen Cooper and Sally Mapstone (eds.), *The Long Fifteenth Century: Essays for Douglas Gray* (Oxford, 1997), 123 n. 2.

[35] The Latin reads: 'Et hora incumbente nona venit super [eos] quidam homo agrestis corpore magnus valde et pilosus erat ut porcus; vox eius ut vox porci. Loquelam non habebat set tanquam porcus alta voce strundebat' (ed. cit. 281, n. to lines 4867–77).

horrible sounds he makes seem to confirm his beastly identity—but there is something disconcerting in their very variety, as though some pressure to communicate lies behind them. However, the narrator forecloses upon this possibility: the creature is 'Dom as a dore-nayle', that is, incapable of speech. The incident with the young girl is not used to demonstrate the wild man's uncontrollable lust, as it is in the prose version—and, for that matter, in various illustrations of the scene, which show his intent to be definitely amorous.[36] Instead, the narrator emphasizes his crude aggression and rage to kill—this wild man 'hissis as a neddire' and 'wald haue strangild hire streȝt ne had stiffe men bene'. This change of motivation is surprising (especially since the wild man's impressively large penis has already been described). Peter Dronke argues that the change is intended to exonerate Alexander from a possible charge of cruelty when he later has the wild man burnt to ashes. As a 'sinister and authentically bestial' creature, he can be seen to deserve his fate.[37] This is certainly true, but the emphasis on murderousness rather than lust can also be seen as a final assertion of that alterity which has been awkwardly under question in the preceding lines. Male readers, after all, might feel some sympathy for a man who tries to make love to a beautiful naked girl suddenly presented to him. What this author does is to make the wild man's action totally *in*comprehensible, by stressing the graciousness ('þat hend') as well as the beauty of the girl. She has done nothing at all to inspire the crazed malice, the snakelike hissing, with which the wild man affronts her. Therefore he is truly other, therefore it is only right that he should be put to death (for humans can dispose of animals, who lack reason, just as they will). In Alexander's last engagement with the living creature, the wild man becomes simply the object of gaze, his 'foule schapp' sustenance for the conqueror's own transcendent selfhood.

The animal comparisons earlier in the passage also help to construct this wild man as non-human. The animals mentioned are either those that naturally come under man's dominion (bulls and oxen), or those he pursues, and battles with, in the chase (the boar, whose bristled coat is like the wild man's skin). There is a similar effect at work in the description of the incident that comes imme-

---

[36] See e.g. BL MS Royal 20. B. XX, fo. 64ʳ, reprod. in Sprunger, 'Wild Folk', fig. 6 (p. 154).

[37] Dronke, 'Poetic Originality', 127–8.

diately before the adventure with the wild man. Alexander and his army arrive at a forest full of fruit-bearing trees. It is inhabited by hosts of wild men, 'whase bodyes ware grete as geaunteȝ, and þaire clethynge ware made of skynnes of dyuerse besteȝ'.[38] These giants, although they live solely on fruit, turn out to be aggressive and attack Alexander's company with large sticks. Alexander marshals his forces and orders them to shout loudly—'sett vp a scharp schoute at all þe schaw ryngis'.[39] The wild men are terrified at the sound and flee hither and thither in the forest, into which Alexander's men pursue them, killing many of them. It would be possible to justify such action by citing the wild men's initial aggression, but the narrators of both texts go further in emphasizing the rightness of Alexander's vengeance by bringing in the metaphor of the hunt as a potent subtext. The wild men, flitting panic-stricken between the trees, become the deer, the huntsman's quarry. Their flight is prompted by the kind of explosion of noise that scatters the deer in *Gawain*—'At þe fyrst quethe of þe quest quaked þe wylde', line 1150—and the final tally of bodies ('And sex hundreth was slane & sesid with oure kniȝtis'[40]) resembles the heaps of slain animals at the conclusion, for instance, of one of Henry VIII's royal hunts.[41] Through such equivalences, these texts 'solve', for the occasion, the riddle of the wild man.

When the questing knight Calogrenant first meets the Giant Herdsman in Chrétien's *Yvain*, the same problem of identity arises, but is dealt with in an altogether more playful way:

> Totes voies tant m'anhardi,
> Que je li dis: 'Va, car me di,
> Se tu es buens chose ou non!'
> Et il me dist: 'Je sui uns hon.'

[38] *Prose Life*, 89; *Wars of Alexander*, lines 4848–9, 4853: 'ᵭit wont men in þa woddis, as þe [writt] tellis, | Of ioynttours as ieants in iopons of hidis ... Þai ware as rughe as a resche, þe [rige] & þe sidis.'

[39] Ibid., line 4857.

[40] Ibid., line 4860.

[41] 'Wherever there are large numbers of deer the manner of proceeding is to have two or three hundred rounded up and then to set greyhounds upon them to kill them, so that he [i.e. Henry VIII] may have commodity of them to present to the gentlemen of that country when he departeth thence' (Letter of Charles de Marillac, the French ambassador, quoted in *The Lisle Letters*, ed. Muriel St Clare Byrne (Chicago, 1981), vi. 177). On another day, in Hatfield, 240 stags and does were killed, and the same number the next day with greyhounds (ibid.).

'Ques hon ies tu?'—'Tes con tu voiz.
Je ne sui autre nule foiz.'[42]

Nevertheless, I was bold enough to say to him, 'Come, tell me if you are a good thing or not.' And he said to me, 'I am a man.' 'What kind of man are you?' 'Such as you see. I am never any different.'

The knight's use of the word *chose* suggests that he has no idea of what the creature facing him might be. The Herdsman appears to answer the question: he is a man. Yet that does not resolve Calogrenant's dilemma: as we have seen, a being might be a 'man' and still not be fully human. What *kind* of man is he? The Herdsman teases his inquisitor by simultaneously giving, and withholding, an answer: 'Tes con tu voiz.' Calogrenant should trust the evidence of his eyes—but we know that sense impressions alone cannot resolve the crux of humanity. But perhaps Calogrenant *has* been given the answer he needs—for the Herdsman's assured verbal play, and, subsequently, his helpful advice, surely mark him as human, beyond any questions raised by his fearsome shape. In the English version of the story, *Ywain and Gawain*, Colgrevance appears equally bemused by the Herdsman's appearance:

> To him I spak ful hardily
> And said, 'What ertow, belamy?'
> He said ogain, 'I am a man.'
> I said, 'Swilk saw I never nane.'
> 'What ertow?' alsone said he.
> I said, 'Swilk als þou here may se.'[43]

His 'belamy' allows for the possibility that the Herdsman is not only human, but fully capable of social intercourse. So it proves, and Colgrevance acknowledges this by joining in the rally of questions about identity—he himself, he says, is simply (but, of course, hardly 'simply') what he appears to be.

In the romance of *Sir Orfeo*, the king, hairy and lacerated from his years in the wilderness, approaches dangerously close to the *visual* prototype of the wild man. Yet we, as readers, must never be allowed to doubt his humanity. One or two details in the story seem designed to remind us of this: his harp, for instance, which he

[42] *Yvain*, lines 327–32.
[43] *Ywain and Gawain*, ed. Albert B. Friedman and Norman T. Harris, EETS os 254 (1964), lines 277–82.

takes with him on his journey into exile, and continues to play, occasionally, to the wild animals, acts as a pledge of his fully human capacity. Appropriately, it enables him to recover his wife, and is the means by which, in the final scene, he resumes his kingly role. Before this, when Orfeo walks through the streets of his city disguised as a beggar, we are told:

> Erles and barouns bold,
> Burjays and levedis him gan bihold:
> 'Lo,' thai seyd, 'swiche a man!'[44]

The nobles are amazed at his shrivelled appearance and at the length of his hair ('Hou long the here hongeth him opan!'), but they are never in any doubt that this is a *man* they are looking at and not a beast. Their comment—in which *man* receives rhythmic emphasis—seems designed to foreclose on other possibilities. In doing so, it reminds us once again of the ambiguity associated with the figure of the wild man, and the importance which various texts accord to the resolution of his identity.

WILD BODIES

As we have seen, wild men in literature and art are attributed bodies that are different from human bodies in various important respects. In this section I look more closely at the construction of this difference, with especial reference to the wild man's most striking feature, his hairiness.

The physical characteristics which the wild man exhibits always bear a particular relation to their human equivalents. This can be seen, for example, in the portrait of the compendiously ugly Giant Herdsman in Chrétien's *Yvain*:

> Un vilain, qui ressanbloit mor,
> Grant e hideus a desmesure,
>
> .   .   .   .   .   .
>
> Si vi qu'il ot grosse la teste
> Plus que roncins ne autre beste,
> Chevos meschiez et front pele,

---

[44] *Sir Orfeo*, in *Middle English Romances*, ed. A. C. Gibbs, York Medieval Texts (London, 1966), lines 489–91.

> S'ot plus de deus espanz de le,
> Oroilles mossues et granz,
> Autes come a uns olifanz.
> Les sorciz granz et le vis plat,
> Iauz de cuete et nes de chat,
> Boche fandue come los,
> Danz de sangler, aguz et ros,
> Barbe noire, grenons tortiz,
> Et le manton aers au piz,
> Longue eschine, torte et bocue.[45]

I saw that his head was larger than that of a packhorse or any other beast. His hair was in tufts and his bald forehead was more than two spans wide; he had big shaggy ears like an elephant. He had heavy eyebrows and a flat face, owl's eyes and a cat's nose, a cleft mouth like a wolf's, the sharp yellow teeth of a wild boar, a black beard and a twisted moustache, a chin that met his chest, and a long spine, crooked and humped.

It is impossible to project an internally coherent body from this mass of grotesque details, which come from all corners of the animal kingdom and also involve textures suggestive of vegetable growth (the twisted moustache, the ears *mossues*). The English version is more concise, but still conveys this fantastic mingling:

> His browes war like litel buskes,
> And his tethe like bare-tuskes.[46]

Just as in Roland Barthes's *S/Z* the promised subject, 'beauty', can never be delivered through the anatomization of the *blazon* but merely joins the list as a further fetishized attribute, so the 'ugliness' of the Herdsman fails to emerge from the description of him, since this is so obviously (again in Barthes's phrase) 'a division and dissemination of partial objects'.[47] Essentially, he is a gathering together of statements of oppositional identity. Each of his features is selected

---

[45] *Yvain*, lines 288–9; 295–307.   [46] *Ywain and Gawain*, lines 261–2.

[47] Roland Barthes, *S/Z*, trans. Richard Miller (Oxford, 1990; first pub. Paris, 1973), 112. Barthes's text is suggestive about the way the 'cumulative' descriptions of ugly wild men do, or do not, work. For example: 'language undoes the body, returns it to the fetish. This return is coded under the term *blazon*. The blazon consists of predicating a single subject, beauty, upon a certain number of attributes: *she was beautiful for her arms, neck, eyebrows, nose, eyelashes, etc.* ... [O]nce this enumeration has been completed, no feature can reassemble it—or, if this feature is produced, it too can only be *added* to the others. Thus with beauty: it can only be tautological (affirmed under the very name of beauty) or analytic (if we run through its predicates), never synthetic' (pp. 113–14).

not to be compatible with its neighbours but to provide a contrast to a particular aspect of 'right-looking'—a negative image against a positive one. So, the *vilain* is black, like a Moor, and has dishevelled hair, 'mossy' ears, and a flat face, whereas a properly handsome man would have white, smooth skin, combed hair, and an angular profile. The lack of proportion between the various parts of the Herdsman's body is also emphasized—his huge head and ears, and fearsome boar's teeth, seem to be on a different scale from his 'cat's' nose. As the English version concisely puts it, 'Þare was noght made withowten lac.'[48]

What role does hairiness play in this dialectic between the socially approved body and the body of the Other? Body-hair is certainly the wild man's chief defining characteristic, becoming, from the twelfth century onwards, an indispensable part of his iconography. The convention becomes so preponderant, in fact, that even wild men who within their texts bear a variety of grotesque features often appear in the accompanying illustrations as hairy, but otherwise normal, human beings. The wild giant who attacks the naked girl in the Alexander romance is described as having the head of a swine, yet most of the illustrators show him with a human head and body, covered thickly with hair.[49]

The cultural significance of hair obviously varies from one society to another.[50] It is also influenced by gender: in the Middle Ages, for instance, male hairiness was linked to sexual prowess.[51] This connects with the image of the wild man as a being of super-virility, and with the many stories and pictures in which he abducts women in order to have sex with them.[52] More generally, hair that flows wild, or covers the body, presents an antitype to civilized, disciplined restraint. Such wildness might, of course, have its own rationale,

---

[48] *Ywain and Gawain*, line 264.

[49] See e.g. BL MS Roy. 19 D I, fo. 31^r; BL MS Roy. 20 B XX, fo. 41^v (reprod. in Doob, *Nebuchadnezzar's Children*, pl. 11, and in Husband, *Wild Man*, fig. 24).

[50] For a discussion of the symbolic uses of hair, see Raymond Firth, *Symbols Public and Private* (London, 1973), ch. 8.

[51] See Joan Cadden, *Meanings of Sex Difference in the Middle Ages: Medicine, Science, and Culture* (Cambridge, 1993), 181–3.

[52] See e.g. Bodleian Library, Oxford, MS Bodley 264 (a lavishly illustrated copy of the romance of Alexander, *c.*1338–44), fo. 69^v: wild man mounted on a stag abducting a lady; Bernheimer, *Wild Men in the Middle Ages*, pls. 26 (the Taymouth Hours), 31, 32, 33, 37, and ch. 5: 'The Erotic Connotations'.

as it does, for instance, in the biblical figures of Samson or John the Baptist, or St John Chrysostom, who grew a thick coat of hair in the course of long years living like a beast in the forest as penance for the murder he believed he had committed. When he was brought back to human society, his hairy covering fell away from him, revealing skin as pure and soft as a young child's.[53] In that story, a hair-coat is part of the saint's penitential suffering; elsewhere, hairiness is unequivocally linked with sin: St Jerome, in his translation of Isaiah, had called the demons haunting a ruined city *pilosi* ('hairy ones'), glossing these as 'incubi or satyrs or a certain kind of wild men whom some call *fatui ficarii* and regard as of the nature of demons'.[54] Cain, the first murderer, was hairy too, according to one popular tradition.[55] Most obviously, perhaps, body hair aligns the bodies of humans with those of animals: at one point in the Alexander romance, the king encounters naked wild men and women living a semi-aquatic life by a river: 'And þay ware als rughe of hare as þay hade bene bestes.'[56]

Within literary texts, and in art, in the Middle Ages as in every other historical period, hair is treated as an expressive medium. It is something that we all (or nearly all of us) have, a vestige, and a reminder, of unsuppressed animality. What we do with it sends out messages about our accommodation with that quality. There can be too much disciplining of hair as well as too little. In an illustration in a fourteenth-century copy of the *Speculum humanae salvationis* Eve has loose flowing locks but the woman-headed serpent has hair that is neatly braided: 'she' 'wears the demure but intricate fillet and braid of an aristocratic maiden'.[57] She is tempting Eve to rise above her station, to adopt a level of artifice that God never intended for

---

[53] For St John Chrysostom, see Charles Allyn Williams, 'Oriental Affinities of the Legend of the Hairy Anchorite, Part I: Pre-Christian', *University of Illinois Studies in Language and Literature*, 10 (1925), 9–13.

[54] Isa. 13: 21 (Douai version). Cf. 34: 14: 'et pilosus clamabit alter at alterum', and see Bernheimer, *Wild Men in the Middle Ages*, 96–8. Wyclif, in his translation, rendered *pilosi* as 'wodewoses' (the usual English word for 'wild men').

[55] See Ruth Mellinkoff, *The Mark of Cain* (Berkeley and Los Angeles, 1981), 70–2.

[56] *Prose Life*, 75–6.

[57] Nona C. Flores, '"Effigies Amicitiae . . . Veritas Inimicitiae": Antifeminism in the Iconography of the Woman-Headed Serpent in Medieval and Renaissance Art', in Flores (ed.), *Animals in the Middle Ages: A Book of Essays* (New York and London, 1996), 179; the picture is reproduced on p. 178.

her. Women, in fact, were often criticized by preachers for their elaborate dressing and tending of their hair.[58]

As the examples above suggest, the treatment of hair in texts is often socially marked as well as marked by gender. Chaucer's 'gentil' characters, for instance, frequently have hair that has been combed and tressed so scrupulously that it has become an artefact, its basic material burnished to a new substance. There are the Squire's locks, 'crulle as they were leyd in presse' (line 81), where the emphasis is not on natural curliness but on one created by art, or there is Emetreus, king of Inde, in *The Knight's Tale*:

> His crispe heer lyk rynges was y-ronne,
> And that was yelow, and glytered as the sonne.   (2165–6)

Characteristic adjectives are *crispe*, *gilte*, *clere*, and *oundy* (i.e. *undé*, 'wavy', a heraldic term). The overall effect is a sculptural one, where no individual filaments can be seen to move—when we *do* see hair in a more natural state the purpose is usually expressive: of enhanced emotionality, perhaps, or of comedy. Criseyde, weeping because she has heard she is to be exchanged for Antenor, allows her beautiful hair, usually bound with a golden thread, to hang loose:

> The myghty tresses of hire sonnysshe heeris
> Unbroiden hangen al aboute hire eeris,
> Which yaf hym verray signal of martire
> Of deth, which that hire herte gan desire.
> (*Troilus and Criseyde*, 4. 816–19)

Such a dishevelment pleads for—and receives—an interpretative reading: Criseyde as love's martyr. In contrast, Absolon's hair in *The Miller's Tale* is properly curly and shines like gold—but comedy springs from our awareness of all the effort that has gone into making it so:

> Crul was his heer, and as the gold it shoon
> And strouted as a fanne large and brode;
> Ful streight and evene lay his joly shode.   (3314–16)

Fatally, we can see his parting!

---

[58] e.g. 'Wommen with here hedes y-horned, schort clokes unnethe to the hupes, with bendels, chapellettes and frontelles y-set above the heued y-lyche to a wylde beste that hath none resoun' (BL MS Harl. 2398, fo. 9, quoted in G. R. Owst, *Literature and Pulpit in Medieval England*, 2nd edn. (Oxford, 1961), 401).

Hair that is untended, that erupts randomly, has affinities with Bakhtin's image of the grotesque body, whose logic 'ignores the closed, smooth, and impenetrable surface . . . and retains only its excrescences (sprouts, buds) and orifices, only that which leads beyond the body's limited space or into the body's depths'.[59] In contrast to the finished, flawless surface of classical portraiture, the grotesque body 'is not separated from the rest of the world',[60] but allies itself with processes of change, decay, and regeneration. No fixed line divides it from its environment. Indeed, in Chaucer's work, unruly hair is often twinned with bodies that display other forms of Bakhtinian grotesqueness: protruding lumps or gaping cavities. The Miller, with his tufted wart, and cavernous nostrils and mouth, is a case in point:

> Upon the cop right of his nose he hade
> A werte, and theron stood a toft of herys,
> Reed as the brustles of a sowes erys;
> His nosethirles blake were and wyde.
> A swerd and a bokeler bar he by his syde.
> His mouth as greet was as a greet forneys.   (554–9)

The consummate statement about 'natural' hair is made by Alison, in the tale the Miller tells:

> Abak he stirte, and thoughte it was amys,
> For wel he wiste a womman hath no berd.
> He felte a thyng al rough and long yherd,
> And seyde, 'Fy! allas! what have I do?'   (3736–9)

Alison's hair is not, of course, 'out of place' in the way the Miller's is, but it performs a Bakhtinian function within the text by disabusing Absolon of his closed, conventionalized picture of womanhood ('For som folk wol ben wonnen for richesse, | And somme for strokes, and somme for gentillesse', lines 3381–2). Alison herself, he painfully discovers, is not the 'faire bryd', the 'swete cynamone' he had serenaded, but a 'body' playfully open to all kinds of experience, proper or not.

How does the wild man fit into this picture? In fact, his hairiness, that feature allying him most closely with 'nature' and 'the wild', is

[59] Mikhail Bakhtin, *Rabelais and his World*, trans. Hélène Iswolsky (Bloomington, Ind., 1984), 317–18.
[60] Ibid. 27.

the object of as much expressive reworking as the hair of any Chaucerian character, tended and modified in a variety of ways. As G. C. Druce observed, the visual appearance of the wild man changes during the first half of the fourteenth century:

He suddenly becomes conventionalized, we may say almost standardized in appearance, and blossoms out into great prominence under his English name of 'wodewose'. Instead of being naked or covered with rough hair, he appears as if clothed in tightly-fitting sheep-skins, and generally bears a knotted branch or a club.[61]

An example are the wild couple who appear on the verso of folio 64 of the Treatise of Walter de Milemete (Christ Church, Oxford, MS E II). Their combed coats have the appearance of a costume rather than hair naturally erupting from the skin, and their legs below the knees are bare and smooth. They are partly hairy, partly not, and their liminal identity also appears in their stance (bent over, but without the knees touching the ground), their juxtaposition (facing each other, with hands extended in expressive gestures, so that there is the hint of interaction, of relationship), and in the fact that their bodies marginally transgress the picture frame that encloses them.[62]

One tradition about the wild man had him clothing himself in the skins of animals he had killed.[63] As Larry D. Benson points out, human ingenuity quickly got to work on this vestigial 'garment'.[64] The *vilain, lais et hidex,* in *Aucassin et Nicolete* wears his hides as a sort of double-folded cape ('Et esttoit afulés d'une cap a deus envers'),[65] while the Giant Herdsman in *Yvain* suspends his from his neck:

> Apoiiez fu sor sa maçue,
> Vestuz de robe si estrange,
> Qu'il n'i avoit ne lin ne lange,

[61] G. C. Druce, 'Some Abnormal and Composite Forms in English Church Architecture', *Archaeological Journal*, 72 (1915), 165.

[62] *The Treatise of Walter de Milemete De nobilitatibus, sapientiis, et prudentiis regum,* introd. M. R. James, Roxburghe Club (Oxford, 1913), 28. The picture is also reproduced in Randall, *Images*, CXLV. 694.

[63] See e.g. the description of the wild man in Paris, Bibliothèque de l'Arsenal, MS 3516, translated in Druce, 'Abnormal Forms', 160: 'The savage man is quite naked, unless he has at some time or other fought with a lion and killed it, and has clothed himself with the skin of the lion.'

[64] Larry D. Benson, *Art and Tradition in Sir Gawain and the Green Knight* (Cambridge, Mass., 1965), 77–8.

[65] *Aucassin et Nicolete*, ed. F. W. Bourdillon (Manchester, 1970), 24. 13–21.

> Ainz ot a son col atachiez
> Deus cuirs de novel escorchiez
> De deus toriaus ou de deus bués.[66]

He leant on his club, dressed in very strange clothing which contained no linen or wool: instead he had, fastened at his neck, two hides newly flayed from two bulls or two oxen.

The word *atachiez* suggests just the merest trace of artifice—the Herdsman has not simply covered his nakedness with the hides: he has dressed himself in them.

Benson goes on to show that, in later developments (and particularly, it seems, in English texts), the 'cape' of hides is replaced by the bushy hair that grows from the wild man's head—but this hair is now clipped and shaped into something that itself resembles a garment. The English author of *Ywain and Gawain*, usually faithful to Chrétien's original, substitutes such a covering for the Giant Herdsman's 'robe . . . estrange':

> Unto his belt hang his hare,
> And efter þat byheld I mare.[67]

And in *Sir Gawain and the Green Knight* the Green Knight's luxuriant hair and beard are composed into a 'kyngez capados', which even seems to be fastened at the neck as a real hood would be:

> Fayre fannand fax vmbefoldes his schulderes;
> A much berd as a busk ouer his brest henges,
> Þat wyth his hiȝlich here þat of his hed reches
> Watz euesed al vmbetorne abof his elbowes,
> Þat half his armes þer-vnder were halched in þe wyse
> Of a kyngez capados þat closes his swyre . . .   (181–6)

In such 'dressing' of the wild man there is play with his liminal identity, poised between animal and human. Clothes are disguises: they stop us seeing what lies underneath. As the wild man's body hair modulates into the combed or curled garment of late-medieval iconography—which is also his garb as the guardian or herald in Renaissance pageants—so the nature of his body, and of his real self, becomes obscured. Questions about his ultimate humanity remain unanswered.

---

[66] *Yvain*, lines 308–13.   [67] *Ywain and Gawain*, lines 253–4.

CHAPTER EIGHT

The Wild Man 2:
The Uncourtly Other

WILD MEN DERIVE their identity from what they are *not*. The lustful wild man in the prose life of Alexander fails his test because his behaviour towards the woman breaches cultural norms (not, as the knights think, because it shows he lacks reason and restraint—he could, after all, have come from a society in which women were objects of barter and rape was not accounted a crime). The wild man is composed of oppositional features—but what exactly is he opposed *to*? The figure most often invoked is that of the knight. Larry D. Benson argues that the wild man, in whatever role he appears, 'always represents a mode of life completely opposed to that represented by the knight', and that, when the two are shown fighting each other, 'The wild man is interpreted as a symbol of unruly passions while the knight is consciously treated as a protagonist of an opposite way of life'.[1] So the 'wodwos' in *Sir Gawain and the Green Knight* who rush down from the hills to attack Gawain are fulfilling their expected role—as creatures of wild nature, they batter against the civilized values of Arthur's court.

Wild men and knights are the theme of this chapter, but in it I would like to complicate the relationship of straightforward opposition that Benson proposes. Neither 'wild man', nor 'knight' are stable terms, for each draws upon the other for confirmation of its identity. And, as the two sides skirmish, the boundary between them becomes fluid, and is re-invented as a site of play. In the first section below, I sketch the different kinds of bodies inhabited by wild men and by knights. The next section considers the case of the wildmen/knights—the romance characters who venture out into the

[1] Larry D. Benson, *Art and Tradition in Sir Gawain and the Green Knight* (Cambridge, Mass., 1965), 80, 81.

wilderness and, for a time, live like wild men themselves; lastly, I discuss the late romance of *Valentine and Orson*, in which knightly bodies and wild ones come together in an especially interesting way.

WILD MEN AND KNIGHTS

Mikhail Bakhtin's analysis of the 'grotesque' body is well known and widely quoted, and has obvious application to the figure of the wild man. Against this body, Bakhtin sets another one:

> an entirely finished, completed, strictly limited body. . . . All orifices of the body are closed. . . . The opaque surface and the body's 'valleys' acquire an essential meaning as the border of a closed individuality that does not merge with other bodies and with the world.[2]

Such 'opacity' is entirely characteristic of the figure of the knight, who is most often shown encased in armour, literally sealed against the world's incursions. Behind the armour, individual emotions—even identity, as in the favourite ploy of the disguised knight at the tournament—are kept hidden from the common gaze. We do not see either the face or the body of Chaucer's Knight—although we are told about the many battles he has participated in, the only sign of wear and tear, of attritive action upon him, is his tunic, stained with rust from his coat of mail. Nor do we know what Gawain looks like, although we know a great deal about the physical singularity of his opponent, the Green Knight. The contrast between two different sorts of bodies appears vividly in an illustration to a French manuscript of the Alexander romance, *Le Livre et la vraye histoire du bon roy Alixandre*, which shows the king and his army warring against a host of wild men and women and giant wild boars. The knights, fully armoured, have blank expressions, while their wild enemies grimace and yell. The same manuscript shows the solitary giant seizing the damsel: his eyes are wide open and his mouth stretched; by contrast, the knights who watch him show no flicker of a reaction.[3]

---

[2] Mikhail Bakhtin, *Rabelais and his World*, trans. Hélène Iswolsky (Bloomington, Ind., 1984), 20.

[3] See Timothy Husband, *The Wild Man: Medieval Myth and Symbolism* (New York, 1980), no. 5 (colorplate III) and fig. 24.

As Bakhtin suggests, different sorts of bodies presuppose different sorts of demeanour *vis-à-vis* the world. The hallmark of knightliness is *mesure*, 'that inward restraint, imposed by individual reason, which leads to a virtuous life'.[4] Its opposite—lack of self-control, rudeness, 'churlishness'—may be displayed by any one of a number of other characters, against whom, in one sense or another, chivalric courtliness is pitched. If the wild man is at one end of the continuum, his affines include the giant, the heathen enemy, the low-born *vilain*, and even—in so far as *vilainie* may be defined as a cast of personality rather than an accident of birth—an ill-mannered person within the knightly fold itself, such as Sir Kay. These individuals may exhibit a number of 'wild man' attributes: for example, the heathen giant Alagolofur in the romance of *The Sowdone of Babylone* shares the wild man's fertility of gesture, as well as his tough, discoloured skin—the latter quality itself correlating with the crassness and lack of sensitivity which was thought to typify the *vilain*:

> Alagolofur rolled his yen
> And smote with his axe on the stone . . .
>
> . . . .
>
> This geaunte hade a body longe
> And hede, like a libarde,
> Ther-to he was devely stronge,
> His skynne was blake and harde.[5]

There is no point in pulling apart such descriptions in order to discover whether they are of true 'wild men' or of something else—a giant, for instance.[6] The 'wild man' in this context simply summarizes a whole repertoire of fallings away from that state of perfected courtliness which the truly *gentil* knight represents.

In principle, though, it should always be easy to tell the difference between a knight and a wild man, since they stand at opposite ends of the spectrum. But is it? In *Sir Gawain and the Green Knight*, the physical attributes of the two types are subtly played off against one

---

[4] David Burnley, *Courtliness and Literature in Medieval England* (London, 1998), 69.

[5] *The Sowdone of Babylone*, ed. Emil Hausknecht, EETS es 38 (1881), lines 2175–6, 2191–7. On hardness of skin as a marker of *vilainie*, see Burnley, *Courtliness*, 84–8.

[6] For an example of overlap between 'giant' and wild man, see John Finlayson, 'Arthur and the Giant of St Michael's Mount', *MÆ* 33 (1964), 112–20.

another. When he first bursts upon the scene, the Green Knight displays all of the wild man's expansive gesturing:

> And runischly his rede yȝen he reled aboute,
> Bende his bresed broȝez blycande grene,
> Wayued his berde for to wayte quo-so wolde ryse.   (304–6)

Bertilak, too, is vividly active and demonstrative:

> Þe lorde luflych aloft lepez ful ofte,
> Mynned merthe to be made vpon mony syþez,
> Hent heȝly of his hode, and on a spere henged,
> And wayned hom to wynne þe worchip þerof,
> Þat most myrþe myȝt meue þat Crystenmas whyle . . .   (981–5)

Although what Bertilak conveys is not threat but seasonal celebration and hospitality, his manner still evokes a contrast to Gawain's behaviour. Gawain (as Larry D. Benson observes) only raises his voice once (to summon the Green Knight at the Green Chapel), and his movements from place to place are described with plain, neutral verbs—*gotz*, *boȝez*, *walkez*, *romez*. It is in keeping with this picture that, while Bertilak is out actively hunting the deer, Gawain should be within the closed space of his curtained bed, reacting with only the tiniest of movements to what he hears outside:

> And as in slomeryng he slode, sleȝly he herde
> A littel dyn at his dor, and dernly vpon;
> And he heuez vp his hed out of þe cloþes,
> A corner of þe cortyn he caȝt vp a lyttel,
> And waytez warly þiderwarde quat hit be myȝt.   (1182–6)

This mode of smooth, unfurrowed demeanour correlates with the poem's code of chivalry. As Ad Putter has pointed out, Gawain's challenge in the bedroom scenes is not simply to resist the sexual temptations of the Lady but to decline her invitations in such a way that neither his courtesy nor her dignity are compromised.[7] Knights do not merely have to act: they have to attune their actions to a specific social code. And the key to that code is restraint. Gawain, for instance, is required to perform a particular action (seeking out the Green Chapel) on a particular day in the year. The narrowness of his purpose is pointed up by the festive merriment in Bertilak's castle, which he could continue to be part of if only he would forget

---

[7] Ad Putter, *'Sir Gawain and the Green Knight' and French Arthurian Romance* (Oxford, 1995), esp. ch. 3.

about his quest. Later, the Green Knight offers to reawaken this jollity if Gawain will come back to the castle with him—but the knight, honour-bound, refuses. As Bakhtin's 'finished, completed man, cleansed as it were, of all the scoriae of birth and development',[8] he cannot allow himself to descend once more into the carnivalesque time of Bertilak's domain.

However, the strategies of gesture that keep knight and wild man—Gawain and the Green Knight/Bertilak—apart also occasion play across the boundary. Bertilak's expansive conviviality, as well as certain aspects of his appearance—his huge size, and his face, 'Felle ... as þe fyre' (lines 844, 847)—might lead us to recognize him at once as a wild man, the Green Knight's *alter ego*, but other details work against this: for example, after the physical description quoted above, we are given Gawain's assessment of his host:

> And wel hym semed, for soþe, as þe segge þu3t,
> To lede a lortschyp in lee of leudez ful gode.   (849–50)

In Gawain's eyes, Bertilak happily 'fits' his role high in the feudal order, so our response is once again complicated. The Green Knight himself, when he first appears, is also presented in a teasingly ambiguous way. While certain of his features suggest the unseemly bulk and proliferating vegetable growth of the archetypal wild man, others imply minutely disciplined human artifice. On the one hand, he is 'Fro þe swyre to þe swange so sware and so þik' (line 138) and has a 'much berd as a busk' (line 182) spreading over his breast; on the other, the trappings of his horse shine like polished jewels and he himself is arrayed in delicate embroidery:

> Þat were to tor for to telle of tryfles þe halue
> Þat were enbrauded abof, wyth bryddes and fly3es,
> With gay gaudi of grene, þe golde ay inmyddes.   (165–7)

As Benson has shown, the mixing of details actually produces incompatibility, for the hood the Green Knight wears 'layde on his schulderes' (line 156) cannot be reconciled with the great 'cape' of his hair shorn at the level of his elbows, which would hide such a hood completely.[9] Significantly, it is with *hair*, the wild man's prime signifying feature, that the two sides of the portrait—wild and human, unkempt and tamed—are quite literally woven into each

---

[8] Bakhtin, *Rabelais*, 25.   [9] Benson, *Art and Tradition*, 59–62.

other. In the tail and mane of the Knight's horse, natural hair and golden thread are laced together, and then bound with a jewelled band set with ringing bells:

> Þe mane of þat mayn hors much to hit lyke,
> Wel cresped and cemmed, wyth knottes ful mony
> Folden in wyth fildore aboute þe fayre grene,
> Ay a herle of þe here, an oþer of golde;
> Þe tayl and his toppyng twynnen of a sute,
> And bounden boþe wyth a bande of a bry3t grene,
> Dubbed wyth ful dere stonez, as þe dok lasted,
> Syþen þrawen wyth a þwong a þwarle knot alofte,
> Þer mony bellez ful bry3t of brende golde rungen.   (187–95)

The body of the Green Knight is framed to tease us about his identity: like Arthur and his court, we are meant to be genuinely puzzled about who, or what, he is—and so it is wonderfully appropriate that the *gomen* he contributes to the feast should be such an outrageously 'bodily' one.

Other romance characters show this mixing of elements, albeit without the *Gawain*-poet's wit and subtlety. King Claudas ('Claudas de la terre desert'), Arthur's foe in the Vulgate prose *Lancelot*, sports a medley of oppositional features similar to those of Chrétien's Giant Herdsman: a black complexion, bushy eyebrows, black, wide-set eyes, a short, ugly nose, red beard, large neck, large mouth, and sharp teeth. But the rest of his body, far from being deformed, is handsome and well proportioned.[10] The carl in *The Carl of Carlisle* (a partial analogue of the *Gawain* story) is the lord of a fine castle, but still has several wild-man characteristics: he has power over wild animals (his pets are a bull, a lion, a bear, and a wild boar), and a mane of hair spreads over his breast 'As brod as anny fanne'.[11]

Wild men in art are also involved in this dialectic. Sometimes, of course, they are simply presented as foils to knightly valour, as in the series of marginal scenes in the Smithfield Decretals and the Taymouth Hours, in which a hairy wild man seizes a lady in the woods, prompting her rescue by a knight.[12] Elsewhere, however, they step

---

[10] *Lancelot*, in *The Vulgate Version of the Arthurian Romances*, ed. H. O. Sommer (Washington, 1908–16), 26–7, quoted with a translation in Benson, *Art and Tradition*, 82–3.

[11] *Sir Gawain and the Carl of Carlisle in Two Versions*, ed. Auvo Kurvinen, Annales Academiae Scientiarum Fennicae, Series B, 71 (Helsinki, 1951), line 255.

[12] See n. 75 to Ch. 5, above.

into the knights' own role, storming the castle of love,[13] or usurping courtly privilege as the successful wooers of ladies. In a series of scenes carved on a German *Minnekästchen* of the later fourteenth century, the wild man first appears sitting pensively on a tree stump; next, he rides off on a horse and seizes a maiden, to whom a knight, on the other side of the picture, is offering a ring. The knight and a companion ride in pursuit, but the final scene shows wild man and maiden playing chess together—the wild man elegantly posed with crossed legs and a falcon upon his wrist.[14] A French Book of Hours, *c.*1500, is illuminated with a whole series of marginal scenes, described by Timothy Husband as follows:

With few exceptions, only knights and damsels are portrayed. In many cases the activity of a knight is countered directly by that of a wild man. The wild man who shoots a heron (fol. 61[v]) is faced on the opposite folio by a knight who kills a stag (fol. 68[r]). Two wild men spirit away a captive knight, while his elaborately caparisoned, mountless horse, led by a third wild man, ends the procession (fol. 17[v]...). Opposite this scene a wild man heralds a procession of a wild man 'lord' who proudly rides an unadorned goat (fol. 18...). In other scenes, wild men enthusiastically portray the spirit and activities of medieval knights.[15]

A real-life example illustrates this sort of play in action. To celebrate a marriage in 1392, the French king, Charles VI, together with four lords and a squire (whose idea the entertainment was), dressed themselves in 'cotes made of lynen clothe, covered with pytche, and theron flaxe lyke heare',[16] and entered the hall so disguised. The duke of Orléans, curious to see who the 'wild men' really were, held a torch too near the costume of one of them; the flax and pitch ignited, and all, except the king, who was shielded by the duchess of Berry, and one lord who managed to plunge into a water-butt, were burnt to death. Richard Bernheimer sees the king's participation in such a masquerade (this was the second in which he is known to

---

[13] See e.g. Husband, *Wild Man*, nos. 12 (fig. 37), 13 (fig. 40); Richard Bernheimer, *Wild Men in the Middle Ages: A Study in Art, Sentiment and Demonology* (Cambridge, Mass., 1952), fig. 34.

[14] See Husband, *Wild Man*, no. 16 (fig. 49) and p. 88.

[15] Ibid. 145. Scenes from this MS are reproduced in colorplate XI, a–d. See also figs. 87 (engraving by Israhel von Meckenem, Lower Rhineland, *c.*1480) and 88 (tapestry, Alsace, 1390–1410), in both of which wild men take part in parodic jousting scenes.

[16] *The Chronicle of Froissart*, trans. Sir John Bourchier, Lord Berners, introd. W. P. Ker, 6 vols. (London, 1901–3), vi. 96.

have taken part) as an escape from the stifling demands of courtly etiquette: 'it is a gauge of the pressure of formalized living upon those who were supposed to be its foremost paragons, that it seems to have been necessary at times to open the valves and to let the agonized fury of "natural man" take its unhampered course'.[17] However, the situation at the Bal des Ardents was not quite so simple. Far from 'natural man' being allowed an entirely free rein (which would have entailed the setting aside of all marks of status and degree), the king entered the hall ahead of the others and, unlike them, was not bound by a chain. As Froissart describes it, 'Fyve of them were fastened one to another; the kyng was lose, and went before and led the devyse.'[18] Charles and his companions preserved their places within the social hierarchy even within their masking uniforms of linen and flaxen 'hair'. Indeed, we could even say that the king owed his survival precisely to the maintenance of these distinctions.

KNIGHTS IN THE WILDERNESS

Several romances feature knights who live *as* wild men for a time: Orfeo, Partonope of Blois, Orson, Merlin, Lancelot, and Yvain.[19] We may see these episodes as a further dialectical enterprise: through *becoming* 'wild', these heroes will discover what it is that constitutes truly human living. Explorers at the edge, they will bring back reports of how 'wildness' may properly be imagined, and in doing so they will clarify the assumptions and values of their own environing society.

In each of the cases I have listed above (with the exception of Orson, who is savage from childhood because he has been brought up by a bear), the romance hero's flight from civilization is triggered by the breaking of a particular relationship. Orfeo loses his beloved wife Heurodis to the Fairy King, while Yvain is stricken with

---

[17] Bernheimer, *Wild Men in the Middle Ages*, 67.

[18] *Chronicle of Froissart*, vi. 97.

[19] The list is not exhaustive, and there are other occurrences in romance literature of the same theme. The lord in the Gelert story mentioned above (see n. 76 to Ch. 5) is one example; another is Owein in the story of 'The Lady of the Fountain' in *The Mabinogion* (trans. Gwyn Jones and Thomas Jones, Everyman's Library, rev. edn. (London, 1989), 155–82).

madness when he is suddenly reminded that he has broken faith with Laudine. From that lost relationship, and implicitly too from all the attachments and obligations of a courtly way of life, the knight flees into the wilderness.

The movement outwards, into a state radically different from the previous one, is deliberately modulated, to show the experiential, if not the actual, length of the journey. Orfeo's departure is one of the simplest, yet it is still presented in successive stages: he first passes through the 'gate', and so out of town, then across the bordering territory of wood and heath, and finally arrives in the wilderness:

> he that hadde ben king with croune
> Went so poverlich out of toun!
> Thurch wode and over heth
> Into the wilderness he geth.[20]

Partonope seems to begin his movement away from a wholly civilized life while he is still physically within the bounds of the court. Disappointed in love, he enters a liminal state in which he takes upon himself the privations he will soon have to suffer:

> Lytill he etith and lasse drynkeþ he.
> Thries in þe weke he doþe ete;
> His fode is not deynte mete:
> Brede made of barly or elles of oote,
> This is his mete, and watir sode
> His his drynke two dayes or þre,
> That in þe weke now taketh he.
> That is his sustenaunce and levyng;
> In oþer rule may no man hym bryng.
>
> .   .   .   .   .   .
>
> His nayles growne and all forfare,
> He martreth his body with sorowe and care,
> He is for-growen with his heere.[21]

Even before he leaves the court, Partonope's body is shading into that of the wild man—in this case an image of debilitation produced by complete indifference to his own welfare. Once in

---

[20] *Sir Orfeo*, in *Middle English Romances*, ed. A. C. Gibbs, York Medieval Texts (London, 1966), lines 221–4. Subsequent references are included in the text.
[21] *Partonope of Blois*, ed. A. Trampe Bödtker, EETS ES 109 (1912), lines 6644–52, 6655–7. Subsequent references are included in the text.

the wilderness, he will lapse into such extreme weakness that Urake will find him barely able to crawl along on knees and elbows (line 7500). Yet, importantly, the description also imposes a reading on Partonope's state: like the dishevelled Criseyde, he is love's 'martyr', and so, it is suggested, his behaviour will continue to be ruled by human motives even when he appears most animal-like.

Partonope's actual departure from the court is explicitly away from his 'frendes', who represent his discarded way of life:

> Forthe now rideþ Partonope
> Into þe forest þat neuer he
> Spareth to ryde, day ne nyght,
> Till he passe knowleche and sight
> Of all his frendes, more and lasse.   (7073–7)

Chrétien's *Yvain*, too, first removes himself from his peers, the 'barons'. Jacques Le Goff has traced and analysed the various ensuing stages in his journey to the wilderness:[22]

> D'antre les barons se remue;
> .   .   .   .   .
> Et il va tant, que il fu loing
> Des tantes et des paveillons.
> Lors li monta uns torbeillons
> El chief si granz, que il forsane,
> Lors se descrire et se depane
> Et fuit par chans et par arees
> Et leisse ses janz esgarees,
> Qui se mervoillent, ou puet estre.
> Querant le vont par trestot l'estre,
> Par les ostes as chevaliers
> Et par haies et par vergiers,
> Sel quierent la, ou il n'est pas.[23]

He leaves the company of the barons . . . He went away, until he was far from the tents and pavilions. Then so violent a whirlwind assails his head that he goes mad. He rips his clothes and flees across fields and ploughland, leaving his men bewildered, and wondering where he can be. They search

---

[22] Jacques Le Goff, 'Lévi-Strauss in Broceliande: A Brief Analysis of a Courtly Romance', in *The Medieval Imagination* (Chicago and London, 1988; trans. of *L'Imaginaire médiéval: Essais*, Paris, 1985), 107–31.

[23] *Yvain: Le Chevalier au lion*, text W. Foerster, introd. T. B. W. Reid (Manchester, 1942), lines 2796, 2802–12. Subsequent references are included in the text.

for him through the whole neighbourhood, in the knights' lodgings, and in hedgerows and orchards, looking for him where he is not to be found.

Le Goff points out that Yvain's flight takes him past the various 'outposts' of civilization. He first leaves behind him the members of the court, and then all the signs of human settlement or cultivation—fields and furrows, tents, orchards, hedgerows. In a 'parc', an area enclosed for grazing animals, he finds a boy and takes his bow and arrows from him. He is now equipped for his life in the wild, and it is as a hunter, not as a knight, that he enters the forest.

To become a 'wild man', therefore, a knight has to take those steps that lead him outside the boundaries of his own society. He has to move *away*, successively discarding things as he goes. The privileged identity that once encased him like his armour has cracked, and he has to find new clothing, both metaphorically and literally. Orfeo, for instance, exchanges his kingly robes for a simple pilgrim's 'sclavin'. In the version of the Gelert story in *The Seven Sages of Rome*, mentioned above in Chapter 5, the repentant lord takes off his shoes before disappearing into the forest.[24] Yet, while one kind of identity is being set aside, there is often a concomitant emphasis on continuing human purpose and integrity. Orfeo's 'sclavin', his bare feet, and the fact that he takes not even a shirt for his back, are suggestive of penance, as well as of Christ's prescription of poverty for the twelve apostles.[25] And Yvain is not so lost in wit that he cannot equip himself with the bow and arrows he needs to survive in the wilderness (and which he wields with great efficiency, as it turns out).

Having entered the wilderness, the wild-man/knight must begin his new life there. As I suggested earlier, this 'wilderness' is not an unpeopled wasteland: although the lovelorn knight may originally have craved solitude, solitude is precisely what he does not get. Partonope's massive forest of the Ardennes is still a place where the courtly activity of hunting goes on—indeed, Partonope himself, at the beginning of the story, was seen participating in just such a hunt (lines 524 ff.). Orson's forest is similarly an area of human thoroughfare, so that even though his dwelling is said to be a 'pitte obscure &

---

[24] *The Seven Sages of Rome*, ed. Karl Brunner, EETS os 191 (1933), 27–32.

[25] 'Nyl 3e welden gold, nether syluer, ne money in 3oure girdlis, Not a scripe in the weye, nether two cootis, nether shoon, nether 3eerd; for a workman is worthi his mete' (Matt. 10: 9–10; trans. Wyclif).

tenebrous' he is frequently brought into conflict with both men and animals: 'He became so great and strong, that none durste passe through the forest for hym, for bothe men and beastes he put vnto death, and eate their flesh al raw as the other beastes did . . . '[26] Even Orfeo's wilderness, which is perhaps the most compellingly remote from civilization, since Orfeo does not speak to another human being there, is haunted by simulacra of his former way of life—horns blowing, dogs barking, the fairy court dancing together or riding hunting.

While the terrain of the wild-men/knights is modelled to provoke human encounters, it is also a place where they will meet animals of various kinds. Interaction with animals is carefully structured within the texts, with some potential readings being screened out. Why? The reason, I suggest, is that one strand of wild-man mythology has him closely allied with the beasts, exercising a quasi-magical power over them. The Giant Herdsman in *Yvain* is such a character; Maruk, the wise old sailor on board the ship that brings Urake to the rescue of Partonope, although he is not a wild man as such, is a close literary relative:

> 'I shall you shew
> Merva[y]lles many, and not few,
> Of lyons, apes, and eke berys,
> Dragons, olifauntez, and gwy[v]ers,
> Beres, wolfes, and eke Serpentes,
> And shall I wyth myn experymentz
> Make hem be-fore yow for fere quake
> And whan me lust I [shall] hem make
> Ryse and walke where-euer hem lust,
> Thorw the forest were hem lyketh best.'
>
> .   .   .   .   .   .
>
> Maruk shewed hir grete lyons,
> Beres, apes, and also gryffouns,
> Dragons, Wyuers, and eke serpentes,
> That be crafte of his experimentes
> Oute of hir place durst not stirre.
>
> (7212–21 (University College MS); 7252–6)

---

[26] *Valentine and Orson*, trans. Henry Watson, ed. Arthur Dickson, EETS OS 204 (1937), 38. Subsequent references are included in the text.

A magical relationship with animals may hint at some sharing in their nature, and thus some blurring of the boundary line between animal and human. This, in the case of the wild-men/knights, the texts cannot allow. Of course, it is acceptable for animals to befriend, amuse, or assist the new entrant into their wilderness. Partonope wishes that a fierce beast would kill him, since he cannot bear to live without Melior, yet, although the forest of the Ardennes is full of savage animals (such as the lion that later attacks his horse), none of them does him any harm. Geoffrey of Monmouth's Merlin marvels at the wild creatures grazing in the glades and chases after them in play; at other times he sits by a fountain and watches them frolicking around him. In the lament that is overheard by a traveller he speaks of a wolf-companion who shares his wintertime privations, suffering even more acutely than he does himself. Later, Merlin leads a herd of stags, deer, and goats to his former wife's wedding, and makes them accomplices in his revenge since he kills the new bridegroom with a well-thrown antler. But there must be clear boundaries to each encounter. When Orfeo plays his harp to the wild animals, and they gather round joyfully to listen to him, there is perhaps the hint of a relationship too ambiguous for comfort, a suggestion that player and audience have begun to partake of the same nature. And so we are told that the spell—if spell it is—only lasts while Orfeo is actually playing: as soon as he stops the creatures vanish:

> And when he his harping lete wold,
> No best bi him abide nold.   (265–6)

Orson, the most beast-like of all the wild-men/knights, still has to be seen as an empress's son and a future champion of the French court. Despite the accidentals of a shaggy pelt, and the ferocity he has sucked in with his foster-mother's milk, he cannot be seen to be a bear and to have a bear's complicity with other animals. The solution is to have him dominate the other forest creatures through sheer brute strength, literally forcing a space between them and him: '[He] began for to smyte the other beastes of the forest, in suche wyse that they all douted hym, and fledded before him' (p. 38). Thus, in their relationships with animals, the wild-men/knights, although they stand upon the boundary, are seen never to lose their footing in the human world that is their real home.

To survive in the wilderness, the wild-men/knights need to be able to feed themselves. The theme of diet is an important one, for food not only ensures physical survival but validates a particular identity.[27] Partonope's near-starvation diet not only induces bodily weakness but also acts to create in him the image of the wild man he will later become. And, towards the end of the romance of *Valentine and Orson*, the knight Valentine, who has accidentally killed his own father in battle, prepares to undergo a seven-year penance as a beggar underneath the palace stairs: 'Valentine entred in to a wode after that he hade shorne his hear, and was there eating rotes so longe that none coude knowe him' (p. 313). Since diet sustains identity, when diet changes identity changes too. Consequently, in the romances of the wild-men/knights, the methods by which the protagonists obtain their food are typically related to the wider concerns and patterns of the narrative. For example, both Orfeo and Partonope subsist on wild vegetation, but there is an important difference between them. Partonope, wishing to die, makes no effort to seek out his own food, taking only what he sees in front of him. He tells Urake:

> I am ouercome with ffeblenesse;
> For be þe Rotes of þe grasse,
> Sith I come hidder, haue ben my levyng.   (7498–500)

Later, Urake comments, 'Of mete ne drynke taketh he none hede.' Orfeo, on the other hand, is tirelessly active in his search for sustenance:

> Now may he alday digge and wrote
> Er he finde his fille of rote.   (241–2)

His body begins to be marked by his habitual digging and rooting, blackened, abraded, and scarred by thorns. What he finds is

---

[27] For interesting reappearances of this theme in very different contexts, see Piero Camporesi, *Bread of Dreams: Food and Fantasy in Early Modern Europe*, trans. David Gentilcore (Cambridge, 1989), 169: 'The university culture of [16th-cent.] Bologna . . . had formulated an ideology of class directed at sanctioning the biological inferiority of the humble poor in order to crush them politically. It was an ideology that postulated two distinct diets, depending on membership of a group in power or a class of the destitute'; and Harriet Ritvo, *The Platypus and the Mermaid, and Other Figments of the Classifying Imagination* (Cambridge, Mass., 1997), 200: 'Even in its unsegmented state, meat reflected essential social divisions, some elevated kinds "fit for fine Complexions, idle Citizens," others, like bacon, "gross, tough and hard, agreeing chiefly to Country Persons and Hard Labourers".'

enough to keep him alive and functioning, but it does not nourish him fully—its components are 'bot good lite'. Orfeo's dedicated, self-lacerating activity as he seeks to sustain himself mirrors his later resolution and courage when he sets out in pursuit of the fairy riders, and eventually rescues Heurodis from the fairy court. Conversely, Partonope's feeble refusal of effort correlates with his role as the heartbroken lover, thrown into desolation by the loss of Melior.

To kill animals for food is an obvious alternative to the rigours of a vegetarian diet, and one—we might imagine—that any committed survivalist would quickly adopt. The savage Orson eats the flesh of both beasts and men. Yvain, too, kills deer, shooting them with the bow and arrows he had providentially taken from the boy he passed on his flight into the forest. He eats the venison raw, and in the English version, *Ywain and Gawain*, drinks the deer's blood too. Penelope Doob suggests that this interposed detail both emphasizes Yvain's bestiality and alludes to a popular cure for melancholy madness (which fails to work on Yvain because his malady is spiritual rather than bodily).[28] However, in its context the drinking of blood is not imbued with 'the horror of savagery'—on the contrary, its nourishing properties are stressed:

> He drank of þe warm blode,
> And þat did him mekil gode.[29]

Yvain, his madness notwithstanding, is a practical opportunist, taking from the forest whatever he needs to survive, and using animals in exactly the way they were meant to be used, as supports for human life. He has retained all his hunting skills intact—we are told that during his time in the woods he does not lose a single arrow, recovering each one after it has been shot.

Jacques Le Goff has explored in detail how Yvain's re-ascent to full humanity is imaged in his changing diet.[30] He begins, as we have seen, by killing the deer and eating the meat raw and bloody ('La veneison trestote crue', line 2826). He then comes upon a hermit, a

---

[28] Penelope Doob, *Nebuchadnezzar's Children: Conventions of Madness in Middle English Literature* (New Haven, 1974), 147.

[29] *Ywain and Gawain*, ed. Albert B. Friedman and Norman T. Harris, EETS OS 254 (1964), lines 1669–70.

[30] Le Goff, 'Lévi-Strauss in Broceliande', 113–14.

man, in Le Goff's description, living at a primitive level of technol-
ogy (he has a hut, and a small patch of cleared ground where he digs
for roots). The hermit leaves bread out for the wild man—bread of
such debased quality that it serves to emphasize the hermit's status
on the very margins of the economy. It is the bread of the desperately poor, and Chrétien's audience are invited to savour it with a
sort of fascinated repulsion:

> Ne cuit, que onques de si fort
> Ne de si aspre eüst gosté.
> N'avoit mie cinc souz costé
> Li sestiers, don fu fez li pains,
> Qui plus iere egres que levains,
> D'orge pestriz atot la paille,
> Et avuec ce iere il sanz faille
> Moisiz et ses come un escorce.   (2844–51)

I do not believe he had ever tasted bread so rough or so coarse. The
measure of grain from which the bread was made had not cost five sous:
made of barley kneaded with straw, it was even sourer than yeast and was
actually mouldy and as dry as bark.

Yvain begins to leave the deer carcasses for the hermit to prepare,
and in exchange the hermit supplies him with bread and water, and
with cooked meat:

> S'avoit a mangier et a boivre
> Veneison sanz sel et sanz poivre
> Et eve froide de fontainne.   (2879–81)

To eat and drink he had venison without salt and without pepper, and cold
water from the spring.

Here, Le Goff suggests, 'Communication between the world of the
hunt and the world of agriculture, the raw and the cooked . . . takes
place at the lowest possible level'.[31] The hermit sells the hides of the
deer, and with the money is able to buy bread of better quality,
'D'orge ou d'avainne ou d'autre grain' ('of barley or oats or other
grain', line 2884). Yvain's improving diet mirrors his gradual return
to the higher life from which he had fallen. As his madness began
with the shattering of all attachments, so his recovery of health
begins with the establishment of the simplest of all relationships—

---

[31] Le Goff, 'Lévi-Strauss in Broceliande', 114.

one of basic trading—with another human being. Yet he still has a long way to go. The cooked venison may nourish him, but in *social* terms it is still a deficient diet since it lacks the seasonings (*sel et . . . poivre*) with which it would be enhanced at court. Later, restored to sanity and with a faithful lion as his companion, Yvain himself roasts the meat the lion catches for him, but, again, he does not really enjoy his meal since he has to eat it without the proper accompaniments:

> Mes del mangier fu nus deduiz;
> Qu'il n'i ot pain ne vin ne sel,
> Ne nape ne coutel ne el.   (3468–70)

But he took no pleasure in his meal, for he had no bread, wine, or salt, no tablecloth, no knife, nor anything else.

Yvain's changing diet therefore images his will to return from his wild-man condition to his former knightly status—a will that is operative even when he appears most deranged and alienated. As Le Goff points out, the very moment when he runs wild is also the moment which marks the start of his long journey back to sanity. It is not enough for him simply to 'survive' in the wilderness, as Orfeo does—every one of his actions predicates his eventual repossession of his true identity.

All of the wild-men/knights, like Yvain, regain their previous status, and are granted full healing of the broken relationship that prompted their flight. Orfeo returns triumphantly from the fairy court with his wife Heurodis, Partonope and Melior are reunited, and so are Yvain and Laudine. The movement back is often instigated, or assisted, by female characters. Yvain is restored to sanity when a damsel anoints him with some magical ointment prepared by her mistress. Partonope is brought back to civilized society by two women, Urake and Persevis. He surrenders himself entirely to their care:

> Partonope hath now clene forsake
> The wodwose life, and haþe hym take
> To þe governaunce all fully
> Of fayre Wrak and of Persewy.   (7690–3)

Urake in turn mediates between Partonope and Melior, interpreting his strange behaviour to her and supplying it with a meaning:

> So moche sorowe for you hath he take,
> Horne-wode he renneth for your sake.

> And ye will hym hele or elles fynde,
> Go seke hym vnder þe wode lynde.
> Ther he renneth wode as any hare.   (7844–5, 7932–4)

Geoffrey of Monmouth's Merlin is first soothed by music and then becomes sane again when he thinks of his sister and his wife. Women as 'others'—standing aside, in some sense, from the dominant culture (a theme that is explored in more detail in the next chapter)—appear to be particularly suited to mediate in this way. With their aid, the hero is drawn back into the sustaining network of relationships he had previously abandoned.

As the wild-man/knight moves back within the bounds of civilization, his former life becomes more strongly imaged in terms of deficiency. King Rodarch, having brought Merlin back to the court once more, pleads with him not to leave, pointing out that life beneath the trees as a wild beast bears no comparison with the personal power he might exert, ruling with royal sceptre over his warlike subjects.[32] In *Valentine and Orson*, Valentine, having battled with his ferocious brother in the forest, describes for him all the benefits of a civilized, Christian life, which can be his if he will only submit and allow himself to be taken back to court:

Alas wylde man, wherfore doest thou not yelde the vnto me thou lyuest here in this wodde lyke a beaste, and hathe no knowledge of God, nor of his blyssed mother saynt Mary, nor of his holy fayth, for the whiche thy soule is in great daunger. Come on thy way with me & then shalt thou do wysely. I shall make the be baptized, and shall teache the, the holy fayth. And shall geue the flesh and fysshe, bread and wyne ynough for to eate, and clothes and all maner of thinges that appertayneth vnto a mannes body, and shalt vse thy lyfe honestly as euery naturall body should doo. (pp. 69–70)

Valentine has answered for himself the crucial question, 'Is he a man?', and from his acknowledgement that Orson, shaggy and bestial, *is* in fact a man, all the rest inevitably follows. If a man,

---

[32] *Life of Merlin*, ed. and trans. Basil Clarke (Cardiff, 1973), lines 227–31: 'astabatque dolens verbisque precantibus illum | orabat ratione frui secumque manere | nec captare nemus nec vivere more ferino | velle sub arboribus dum regia sceptra tenere | posset et in populos jus exercere feroces.'

then a soul in crying need of salvation. In realistic terms it is not clear *how* Orson understands what Valentine is saying to him (unless the knight's courtly fluency of speech is matched by a prodigious talent for sign-language). However, the text requires that the dominant code should be seen to penetrate even Orson's beastlike mind. '[A]fter the course of nature that can not lye', Orson comprehends all this talk of God and the Blessed Virgin, as well as the workings of the feudal society he is about to enter, and, falling to his knees (a nicely proleptic gesture), declares himself to be wholly Valentine's 'man':

Orson fell downe vpon both his knees, & stretcheth forth his handes towarde his brother Valentyne, in makyng hym signe that he woulde forgeue hym, and that he would obeye vnto hym in al maner of thynges for the tyme to come. And he shewed vnto him by sygnes that neuer the dayes of his life he should fayle him, neyther with body nor goodes. (p. 70)

How Orson manages to pledge the 'goods' he has never known possession of is, again, something of a mystery. However, the message is clear. The wild-men/knights return from their proving-ground, the wilderness, and, to a man, re-embrace, and so reaffirm, the values of their native society.

VALENTINE AND ORSON

Knight and wild man are inextricably linked, each drawing his identity from his shadow 'other'. In real life, we can see that a knight of perfect *politesse*—like Gawain, perhaps—would never actually do any fighting and would thus forfeit his *raison d'être*. Knights *need* an infusion of wild-man blood to launch them into battle. It is in this light that I now turn to the late romance of *Valentine and Orson*, which provides a fascinating commentary on several of the themes explored in this chapter.

The surviving English version of the story of the knight Valentine and his savage brother Orson dates from about 1510, and is a close translation of the French prose *Valentin et Orson* first printed in 1489. No earlier version in French or English survives, but there are earlier German, Swedish, and (fragmentary) Dutch texts of a closely related story, *Valentin und Namelos*, and a common ancestor for this and

Valentine and Orson has been posited—a lost French original, dating from the first half of the fourteenth century.[33] The tale was popular in England, and the twin heroes appeared in pageants, such as the one which greeted the new king Edward VI as he rode through London in 1547. Here Orson, who was 'clothed with mosse and in leves, having in his hand a great clobb of yew-tree for his wepone', played the role of Edward's champion:

> For I wylde Urson dothe here syngnefye
> an emperour's son of excellent majestye,
> notwithstanding in a forest noryshed by a bere,
> where many knightes I dyd there conquere.[34]

There is no literary evidence that the story was known in England before the early sixteenth century, but the scenes on two misericords suggest that this was at least a possibility. In the first (Gloucester cathedral; fourteenth century) a knight on foot fights with a bearded giant and wounds him in the neck (a tree near the giant may suggest a forest setting), while the second (St Mary's, Beverley; early fifteenth century) shows a meeting between a knight and a wild man.[35] These scenes are similar to—and may actually depict—the first meeting of the brothers, and the fight between them.

Valentine and Orson are twins, the sons of the empress Bellissant, who gives birth to them within the forest of Orleans, through which she is travelling after having been unjustly banished from the court of her husband, the emperor of Greece. One son is stolen by a bear, and while his mother is vainly trying to save him the other is taken up by king Pepin of France, who is Bellissant's brother and to whom she had been making her way. Pepin adopts Valentine, and brings him up within the court, although he does not know he is his own nephew. Orson, however, is raised by the bear with its own cubs, and grows up hairy, ferocious, and unable to speak. He lives a totally bestial life, eating raw flesh and attacking any creature that ventures

---

[33] For a full discussion of sources and analogues, see Arthur Dickson, *Valentine and Orson: A Study in Late Medieval Romance* (New York, 1929).

[34] Sydney Anglo, *Spectacle, Pageantry, and Early Tudor Policy*, Oxford-Warburg Studies (Oxford, 1969), 285, 286.

[35] Gloucester: see G. C. Druce, 'Some Abnormal and Composite Forms in English Church Architecture', *Archaeological Journal*, 72 (1915), 140 n. 1; Beverley: see G. L. Remnant, *A Catalogue of Misericords in Great Britain*, with an Essay on their Iconography by M. D. Anderson (Oxford, 1969), p. xl.

into his domain. The people at Pepin's court are aware of his nature and his activities, and give him the name 'Orson', itself a sort of proprietorial outreach since it implies understanding of his history. The contrast between the brothers' lives is strongly emphasized:

Valentyne bare hym so meke and so gentyll in kinge Pepyns courte that he was beloued of lordes, ladyes, knyghtes, and squyers, and euery body sayd good & honour by hym. And hys brother Orson is within the forest, roughe & couered with heer as a bere, ledynge a wylde bestes life. (p. 54)

During this period of his bestiality, Orson, despite having a name, is treated as a wild animal—a dangerous and unusual quarry, like the cornered wild man in Queen Mary's Psalter. King Pepin, eager to see him, gathers his company together to go in search of him. 'The chace was ordeyned & they entred in to the wodde. They toke dyuers wylde beestes, but to finde Orson euery body was a ferd' (p. 55). The expedition is a hunting foray, and Orson's eventual discovery, in a 'pitte obscure & tenebrous', resembles the rousing of the great boar in the second of the hunts in *Gawain*. Cornered, Orson fights like a wild beast, attacking first the king and then the knight who comes to his aid: 'whan Orson sawe the naked swerd flambing, he left the kynge and ranne to the knyghte and tooke hym in hys armes and held hym so hard that he threw doune both hors and man. . . . And Orson held the knight the which with his sharp nailes strangled hym, and pyteouslye pulled him in pyeces' (p. 56).

At this point, Orson is the antitype to the values represented by the court—the alien challenger whose function is to test the knights' valour. 'You knowe well ynoughe', Pepin tells Valentine, 'that by hym is deed many valyaunt men, and that some noble champyons hathe lefte this enterpryse' (p. 66). Nothing daunted, however, Valentine sets out to conquer him. In the encounter between the two, we see Orson irresistibly drawn to all the gear and trappings of chivalry. He is first attracted to Valentine's horse: 'And whan he sawe hym so fayre and so plesaunt, he combed hym a paas weth his roughe handes, in makynge him chere. For he had neuer sene so fayre a beest' (p. 67). Later, he is distracted by the brightly coloured shield his opponent wears around his neck:

And when that he had taken it from hym, he behelde it ryght strongly, because of the beautie of the colours that he was not accustomed for to se, and then he cast it strongly against the earth, and incontinent retourned vnto valentyne. (p. 69)

Which will prove better, a wild body, or weapons? In the battle that ensues, Orson fights with all his tremendous strength, clawing and tearing at his enemy with his nails and wielding a torn-up tree as a club. However, Valentine prevails by means of his knightly armoury—his shield, his sword, which daunts Orson, and the sharp knife with which he eventually manages to wound him:

When valentyne sawe that by strengthe of bodye he myght not wynne hym, he drewe out a sharpe poynted knyfe and smote Orson in to the ryght syde, in suche wyse that the bloude yssued out by great haboundaunce. Then Orson ster[te] vp when he felte himselfe wounded And for the dolour that he felte, as all in a rage he gaue suche a crye that all the wodde sowned therof. (p. 68)

It is not weaponry that finally overcomes Orson, however, but Valentine's discourse on the benefits of a Christian life, which I quoted above. His submission to the dominant code was prefigured by his attraction to its talismans—sword, shield, warhorse—now, as he enters into the milieu of the court, he will conduct his own dialogue with the new way of life offered to him. The court, in turn, views *him* dialectically, seeing both the present wild man and the 'fair knight' he will later become. King Pepin remarks: 'Lordes by god almighty it is a meruayllous thinge to se this wylde man, he is right well made and of a fayre stature. And how wel that he is roughe, yf he were clothed as we be, he wolde seme a right fayre knyght' (pp. 73–4). Meanwhile, the wild man must be baptized: 'And other name they gaue him not saue that whiche he had taken in the forest' (p. 74).

The new life Orson is entering upon is one that is governed by various conventions of social behaviour. But have these conventions expunged the basic bodily appetites that Orson gave rein to so uninhibitedly in his wild state? Several of his escapades seem designed to provide an answer. For example, when the two, on their way to court, are refused shelter by terrified villagers, Orson breaks down the gate of an inn with a massive piece of wood so that they can enter and spend the night there. At court, he grabs hold of a peacock being carried on a dish to the king's table, and devours it greedily. Such actions obviously transgress the rules of polite behaviour (after Orson's food-stealing, Valentine 'shewed hym by sygnes that he gouerned hym not wyll', p. 74), yet it is clear that the needs that prompt them—for food, for shelter—are shared by all creatures, knights and wild men alike. Later, Valentine takes Orson into the chamber of Eglantyne, Pepin's daughter and his own love:

in the whiche was dyuers ladyes that gladly behelde Orson. And Orson in laughynge lepte vpon the bedde, & sate there makynge dyuers sygnes that was ryghe pleasaunt vnto the ladyes. But the whiche he dyd they vnderstode not, of the whiche they were much displeasaunt. So they called Valentyn and demaunded hym what it was that the wylde man shewed them by sygnes. And Valentyne sayd to them. My ladyes knowe for a trouthe that the wylde man sheweth you by his sygnes that he wolde gladly kysse and colle the damoyselles that be here, wherat they began for to laughe & to beholde eche other. (p. 75)

In so far as Valentine and Orson are both *male* (beyond being knights, or wild men), they share a knowledge, and a secret, 'signed' code. Therefore Valentine understands exactly what Orson's gestures mean, and can interpret them—with the proper gloss of courtly euphemism—to the ladies of the chamber. The complicity of the worlds of the two men could be shown in a diagram.[36]

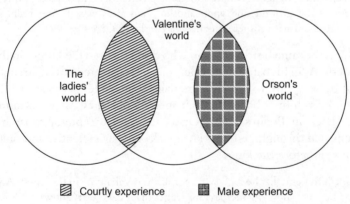

Valentine's world

The ladies' world

Orson's world

▨ Courtly experience   ▦ Male experience

[36] My diagram has obvious affinities with the Ardeners' model of the relationship between dominant (male) and muted (female) groups, in which a shadow crescent, the only part of the circle that is not eclipsed, signifies the 'wild zone' of women's culture. See Edwin Ardener, 'The "Problem" Revisited', in Shirley Ardener (ed.), *Perceiving Women* (London, 1975), 23. In my version there are, from Valentine's point of view, *two* 'wilds' (the ladies', and Orson's) which he cannot access. Some of the questions this raises about the role of gender in the construction of 'the wild' are considered in the next chapter.

However, perhaps things are not quite so simple. The ladies declare themselves innocent of Orson's meaning, yet they look at him with evident pleasure, and when Valentine has translated for them laugh and exchange glances among themselves. Those glances constitute another code, which may be much more cognizant of the first sign-system than its (male) users would like to admit. So, female sexual desire finds its expression in the evanescent, voiceless language that Orson, the wild newcomer to the court, inaugurates. He can be said to speak *for* Valentine in a more particular sense too, since his message of direct, physical passion is heard against his brother's frustrated love for Eglantyne, whom he is forbidden by social convention to approach. Although he is dumb, Orson manages to speak effectively about what lies underneath the civilized façade.

In the episode in which Valentine is attacked and captured by the traitor Grygar, Orson's animal nature becomes dominant as he tries to protect his brother:

[He] sterte forthe as halfe afrayde with his rough handes, and tore and rent all them that he founde in his waye, soo that with his sharpe nayles he pulle[d] them in peces, & bote and strangled them with his teeth. He threw them to the ground one vpon another, and after passed ouer them in smiting them with his fete muche vylaynosly. (pp. 86–7)

This is the same bearlike Orson who dismembered the knight in the woods. As in his battle with Valentine, he is defeated not by strength but by weapons, to which he remains vulnerable—Grygar and his men keep him at bay with their spears while they carry Valentine off. Back in Pepin's court, Orson manages to convey what has happened through gestures. He attacks Grygar violently, and then, brought before the king,

made him signe that he had slayne & murdred Valentyne in the forest. And after he went shewyng meruaylous sygnes that he wolde fyght wyth Grigar for that thynge by the lawe of champion, & make him confesse his cursed enterpryse and dampnable treason. (p. 90)

Orson succeeds in communicating not merely intentionality (he wants to fight Grygar) but obedience to the court's particular ritual for combat ('by the lawe of champion'). In a telling gesture (especially since he is still supposed to be naked), he takes his 'hode' and

flings it 'by great fyer[s]nes vnto Grigar in maner of wage & dyf-
fyaunce' (p. 90).

In the battle with Grygar, Orson displays his full animal ferocity,
but now he also begins to make use of the resources of chivalry.
When he first confronts his enemy, he appears more like a bear than
a man: 'he ... stratched forth his armes, and shewed his nayles and
his teeth, grennyng full hugely' (p. 92). When Grygar fails to strike
him with his spear, Orson grabs the spear himself, and 'gaue hym so
great a stroke that he loste witte and vnderstanding in such wyse that
he wiste not where he was' (p. 93). Once Grygar has mounted on his
horse, Orson pursues him round the field, 'makyng a grymly countenaunce, and shewyng the kyng that he woulde yelde hym matte
anone' (p. 93). Orson succeeds in catching the horse, and spins it
about so that Grygar is thrown, losing his shield in the process.
Orson then mounts the horse himself and, armed with Grygar's
shield, 'in makyng marueylous sygnes he roode after Grygar that fled
about in the fielde' (p. 93). He finally defeats his opponent by
inflicting mortal wounds upon him with his own sword and dagger.
The fight with Grygar has been a sort of 'jousting by numbers', with
Orson signing his commentary on every step of the action. He
presents the world of chivalry with its own image, writ large. And,
as he begins to bring together in his body the virtues of the wild and
the virtues of knighthood, he is shaping himself into the one
champion who can meet the ultimate challenge the knights have
to face.

This challenge presents itself in the form of the Green Knight, a
merciless foe who has killed 'dyuers valyaunte knyghtes' and caused
their bodies to be hung shamefully from a tree. It is his destiny never
to be vanquished 'but of a kynges sonne that neuer had souked
womans breastes' (p. 95). It is obvious to us that such a role is tailor-
made for Orson, although it is not obvious to the other characters in
the story, who are still ignorant of his parentage. Orson expresses
extreme eagerness, both to fight with the Green Knight and to 'loue
the fayre Fezonne', the beautiful maiden whom he guards. Orson's
signing of his desire to love Fezonne is presumably the same as his
signing to the ladies in Eglantyne's chamber—at least, it is hard to
imagine how it could be different. But it is now read as part of the
courtly code: to battle enemies and to love ladies is exactly what
knights are supposed to do, and Valentine duly responds with 'great

ioye' to his brother's enthusiasm. When he introduces Orson to Fezonne, it is as 'the moste valyaunte and hardy man that is vpon the earthe. . . . If he coulde speake well in all the worlde might not be founde his make' (p. 101). Orson's tough, impervious skin, originally a mark of his wildness, is now read as a sign of his heroic endurance in adversity: 'his flesshe is so harde that he feareth nother wynde nor colde' (p. 101). Fezonne is impressed:

For he is marueylusly well made of his membres, and well formed, streight and hardy of countenaunce, & I beleue that & he were bayned in a hoote house, his flesshe woulde be whyte and softe. . . . Alwayes in speakynge these wordes the excellent Fezonne behelde stron[g]ly Orson & so as it was goddes pleasure, she was enamoured on Orson, and stryken at the harte more ardauntly than euer she was before of any other, howe well that he was not pycked nor gorgyously clothed as dyuers other were for all that it is sayde commonly that there is no foule loues whan the hartes geueth them therto. (p. 101)

To Fezonne, Orson's hard skin is something else again: touchable, strokable, apt to be softened by women's hands. The wild man's body, expressive and unadorned, once more enables the speaking of female sexual desire.

In his confrontation with the Green Knight, wildness and courtliness continue their debate in Orson's person and in his actions. From being dumb, he has now moved to the borderline of human speech: threatened by the Green Knight, he 'began for to momble a peace and makyng sygnes that vpon the morowe he woulde fyghte with hym, and in token of wager he cast the grene knight his hod' (p. 104). Yet he is still engagingly spontaneous, and when he hears the noise of the crowds eager to catch sight of him he leaps up to a window 'for to beholde the people that were without' (p. 104). He spends the night before the battle not in a bed but lying 'platte to the earth as he was accustomed to do in the forest' (p. 105). After Valentine and the Green Knight have fought bloodily but inconclusively, and Orson has been given leave to take up the challenge himself, he is 'ryght Ioyous and lepte and daunced aboute the halle for gladnes' (p. 112). He is persuaded, against his will, to wear armour, and, once armed, 'he was moche loked on of the lordes and barons that was there presente, for he semed ryght well to be a man of grete prowesse and hardynesse, replete with all beaute hye and well formed in all his membres by ryght mesure compassed' (p. 113). Orson's body has shed its wild-man deformities and is now perfectly attuned to the courtly ideal of beauty. In the same way his manners and bearing are being assimilated to the courtly code. However, the revision is incomplete: he still makes people laugh by his menacing gestures ('he made synes with his handes that he wolde strangle the grene knyght or that myd daye were paste before all the courte', p. 113) and by the way he dashes back, at the very last moment, to kiss Fezonne. Fezonne accepts his impulsive kiss and assigns it a meaning within chivalric discourse: as the knight's classic pledge to his lady before he goes out to do battle for her sake:

And Fezonne that was replete wyth al graciousnes in smiling made hym sygne that he sholde beare hym valyauntlye, and than whan he retorned from the batayll she woulde gyue hym her loue. (p. 113)

(Orson, of course, does not look on the battle as a *prelude* to winning Fezonne. For him it is the main event.)

In the fight itself, Orson first bases his technique upon what he has learnt from knights, riding against his adversary with a spear and then attacking him on foot with his sword. Yet once he is wounded his animal nature flashes out decisively:

Whan Orson sawe his bloode renne down alonge hys harme he was more fyerser than a Leoparde, and more courageous than a lyon. He rolled his eyen and shaked his head, and with his bright swearde he gaue the Gyaunte so grete a stroke vpon his head that he touched his naked flesh and bare away a grete quantyte of the flesh & heer withall, and the stroke slyded downe and hyt hym on the arme so that the bloud ranne down haboundauntly. (p. 114)

In his fury, Orson resorts to the extravagant bodily gestures of the wild man, rolling his eyes and shaking his head. However, the animals he is now compared to, the lion and the leopard, are no longer the savage creatures of the wild but those of the heraldic pantheon. And, to inflict final defeat, he needs to ally his native ferocity with the human qualities of reason and intelligence instilled in him during his stay at the court. As he is 'subtyl and well auysed', he realizes he must stop the Green Knight treating himself with his magic balm. Therefore he brings his tremendous strength into play, lifting his enemy in his powerful arms and hurling him to the ground so that he cannot reach for his healing ointment.

The defeat of the Green Knight is Orson's crowning achievement. After it, the last vestiges of his 'wildness' either fall away from him, or are re-interpreted in a different light. His dumbness, for instance, is no longer seen as an animal trait but becomes a mere plot device, on a par with the Sleeping Beauty's coma. Orson is betrothed to Fezonne, the narrator tells us, yet 'shall he not wedde her, nor neuer lye by her sydes tyll that by the wyll of god he shall speke good language' (p. 119). What prevents Orson from speaking has nothing to do now with his upbringing—it is 'a thread that is under his tongue' which Valentine, counselled by a head of brass, finally severs. Once he has done this, Orson is able to speak 'also playnly as ony body' (p. 141).

When Orson at last returns to Fezonne to claim her hand in marriage, she does not at first recognize him—he has lost his 'wild' exterior, with all its ramifying expressiveness, and put on knightly anonymity. When he fights now, he will fight as an ordinary, typical—although, of course, still a valiant—knight. He will become Constable of France, outstanding in piety and in martial Christian allegiance: when the enchanter Pacolet reveals his plan to massacre the Saracens who are being besieged by king Pepin and his army, he responds with unqualified approval: 'By God sayde Orson you speake ryght well and subtylly, and shewe well that you haue a good wil and deuocion for to susteyne and defende oure lawe' (p. 255). The transformed wild man now operates the moral turnstile. It is Pacolet who is the new focus of ambiguity—his schemes are indispensable to the knights, and yet he is involved with necromancy, on one occasion summoning up a devil to tell him the future. Orson himself ends his days as a hermit, back in the forest he had roamed in the years of his wildness. His story has been an interrogation, by a courtly society, of the world beyond its boundaries. If we feel—as we surely do—by the close of the romance that Orson the pious hermit is a much less interesting figure than Orson the wild man or Orson the apprentice knight, it is because the dominant code has triumphed too conclusively: there is no longer that sense of dialectical tension, of the immediacy of questions being presented through the bodily imaging of the central actor. It is this tension that the best of the wild men, in literature and in art, succeed in conveying to us.

CHAPTER NINE

Women and the Wild

IT CAN HARDLY have escaped attention that the human bodies that
have been discussed in the preceding chapters have been, over-
whelmingly, male. Distinctively female bodies, and female bodily
experiences, have been notable for their absence. The few examples
that have emerged reflect familiar tropes: from a male perspective,
women have affinity with various creatures, in a belittling or overtly
sexualized way. They chatter like magpies, and strut abroad with
those birds' insouciance and eye-catching plumage, or they have
bodies whose compliant sensuality is spoken through the stroked
and petted lapdogs that nestle in the crooks of their mistresses' arms.
Alison in *The Miller's Tale* is a 'wezele', her body 'gent and smal' (line
3234)—and again what is imagined is the mock resistance of the
little creature as it tries to squirm its way out of a hold that it secretly
desires.

The discourse of hunting could be seen as a special case, for
women certainly took part in hunts, and may even have contributed
to hunting literature.[1] However, the imaged body of the deer itself,
in its surrender to the delving hands of its hunters, is inescapably

---

[1] Although the identity of 'Julyans Barnes', the author of the hunting treatise in *The
Boke of St Albans*, is not known, Julia Boffey argues that there is no reason why she
should *not* have been a woman, as her name suggests, and points out that the Ménagier
de Paris (ed. G. E. Brereton and J. M. Ferrier (Oxford, 1981)) includes instructions on
hunting and hawking in the advice compiled for his young wife ('Women's Authors and
Women's Literacy in 14th- and 15th-Century England', in Carol M. Meale (ed.),
Women and Literature in Britain 1150–1500, Cambridge Studies in Medieval Literature,
17 (Cambridge, 1993), 143–69). Women hunters quite often appear in marginal illustrations: see e.g. Lilian M. C. Randall, *Images in the Margins of Gothic Manuscripts*
(Berkeley and Los Angeles, 1966), CXLVIII. 707, CL. 714, 715. A sequence of *bas-
de-page* illustrations in the Taymouth Hours (BL MS Yates-Thompson 13) opens with
the title 'Cy comence jeu de dames' (fo. 68ʳ) and includes pictures of women shooting at
rabbits with bows and arrows, coursing hares, riding after a stag, and even impaling a
wild boar on a spear. On fo. 80ᵛ a woman hunter carrying a bow and holding two
greyhounds on a leash kneels to spy out a grazing stag.

feminine—to such an extent that its biological sex becomes irrelevant. Several of the animals discussed by Marcelle Thiébaux as 'stags of love' are actually female, and in cognate versions of the same tale harts and hinds figure interchangeably.[2] The pure white hind who is mortally wounded by Marie de France's Guigemar is clearly female, and is accompanied by its fawn, yet it bears antlers on its head:

> Tute fu blaunche cele beste,
> Perches de cerf out en la teste.[3]

Leslie Brook relates this apparently anomalous feature to the antlered stag in Celtic religion which, although male, was associated with the Mother Goddess[4]—another plausible explanation is that deer were so strongly linked with the feminine that characteristics of both sexes could coexist unproblematically in a single body. This deer, however, although doomed by its hunter, resists the usual sequel of absorption by the human world, since the arrow that kills it rebounds and strikes Guigemar, inflicting a wound which can only be cured by a woman. The passive, objectified body suddenly answers back.

Do female bodies participate in the dialogue about human identity initiated by the wild man? In other words, are there any wild women? St Mary of Egypt, whose legend appears in several medieval compilations, lived alone in the desert for many years, as penance for her insatiable promiscuity.[5] Male anchorites leading similar lives

---

[2] 'Stags' lure the hero 'to erotic adventure' (*The Stag of Love: The Chase in Medieval Literature* (Ithaca, NY, 1974), 109), but the examples given in the accompanying note (from *Graelent* and *Guigemar*) involve hinds. The milk-white deer who guides the hero over a river is a hart in *Firumbras* (ed. Mary Isabelle O'Sullivan, EETS OS 198 (1935), 1055–62) and *Sir Ferumbras* (ed. Sidney J. Herrtage, EETS ES 34 (1879), 3955–66) but a hind in *The Sowdone of Babylone* (ed. Emil Hausknecht, EETS ES 38 (1881), 2809–14). Hunting is punningly associated with male sexuality in some of Henry VIII's poems (see John Stevens, *Music and Poetry in the Early Tudor Court* (Cambridge, 1979), 249–50, nos. H35, H62, H65) and in Wyatt's sonnet 'Whoso list to hunt' (*Collected Poems*, ed. Joost Daalder (London, 1975), no. VII).

[3] *Guigemar*, in Marie de France, *Lais*, ed. A. Ewert (Oxford, 1965), lines 91–2.

[4] Leslie Brook, 'Guigemar and the White Hind', *MÆ* 56 (1987), 94–101.

[5] Medieval versions of her legend, all of which descend from a 7th-cent. Greek text attributed to Sophronius and show little significant variation, include: *Aelfric's Lives of the Saints*, ed. W. W. Skeat, EETS OS 94, 114 (1890, repr. in one vol. 1966), 2. 2–54; *Legends of the Saints in Scottish Dialect*, ed. W. W. Metcalfe, STS 13 (1896), 1. 309; *The Early South-English Legendary or Lives of the Saints*, ed. Carl Horstmann, EETS OS 87 (1887), 261–71; *The Golden Legend or Lives of the Saints as Englished by William Caxton*, ed. F. S. Ellis (London, 1900; repr. New York, 1973), 3. 107. The legend is summarized by

are often described as growing hair all over their bodies,[6] yet there seems to have been a reluctance to endow Mary with such a characteristic. She appears to the monk Zosimas as a recognizably female body, blackened by the sun's heat, and with white hair like wool that reaches no further than her neck.[7] When she realizes she is being observed, she flees, and puts the width of a dried-up stream between herself and the pursuing Zosimas, refusing to turn towards him until he has given her a cloak with which she can hide her nakedness. Her years in the wilderness have not unsexed her: she is still, unmistakably, a woman—her femininity, in fact, enhanced by Aelfric's description of her as 'þæs sweteste wildeor' which Zosimas, the questing hunter, tries eagerly to capture.[8]

A saintly woman covered in hair would perhaps prompt uncomfortable comparisons with the thoroughly monstrous women of folktale and myth, whose hairiness, like that of their wild partners, is linked to a ravenous sexuality.[9] The desirable woman of the romances has a white, soft body, its smooth, caressable surface a metaphor for its uncontested appropriation by the hero. When that surface is broken, the result is not wildness, or the irruption of animal features, but a loss of specularity—the woman no longer reflects back those qualities which both sign her femaleness and

Charles Allyn Williams, 'Oriental Affinities of the Hairy Anchorite, Part II: Christian', *University of Illinois Studies in Language and Literature*, 11 (1926), 107–10, and discussed in Ruth Mazo Karras, 'Holy Harlots: Prostitute Saints in Medieval Legend', *Journal of the History of Sexuality*, 1 (1990), 3–32, and Erich Poppe and Bianca Ross (eds.), *The Legend of Mary of Egypt in Medieval Insular Hagiography* (Dublin, 1996). Mary of Egypt is usually described as a 'prostitute saint' but this is not strictly accurate as we are told that she never asked men for money: her motive in soliciting them was simply the great pleasure she took in sex.

[6] e.g. St John Chrysostom: see n. 53 to Ch. 7.

[7] See e.g. *Aelfric's Lives of the Saints*, 12, lines 176–7: 'and þa loccas hire heafdes wæron swá hwíte swá wull . and þa ná siddran þonne oþ þone swuran'. Williams agrees that authors 'seem to have been reluctant to represent the woman-solitary as hairy like the remote anchorite, her prototype' ('Hairy Anchorite, Part II', 109). He finds a late German prose version which describes Mary as covered in hair like a beast, but points out that by this time there had been some cross-fertilization from the legend of Mary Magdalene, who allowed the hair of her head to grow long to conceal her body. In a sequence of marginal illustrations in the Smithfield Decretals (BL MS Royal 10 E IV, fos. 268^r–290^r) Mary is shown covered in hair, but the story told in this sequence differs in many respects from written versions of the legend.

[8] *Aelfric's Lives of the Saints*, 48, line 734.

[9] See Richard Bernheimer, *Wild Men in the Middle Ages: A Study in Art, Sentiment and Demonology* (Cambridge, Mass., 1952), 33–8.

substantiate male identity. As Susan Crane points out, when the queen Heurodis in *Sir Orfeo* is menaced by the fairy king, she 'undoes' her beauty in her husband's sight, acting out, in bodily terms, the impending destruction of their relationship.[10] Orfeo laments:

> 'O lef liif, what is te,
> That ever yete hast ben so stille,
> And now gredest wonder schille?
> Thi bodi that was so white y-core,
> With thine nailes is al to-tore.
> Allas! thi rode that was so red
> Is al wan, as thou were ded,
> And also thine fingres smale
> Beth al blodi and al pale.
> Allas! thi lovesom eyghen to
> Loketh so man doth on his fo!'[11]

The features that Heurodis mars are those that had previously defined her femininity—smooth skin, rosy complexion, delicate fingers, and demure silence. Her eyes, which had once signalled love, now appear to Orfeo to speak hostility. After her long years in the fairy kingdom, Heurodis's beauty has to be reconstituted by another male, the fairy king ('sche is lovesome, withouten lac'), before she can be handed back into a right relationship.

Women's potential 'wildness' is therefore constrained by the bias of gendered representation. Social factors also work against the effective imagining of a 'wild woman'. The condition of 'liminality', in which subjects discard the props of status or hierarchy to explore a radically different way of living, has been lucidly described by Victor Turner,[12] and has obvious application to the case of the wild-men/knights. Classically, the time in the 'wilderness'—the period of rolelessness—is followed by a return to society which reaffirms the validity of existing forms and structures. However, for this trajectory to 'work' there has to be a sense of real, experi-

---

[10] Susan Crane, *Gender and Romance in Chaucer's 'Canterbury Tales'* (Princeton, 1994), 74–5.

[11] *Sir Orfeo*, in *Middle English Romances*, ed. A. C. Gibbs, York Medieval Texts (London, 1966), lines 88–98.

[12] e.g. *The Ritual Process: Structure and Anti-Structure* (Chicago, 1969); *Dramas, Fields and Metaphors: Symbolic Action in Human Society* (Ithaca, NY, 1974).

ential change—status, in other words, has to be securely established
before it can be set aside. This is certainly so in the romances of the
wild-men/knights, whose authors take pains to stress the contrast
between their subjects' past and present states. Orfeo's displacement
into the wilderness, for example, is lamented by all the court:

> O, way! what, ther was wepe and wo,
> When he that hadde ben king with croune
> Went so poverlich out of toun!
>
> . . . .
>
> He that had y-had knightes of priis
> Bifor him kneland, and levedis,
> Now seth he no thing that him liketh,
> Bot wilde wormes bi him striketh.[13]

Orfeo moves outwards from a society which affirms and celebrates
his high rank to a place where there is not even recognition of his
bare physical presence (as the fluent, untrammelled motion of the
'wilde wormes' shows). The change is so profound because he has
had so far to fall. However, the same narrative involving a woman
would not carry a comparable charge. Women were not on the
status 'ladder' in the same way that men were: they are commonly
absent from the three 'orders' of medieval society classically identified by Georges Duby,[14] and, where they are accorded recognition, they are grouped according to their sexual relationships—as
virgin, wife, mother, nun, or whore.[15] No wonder, therefore, that,
in Caroline Bynum's words, the 'complex imagery of role reversal,
of inversion of power and status . . . appealed more to men, for
whom the precise gradations of society were self-definitions that
might bear down with a psychological weight that demanded peri-
odic release'.[16]

If the motif of going out into the wild and then returning is
strongly gendered, so too is the very concept of 'adventure', in the
sense of seeking out and engaging with the unknown. Susan Crane
briefly considers this question at the end of her *Gender and Romance*.

[13] *Sir Orfeo*, lines 220–2, 235–8.

[14] Georges Duby, *The Three Orders: Feudal Society Imagined*, trans. Arthur Goldhammer (Chicago, 1980), esp. ch. 9: 'Ternarity'.

[15] See Crane, *Gender and Romance*, 97.

[16] Caroline Walker Bynum, *Holy Feast and Holy Fast: The Religious Significance of Food
to Medieval Women* (Berkeley and Los Angeles, 1987), 286.

She argues that adventure is so highly valued in texts because it allows men to step for a moment into the female role of receptivity to chance and change, without in any sense becoming *less* masculine themselves in the process. And in grappling with, and overcoming, the challenges that adventure brings, men become masters over the previously unknown and unexplored—in other words, over terrain which, in its 'otherness', can be construed as feminine. Thus, 'adventure engages the mysterious feminine, not deleteriously but in a positive process of masculine gain and self-definition'.[17] In this context, Crane argues, women's adventures play a subjected and occluded part, being 'peculiarly at odds with, and concealed within, the dominant adventures of their lovers'.[18] Josiane, the heathen princess in *Sir Beues of Hamtoun*, is active, intelligent, and courageous, but there are clear limits to her participation in events. When two lions invade the cave in which she is hiding, and kill her protector, Bonyface, she is able to restrain them because they have no power to harm her, as a king's daughter and a virgin. When Beues returns from hunting, she offers to hold on to one while he dispatches the other, but her lover angrily spurns her help:

> About the necke she toke the one,
> But Beuys bad hyr lat hym gone:
> 'I say, Iosian, let them ben!
> I se, thou art a mayden clene:
> What maystry is it, them to slo,
> In bondes whan thou holdest them so?
> Late them come to me both,
> Or ellys, forsothe, I wol be lothe!'[19]

Josiane's quick thinking and intrepidity are totally discounted by Beues, for whom her action's only point is the proof it gives that she really is a virgin. Otherwise what she does is an impediment to that willed exposure to maximum peril which is the mark of the true hero. Rebuked, Josiane subsides into her proper role, which is to

[17] Crane, *Gender and Romance*, 191.   [18] Ibid. 185.

[19] *Sir Beues of Hamtoun*, ed. Eugen Kölbing, EETS es 46, 48, 65 (1885, 1886, 1894), MS M: lines 2197–2204. In the version in the Auchinleck manuscript, Beues is even angrier and threatens first to desert Josiane if she hinders him again ('But þou let hem goo both twoo | Haue good day, fro þe y goo!', lines 2419–20) and then (when she does) to kill her: 'Beues bad hire go sitte adoun, | And swor be god in trinite, | Boute 3he lete þat lioun be, | A wolde hire sle in þat destresse | Ase fain ase þe liounesse' (lines 2474–8).

reflect back to her lover, in mute, worshipful love, an empowering sense of his own identity:

> Beuys loked on Iosian,
> And suche a confort toke he than,
> That, thoughe the lyons were grym and lothe,
> At one stroke he slewe them both.[20]

Custance in *The Man of Law's Tale* has a series of adventures (dramatic enough, in summary), but her active participation in them is always qualified—most usually by the narrator's insistence that Christ, her champion, stepped in at crucial moments to save her. For example, when Custance is falsely accused of killing Hermengyld, the narrator exclaims:

> Allas! Custance, thou hast no champioun,
> Ne fighte kanstow noght, so weylaway!
> But he that starf for our redempcioun,
> And boond Sathan (and yet lith ther he lay),
> So be thy stronge champion this day!   (631–5)

The narrator's intervention swings the story in an unanticipated direction and re-presents the situation according to the canon of masculine 'adventure'. Before this, there has been no mention of Custance's guilt or innocence being proved in battle—on the contrary, the previous stanza has described the beginnings of a different kind of process: the people's testimony that Custance had loved Hermengyld greatly, and Alla's suspicion that he has not yet been told the whole truth, and determination to investigate further. This process the narrator interrupts—and in so doing he disqualifies Custance from acting in her own defence: as a woman, she naturally cannot take up arms. Luckily, God responds to Custance's prayer, and strikes down the traducing knight—but not before Custance's utter helplessness and desolation have been revealed to us in the image of the pale face of the man being led through a crowd to his death.

The way the tale is told in fact re-emphasizes Custance's passivity: she is often presented as the focus of other people's gaze, an object of wonder, curiosity, or sympathy. The inhabitants of the 'hethen castel' where she lands after being set adrift with her son come

---

[20] Ibid., MS M: lines 2211–14.

down 'To gauren on this ship and on Custance'; earlier, the narrator had solicited queens, duchesses, and other great ladies to look upon her with pity, as an icon of the reversals that fortune can bring ('An Emperoures doghter stant allone', line 655). Custance herself could have participated in the dramatic momentum at various points by telling her own story (after all, it is a tale worth the hearing), but she either remains silent or gives partial, occluded answers. After she has landed in Northumberland, for example, she refuses to identify herself and pleads loss of memory:

> She seyde she was so mazed in the see
> That she forgat hir mynde, by hir trouthe.   (526–7)

Later, taken on board the Roman senator's ship,

> she nyl seye
> Of hire estaat, althogh she sholde deye.   (972–3)

In a curious way, Custance refuses to concretize her own, lived adventures—if, as Susan Crane argues, the romance hero's 'traject-ory towards distinction must be made known to others because identity is finally in the gift of the community', then identity in these terms is a gift Custance consciously rejects.[21]

If the idea of 'women's adventure' proves to be problematic, it is, in a way, only a further sign that women's experience is not central to the majority of medieval texts. From this, it is a short step to making women themselves habitants of the periphery—that area where, I have argued in previous chapters, men locate that which they are not, and into which they make forays, with the aims of engagement and colonization. Such a placing would ally women with animals, and would thus tie in with a persistent strand in medieval thought according to which women's bodies were more labile, less continent than those of men—more inclined to manifest

---

[21] Crane, *Gender and Romance*, 29. Chaucer also minimizes Custance's agency by his refusal to confirm that it was she who persuaded the senator to take her with him to Alla's feast ('*Som men wolde seyn* at requeste of Custance | This senatour hath lad this child to feeste', lines 1009–10, my italics); by contrast, Gower, in his version of the story, makes her positively instruct Moris to make sure Alla notices him (*The Complete Works of John Gower*, ed. G. C. Macaulay, 4 vols. (Oxford 1899–1902), vol. ii: *The English Works*, *Confessio Amantis*, 2. 1365–9). The two women who *do* act effectively within the tale— the Sultan's mother and Donegild—are both presented as dreadful aberrations: the Sultaness is compared to the serpent who tempted Eve (lines 360–1), while Donegild is both demonic (lines 782–3) and 'mannysh' (line 782), i.e. unfeminine.

dangerously liminal characteristics. The supposed wanderings of the womb—that 'animal within an animal'—in hysteric disorders is a well-known example; another is the belief that menstrual blood was poisonous and needed to be expelled by the body (hence the 'venom' stored up in older women who had passed the meno-pause).[22]

Women's bodies therefore represent a falling-away from the paradigmatic male body. They are less self-contained, less stable. The stability they do attain has to be imposed upon them by men—hysteric disorders, for instance, were thought to be caused by lack of regular sex and therefore to be especially common in virgins, nuns, and widows.[23] If women were thus displaced to the periphery, did it mean that they had especial affinity with other creatures similarly displaced—with animals, and with the whole natural world? It is tempting to say *yes*—and Sherry Ortner has argued persuasively that the fact that women are seen as closer to nature than men accounts for their subordination the world over, since it is an essential part of the human enterprise to subdue and manipulate nature through culture.[24] The assumption of kinship between women and animals is made by a number of writers on medieval texts: Susan Crane, for instance, discussing *The Squire's Tale*, considers that 'The sympathy that unites "Canacee and alle hir wommen" with the wronged falcon illustrates both a special feminine capacity for compassion and a certain exoticism that connects women more closely than men to the animal world—so closely, indeed, that a bird can voice feminine positions more vividly than Canacee herself'.[25] However, there is something a little suspect in such straightforward binarism, and not just because any number of counter-examples can be

---

[22] Wandering womb: see Laurinda S. Dixon, 'The Curse of Chastity: The Marginalization of Women in Medieval Art and Medicine', in Robert R. Edwards and Vickie Ziegler (eds.), *Matrons and Marginal Women in Medieval Society* (Woodbridge, 1995), 49–74; Vern L. Bullough, 'Medieval Medical and Scientific Views of Women', *Viator*, 4 (1973), 494–6. 'Dangerous' menstrual blood: see Shulamith Shahar, 'The Old Body in Medieval Culture', in Sarah Kay and Miri Rubin (eds.), *Framing Medieval Bodies* (Manchester, 1994), 163–4.

[23] Dixon, 'Curse of Chastity', 52.

[24] Sherry B. Ortner, 'Is Female to Male as Nature is to Culture?', in Michelle Zimbalist Rosaldo and Louise Lamphere (eds.), *Woman, Culture and Society* (Stanford, Calif., 1974), 67–87.

[25] Crane, *Gender and Romance*, 67.

found—from Beues and his horse Arondel[26] to Yvain and his lion,
and even to Siegfried and the woodbird and beyond. Would Canacee understand a *male* bird half so well? Sherry Ortner, after considering women's alleged closeness to nature in terms of physiology,
social position, and psyche, goes on to propose a more nuanced
picture:

> Shifting our image of the culture/nature relationship once again, we may
> envision culture in this case as a small clearing within the forest of the larger
> natural system. From this point of view, that which is intermediate be-
> tween culture and nature is located on the continuous periphery of
> culture's clearing; and though it may thus appear to stand both above
> and below (and beside) culture, it is simply outside and around it. We
> can begin to understand then how a single system of cultural thought can
> often assign to women completely polarized and apparently contradictory
> meanings, since extremes, as we say, meet.[27]

Since women are intermediaries between culture and nature, their
representation is radically destabilized, lacking definitive grounding:
'Feminine symbolism, far more than masculine symbolism, manifests this propensity toward polarized ambiguity—sometimes utterly
exalted, sometimes utterly debased, rarely within the normal range
of human possibilities.'[28] In the next section I will take this idea of
doubleness, and apply it to a medieval narrative in which a woman
actually appears with a doubled body—the story of Melusine.

First, though, I would like to revise Sherry Ortner's model of a
central hub of 'culture' circled by a larger 'nature'. That model,
although attractive and enlightening in many ways, comes under a
sort of dimensional strain when we are asked to think of women as
both above and below (and beside) culture as well as along its
continuous interface with the world of nature. In important ways,
too, women are *not* 'outside', or 'around' culture but profoundly
involved within it. Rather than giving women a fixed place, or
places, within a two-dimensional schema, I believe it is more
illuminating to think of them as *both* wholly present *and* wholly
absent, from the dominant, male point of view. This mixing of

---

[26] Before a horse-race, for which the prize is a thousand pounds, Beues speaks to
Arondel, promising to raise a castle for him if he wins. Arondel hears, and responds
(*Beues of Hamtoun*, Auchinleck MS: lines 3531–42).

[27] Ortner, 'Female to Male', 85.

[28] Ibid. 86.

presence and absence generates anxiety, since men cannot always be sure which style is operative.[29]

'Presence', of course, does not necessarily mean physical presence, but secure containment within the overarching economy of men's needs and routines. When a knight goes off to seek renown in tournaments, for example, his lady is still highly 'present' to him if he can be sure she is waiting patiently for him to return, ready to reward him with the gift of herself when he does. Beues of Hamtoun hopes that his lady, Josiane, is as faithful to him as his good horse Arondel is, soliciting her 'presence' even though she is far removed from him, and actually entrapped, at that moment, in marriage with another man:

> 'Wer Iosiane,' a þouȝte, 'ase lele,
> Also is me stede Arondel,
> Ȝet sholde ich come out of wo!'[30]

As Susan Crane argues:

In the dominant paradigm of courtship, women attest to their suitors' deeds and reflect back to them an image of their worth. The resistance women may put up to suitors is compatible with the masculine desire for a complex experience of effective subjectivity.[31]

If 'presence' is women's acquiescence in culturally sanctioned roles, and also in the expected progression of romance, 'absence' can take a variety of forms. The desired woman may absent herself by refusing to make herself available for courtship, or she may deliberately reject the currency of knightly worth and make an unexpected, completely illogical choice. This is what Phoebus's wife does in *The Manciple's Tale*—and, interestingly, her taking of

[29] Mark Chinca detects a related theme in the Middle High German *Mären* which tell of the trickiness of wives. In the context of these tales, marriage itself is a problematic institution, for in it 'the distinction between centre and periphery, lord and subject, is lost' (p. 203). Women have to be enlisted as partners, and thus brought in from the periphery, but they use their enhanced status to betray their husbands, displaying 'both a mobile, incontinent use of the body and a mobile use of signs' (p. 201) as they do so ('The Body in some Middle High German *Mären*: Taming and Maiming', in Sarah Kay and Miri Rubin (eds.), *Framing Medieval Bodies* (Manchester, 1994), 187–210).

[30] *Beues of Hamtoun*, lines 2033–5.

[31] Crane, *Gender and Romance*, 13. Also p. 117: 'The admirable women of romance wield their emotional sovereignty in ways beneficial to men and pleasurable to audiences, deferring stasis for a time but finally yielding in harmonious accord with male desire.'

a worthless lover immediately involves her in comparisons with the animal kingdom: with the pet bird which longs to escape from its dainty cage and live 'in a forest that is rude and coold' (line 170), and with the pampered cat whose inborn lust is aroused once it sees 'a mous go by the wal' (line 177). The male nightmare revealed here is that the right words should be said, the right deeds done, *and all for no reward*.

This dilemma of courtship—that, because of women's willed 'absence', apparently purposeful activity may turn out to have been wasted time and effort—generates several of the motifs of romance writing. One line, of course, leads to the 'cruel fair' of Renaissance poetry: the woman who is castigated, whether bitterly or playfully, for withholding her consent. An unforgettable medieval example is Boccaccio's eighth story on the fifth day of the *Decameron*, of Nastagio's vision of the woman whose horrible fate it is to be torn and devoured by dogs over and over again, in punishment for the pride and cruelty which, in life, had led her to reject her would-be lover.[32] Another, less violent response is to invoke accepted conventions of male governance and disposal to take the decision out of the woman's hands altogether—which is what happens to Emily in *The Knight's Tale*. A further variation can be found in the motif of the fairy mistress, who, by surrendering herself immediately and unreservedly, short-circuits the risks of wooing altogether. Or the man may simply turn his back on the game, refusing to set foot in the bloodied arena. This choice, however, is unlikely to be validated in romance writing, as the examples of Marie de France's Guigemar and Chaucer's Troilus show. Both men initially scorn the experience of love, and both are made to suffer as a result.

The option of refusing to love is not a feasible one because a mode of living that permanently excludes women is simply not viable. Women, quite apart from their general role as fuellers and supporters of male activity, give birth to the children on whom men's hopes for the future depend. Any scheme that denies them this centrality is doomed from the start: it will simply run out of bodies very fast. The paradox is that, while it is admirable for men to fill each day with

---

[32] Giovanni Boccaccio, *The Decameron*, trans. and introd. G. H. McWillliam (Harmondsworth, 1972), 457–62.

enterprises that do not involve women (with hunting, for example, which could well absorb all one's waking hours, from sunrise to sundown), in the long view, a life that leaves women out of the reckoning altogether has to be viewed as an unsatisfactory one (I exclude, of course, monks and others whose chastity was a matter of religious idealism). Love and 'chivalry' (in its most extended sense) are therefore profoundly at odds: as Aldo Scaglione puts it, 'the ideal noble knight must be a great fighter to be a worthy lover, but can hardly be both at the same time . . . We must fight to qualify for love, yet we cannot love while we fight.'[33] The very means by which women are won may turn out to be the means by which they are lost, since withdrawal into the world of knightly pursuits opens up, disquietingly, possibilities of absence for the women left behind.

The incompatibility between highly valued masculine activities and involvement with women appears, for example, in Chrétien's story of Yvain, who yields to Gawain's advice to leave his lady behind and ride away with him to take part in tournaments. Gawain weaves a skilful argument, avowing that the lady would quickly withdraw her love if Yvain stopped performing brave deeds, and suggesting that a time of abstinence will in fact make the sensual pleasures he enjoys with her even more exquisite:

> Certes, ancor seroiz iriez
> De s'amor, se vos anpiriez;
> Que fame a tost s'amor reprise,
> Ne n'a pas tort, s'ele desprise
> Celui, qui de neant anpire,
> Quant il est del reaume sire.
>
> .   .   .   .   .
>
> Biens adoucist par delaiier,
> Et plus est buens a essaiier
> Uns petiz biens, quant il delaie,
> Qu'uns granz, que l'an adés essaie.[34]

Indeed, you would be distressed by the loss of her affection if you grew degenerate, for a woman is quick to take back her love—and rightly so—if

[33] Aldo Scaglione, *Knights at Court: Courtliness, Chivalry, and Courtesy from Ottonian Germany to the Italian Renaissance* (Berkeley and Los Angeles, 1991), 11–12; quoted in Crane, *Gender and Romance*, 39 n. 16.

[34] *Yvain: Le Chevalier au lion*, text W. Foerster, introd. T. B. W. Reid (Manchester, 1942), lines 2493–8, 2515–18.

she despises a man who, once he is lord of her realm, becomes worse in any respect.... A pleasure becomes sweeter when it's delayed, and a small pleasure that we have to wait for is more enjoyable than a great one sampled at once.

Yvain fails to keep his lady in his mind once he is away from her—in part because his male companion, Gawain, insists on sticking close to him at all times, substituting *his* presence for that of the absent one. The realization that he has broken his promise to return after a year plunges Yvain into grief and madness—the tension between irreconcilable demands tears him apart. Women and chivalry are again at odds in the English prose *Melusine*, when king Elynas, out hunting, stops to drink at the fountain of the lady Pressyne. He is so enraptured by her beauty and by her singing that the hunt passes instantly from his mind—until two hunting dogs recall him to reality, he is suspended in the alternate world of Pressyne's enchantment:

Thenne the kynge Elynas was so rauysshed & abused that he remembred of nothinge worldly but alonely that he herd & sawe the said lady, and abode there long tyme. Thanne camme rannyng toward him two of hys houndis whiche made to hym greet feste, and he lept & mevyd hym as a man wakynge from slep and thenne he remembred of the chasse . . .[35]

To focus on women is to let other, necessary aspects of one's masculinity slide. Also, it is impossible in practical terms to keep women under continual surveillance and thus convert them, forcibly, into 'presences'. 'Absences'—periods when they are necessarily secluded from the male gaze—are part of the intimate rhythm of women's lives. Menstruation and childbirth both project women as absent in this sense. The absence involved in the latter is particularly charged with male anxiety, since it may mean that the promised heir is not produced. Hence the motif of the woman who is said to have given birth to a monster, which appears, for example, in *The Man of Law's Tale* and in the romance of *Chevelere Assigne*.[36] (In neither case, of course, is the rumour true, but the credence it gains reflects deep-seated fears.)

[35] *Melusine*, ed. A. K. Donald, EETS es 68 (1895), 7–8.
[36] In *Chevelere Assigne* the king's mother, Matabryne, substitutes seven puppies for the six sons and a daughter the queen has just given birth to, and accuses her: 'Bothe howndes and men have hadde þe a wylle' (*Medieval English Romances*, ed. Diane Speed, 2 vols. (Sydney, 1987), line 79).

In *Beues of Hamtoun*, the heroine, Josiane, nicely employs the conventions of womanly *privetee* to elude male control. Travelling through a forest with Beues and his henchman Terri, she begins to suffer labour pains. The two men use their swords to build her a shelter, and then leave her, respecting her desire for privacy:

> Syr Beuys dyd hyr seruyce bede,
> For to helpe hyr at hyr nede;
> 'Gramercy, syr,' she sayde, 'nay,'
> For goddys loue go hens away,
> Go and sport you wyth Terry
> And late me worke and our lady;
> Shal neuer womans pryuete
> To man be shewed for me!'[37]

Josiane summons up a female helper for herself in the shape of 'our lady', and, while the men are away, gives birth to two boys. However, she is then captured by the giant Ascopard with (in the Auchinleck version) a force of forty Saracens. Ingeniously, Josiane pretends she needs to go and relieve herself, calculating that a sense of decorum will stop the men from watching her:

> '. . . i praie on me þe rewe
> And ȝeue me space a lite wiȝt,
> For wende out of þis folkes siȝt,
> To do me nedes in priuite,
> For kende hit is, wimman to be
> Schamfaste and ful of corteisie,
> & hate dedes of fileinie.'[38]

When her request is granted, she disappears into the bushes and picks and eats a herb which gives her the appearance of a leper, so that when she is brought before the king who wants to marry her he is appalled at the sight and orders her to be taken away from him. Josiane uses her 'absence' to mark out for herself a space in which she has freedom to work—and that space guarantees her safety far more effectively than her lover's sword-built shelter.[39]

---

[37] *Beues of Hamtoun*, MS M: lines 3367–74.

[38] Ibid., Auchinleck MS: lines 3658–64. This incident is not related in MS M, perhaps for reasons of propriety.

[39] It is necessary to add, though, that Josiane's goal throughout her exploits is the preservation of her chastity, which Beues has made a condition of their marriage. As

Absences of this kind obviously involve women's bodies—Josiane's withdrawal is predicated on what may not be seen *of her* as well as on what she may not be seen doing. *Privetee* and *privetees* are closely related. And so women, as well as dazingly offering both presence and absence, are never entirely *visible* to men either. This quality finds expression in the stories about women whose hidden parts are really monstrous—for example, in the romance of *Melusine*.

MELUSINE: SHAPE-SHIFTER

There are two medieval English versions of the story of Melusine, the woman whose fate it is to spend one day every week in serpent form. The prose *Melusine*, extant in a single manuscript (*c.* 1500), is a translation of the late fourteenth-century *Mélusine* of Jean d'Arras. The *Romans of Partenay*, in seven-line stanzas, survives in a late fifteenth- or early sixteenth-century manuscript, and is a translation of the other major French version, the *Roman de Mélusine* of Coudrette, composed near the beginning of the fifteenth century.[40] There are other stories about men who marry shape-shifting women, and the motif itself is clearly a very ancient one: as Jacques Le Goff concludes, the literary Melusine 'is the written, high-cultural manifestation of a popular oral phenomenon whose origins are difficult to identify'.[41] I limit my discussion to the two English texts, although I shall also refer to the illustrations of some of the French versions, which have been studied, and helpfully reproduced, by Françoise Clier-Colombani.[42]

Susan Crane points out, this is a very typical motif in women's adventures in romance (*Gender and Romance*, 201).

[40] *The Romans of Partenay, or of Lusignen*, ed. W. W. Skeat, EETS OS 22 (1866). Subsequent references to both the prose *Melusine* and *Partenay* are included in the text. The relation between the two French texts is not clear: Coudrette may have condensed and versified d'Arras's work, or both versions may be based on a lost French tale. See Jacques Le Goff, 'Melusina: Mother and Pioneer', in *Time, Work and Culture in the Middle Ages*, trans. Arthur Goldhammer (Chicago, 1980), 204–22.

[41] Ibid. 216. Le Goff mentions several similar tales, including Walter Map's account of Henno, who married a fairy who was really a dragon in disguise (*De nugis curialium*, ed. M. R. James (Oxford, 1914), pt. 4, ch. 9).

[42] Françoise Clier-Colombani, *La Fée Mélusine au moyen âge: images, mythes et symboles* (Paris, 1991).

Le Goff identifies several problems with the interpretation of the tale. Of these, the chief problem concerns Melusine herself: why, in both the French versions, does her plight arouse sympathy? ('What accounts for this tenderness toward a demonic woman?') A further difficulty concerns the denouement: why does the story have a sad ending?[43] Le Goff solves his first crux by arguing that 'Melusine's *nature* emerges through her *function* in the legend'. Since she is associated with the clearing of forests and the building of castles and cities, she is above all 'the symbolic and magical incarnation of . . . social ambition', and the heroes to whom she links her fortune are that class of upwardly mobile *milites* whose eager desire is 'to push back the boundaries of their little seigneuries'. At the same time that she is amassing riches, she ensures her family's continuing hold upon them through her extraordinary fertility.

Le Goff provides a cogent reason for the accommodation of Melusine—as 'the fairy of medieval economic growth' she can hardly be demonized—and her labours to increase the prosperity of her husband and her sons certainly form an important strand in the story. He does not explore, though, the tension between her benevolent progressiveness as castle-builder and city-founder and the atavistic fears aroused by her 'secret' form, nor does he deal with the story's tragic ending. Susan Crane discusses Melusine as one of a company of 'shape-shifting' women (others include the woman-serpent in *Le Bel Inconnu* and the loathly ladies in *The Wife of Bath's Tale* and its cognates) whose transformations are acts of mystification, cancelling any straightforward correspondence between outward appearance and 'true' identity.[44] Crane points out that conventional 'feminine' traits are still disconcertingly present in the 'loathly' body (such as the vermilion lips of the serpent in *Le Bel Inconnu*) and argues that this complicates our view of what women should be like: 'If both bodies are female, what are the defining characteristics of femaleness?'[45] Shape-shifting thus becomes a female ploy to elude the determinism of gender, a carnivalesque rattling of the categories. Typically, the shape-shifting

---

[43] Le Goff, 'Melusina', 217. The story's unhappy ending is discussed in the context of other prose romances by Helen Cooper in 'Counter-Romance: Strife and Father-Killing in the Prose Romances', in Cooper and Sally Mapstone (eds.), *The Long Fifteenth Century: Essays for Douglas Gray* (Oxford, 1997), 155–7.

[44] Crane, *Gender and Romance*, 84–92.

[45] Ibid. 88.

woman 'makes an exuberant spectacle of herself'—Melusine in her bath 'could not have displayed herself more provocatively'.[46] Crane's thesis is attractive, but is not really faithful to the way Melusine herself is portrayed: as I shall show below, she is far less of a free spirit than that picture suggests.

The story of Melusine, as I read it, expresses the irreconcilable tension between woman present and woman absent—between woman subsumed in the social pattern and woman removed from it. That is why it ends tragically. Melusine's most obvious 'absence' is her withdrawal every Saturday from her husband's view. She withdraws herself, of course, for an extraordinary reason, but her rhythm of phased absences is one that is shared by women everywhere. Clier-Colombani interprets Melusine in her bath as a symbol of the menstruating woman, who regularly secludes herself from men's gaze so that she can cleanse herself from impurity and prepare to re-enter the world as a fertile and nourishing mother.[47] Less contentiously, perhaps, Melusine's withdrawal is prefigured in the story of her mother, Pressyne, who makes her husband, Elynas, promise never to look at her when she is in childbed. When he breaks this promise, and spies on her while she is bathing her newly born daughters, she vanishes. Melusine's weekly absences, therefore, correlate with a more general pattern of female inaccessibility—at the very moments when men might most wish to look at women (for example, to check that they are not engaged in baby-swapping tricks) they are prevented from doing so. Melusine's story is riven with paradoxes of this kind.

Melusine is, of course, the central figure in her tale, but we are also told, at the outset, that she is just one among a number of fairies who made marriages with men. The narrator of *Melusine* explains that the fairies always insist that their husbands should never ask them about their origins, or look at them in childbed—if this promise is kept, the men are happy and prosperous, but if it is broken they become poor and unlucky while their wives turn into serpents (pp. 4–5). Just such a fairy alliance is part of the background of the hero of the story, Raymondin: his father's first wife was a fairy, whom he met by a fountain. Together they cleared land and built castles and towns in their domain, which was called Forest 'bycause

[46] Crane, *Gender and Romance*, 89.   [47] Clier-Colombani, '*La Fée Mélusine*', Part III.

that they founde it full of grett wodes & thikk bushes' (p. 18). However, they quarrelled, and the fairy left her husband, who subsequently married the sister of the earl of Poitiers, the mother of Raymondin and his brothers. Raymondin, therefore, has a Melusine in his lineage as well as awaiting him as his destiny, and the realm of Forest, with its suggestions of untamed wilderness, persists, through his father's line, as his lost domain.

At the opening of his story, Raymondin, as the third son of an earl, has little to rely on and everything to achieve. The change in his fortunes begins when he is taken into the household of his uncle, the earl of Poitiers, and brought up there. However, disaster strikes when he is accidentally responsible for the death of his patron on a boar hunt. Distraught, he wanders through the forest in a fugue state, allowing his horse to take him where it will:

> he layed his foot on the sterop and lepe vpon his hors and departed, holding his way thrugh the myddel of the Forest, moche dyscomforted, & rode apas vnknowing the way, ne whether he went but only by hap & att auenture. . . . And the hors ledd Raymondyn whiche way that he wold, For no heede nor aduys he had of nothing, for cause of the gret dysplaysaunce that he had within hym self. (p. 27)

It is in this condition, physically and psychically distanced from his former life (for he has just killed his lord, and later fears that his uncle's men are coming to kill him), that Raymondin meets Melusine at her fountain. She is, in one sense, the epitome of uncanniness, for she knows both his name and what has happened to him, yet she insists that she has not acquired such knowledge 'be fauntesye or dyuels werk' (p. 31)—on the contrary, she is a good Christian: 'I certyfye the, Raymondyn, that I am of god, and my byleue is as a Catholique byleue oughte for to be' (p. 31). At once she offers to focus her special powers on Raymondin's life, first mending seamlessly the tear he has made in the feudal fabric (for she suggests he say nothing about his uncle's death: his men will then conclude that he died heroically fighting the boar), and then, through their marriage, bringing him prosperity. Yet there is a price: as he enters into, and triumphs over, his social milieu, he will at the same time be estranged from it, for he will be linked with Melusine in a secret pact:

> Ye muste promytte to me, Raymondyn, vpon all the sacrements & othes

that a man very catholoque & of good feith may doo and swere, that neuer
while I shalbe in your company, ye shal not peyne ne force your self for to
see me on the Satirday nor by no manere ye shal not enquyre that day of
me, ne the place wher I shalbe. (p. 32)

For Melusine to be wholly present to him, with all the happy
fortune that that entails, Raymondin has to acquiesce in her absences. Maintaining the integrity of those absences, in the society to
which he introduces her, will eventually prove impossible, and the
consequences will destroy their union.

For the moment, though, everything goes well. In her conjuring
of an idyllic haven, and a court of lords and ladies, in the heart of the
forest, Melusine echoes the creation of the 'gathering' in hunting
ritual—like the hunters, she is remodelling the wilderness to make it
reflect the good things that civilization can bring. Raymondin
marvels at the appearance of 'a hous made of stone in a manere of
a Chapell' (p. 37), and numerous retainers all ready to serve him.
Later, there will be a similar positive conjunction of the fruitful
wild and artifice when, on Melusine's advice, Raymondin claims
from the new earl of Poitiers as much land as the skin of a hart can
cover. Cut into thongs, the hart's skin covers a miraculous acreage,
and where the cut ends meet a fountain springs up. Melusine's
activities, therefore, although they are magical, win approval at
this point through their consonance with the 'high' discourse of
the hunt. The sumptuous 'gathering' which she prepares for her
wedding to Raymondin is richly emblematic of this side of her
character:

Thenne meruaylled therof euerychone, how so sodaynly that might haue
be doo. And they yede fourth and biheld dounne toward the medowe and
sawe grete plente of fayre & riche pauillons or tentes, righ[t] high so grete,
so noble, and so meruayllously facyoned that euery man awondred therof. . . . And also might they see there right grete foyson of ladyes & damoyselles richely apparayled & arayed, many horses, palfreys, & coursers
were there. Ther might they see kychons & Cookes within, dressing
meetes of dyuerse maneres. (p. 50)

Melusine's willing compliance with the conventions and bonds of
her husband's society is also shown by her determination to 'do
everything right'. A bishop performs the marriage ceremony, and
blesses the bed, and the wedding feast is followed by jousting, and,

the following morning, by the distribution of rich gifts. Previously, she had insisted that Raymondin's possession of the land enclosed by the hart's skin should be fully endorsed by all his fellow nobles:

'In so moche that none shal now lette nor empesche you therof, by reason of homage, nother by charge of rente or other ordynaunce, and whan he shall haue graunted it to you, take þerof his lettres, vnder hys grete Seele, and vnder the seelles of the peris, or lordes pryncipal of the land.' (p. 39)

We may think that Melusine—and the narrative—protest too much, and it is indeed at this point that the first seeds of future discord are sown. The earl of Poitiers is curious about Melusine and where she comes from—to him, her apparent lack of a family history constitutes an 'absence', a hiatus where knowledge ought to be.

'Forsouthe,' sayd the Erle, 'it is grett meruaylle. Raymondyn taketh a wyf that he knoweth not, ne also the lynage that she commeth of.' (pp. 48–9)

The earl's continued attempts to find out more finally anger Raymondin and almost cause a breach between the two cousins. They are reconciled when the earl promises not to enquire any further, but the damage has already been done, and tragic consequences set in train:

But, helas! he [the earl] aftirward faylled Couenaunt. wherfore Raymondyn lost his lady, and also the Erle of Forest toke deth therfore by Geffray with the grete tothe. (p. 61)

Meanwhile, Raymondin and Melusine consummate their marriage, in a closed pavilion ('the stakes of hit joyned & shette', p. 57) which symbolizes both the rare quality of their love and the less auspicious 'covenant' they have made with each other. Melusine clearly explains its terms:

'My right dere lord and frend, I thank you of the grete honour that hath be doo to me at this day of your parents & frendes and of that also that ye kepe so secretly that which ye promysed me at oure first couuenaunte, and ye moste know for certayn that yf ye kepe it euer thus wel, ye shalbe the moost mighty & moost honoured that euer was of your lynage. And ye doo the contrary, bothe you & your heyres shall fall litil & litil in decaye & fro your estate.' (p. 57)

On that night, Melusine conceives her first child, Urien, and the following years are taken up with the production of a succession of (male) children interspersed with the equally prolific building of castles. The first of these is Lusignan, which, prompted by the earl of Poitiers, she christens after herself:

'But my feyth,' said the Erle, 'the name setteth full wel to it for two causes, First bycause ye are called Melusyne of Albanye, whiche name in grek language is as moch for to say as thing meruayllous or commyng fro grete merueylle, and also this place is bylded and made meruayllously.' (p. 64)

The ambiguity in the earl's last phrase rings true: Lusignan is not only an exceedingly strong and well-made castle, but owes its construction to its mistress's supernatural powers. The workmen who build it are generously treated ('euery Satirday Melusyne payed truly her werkmen and meet & drynke they had in haboundaunce', p. 62), but their origin is a mystery ('but trouth it is that no body knew from whens these werkmen were'). Melusine herself is clearly an efficient hands-on manager, as shown by her organizing of payment and provisions; yet uncanniness underlies her practical skill, emblematized by illustrators of Jean d'Arras's French text in the little dragon that accompanies her on her visits.[48] Her beloved Lusignan is the cornerstone of her family's power, yet it is also lastingly 'signed' by her ambiguous body: in *Partenay* she refers to it as her 'goddoughter' ('For with my name baptised was she', line 3720), and in *Melusine* she leaves the imprint of her foot on a window-ledge when she finally departs from it in serpent form ('And wete it wel that on the basse stone of the wyndowe apereth at this day themprynte of her foote serpentous', p. 320).

Melusine's sons, from Urien to the rightly named Horrible, are disfigured by a variety of odd features. Urien has one blue eye and one red eye and ears 'as grete as the handlyng of a fan' (p. 65), while Anthony has 'a token along his chyk, that was the foot of a lyon, wherof they that sawe hym wondred, & moche were abasshed' (p. 104). Such traits, in their disproportion and their suggestion of the animal breaking through, ally the sons with wild men and beasts, creatures of the periphery—yet other comments work to assimilate this wildness, to bring it within the chivalric fold. Therefore we are told of Anthony that, despite his lion's claw, 'none fayrer was seen

---

[48] Clier-Colombani, '*La Fée Mélusine*', Part III, fig. 12 (Ars MS fr. 3352, fo. 22ᵛ). Clier-Colombani describes the dragon following Melusine 'comme un petit chien familier, le nez dans la traîne de sa robe' (p. 42), and suggests that it functions as a symbol of both her true nature and her destiny.

before that tyme'; in *Partenay* he himself accommodates his deformity by choosing to bear a lion on his shield (lines 2045–51).

The sons (apart from Horrible, and Froimond, who becomes a monk) are all notable for their warlike prowess, and travel far and wide defending Christian monarchs against encroaching pagans. Melusine strongly encourages their enterprises, provisioning their fleets and sending them off with long lectures which begin with pious admonishments to serve God and move on to give practical advice about the arts of lordship (for example, do not tax your people too heavily). Her sons, ranging the world and winning for themselves kingdoms and princesses, can be seen to be re-enacting their mother's clearing and colonization of domestic terrain. Their bodies, unlike hers, are visibly aberrant, yet no suspicion or obloquy seems to attach to them—the strongest reaction they arouse seems to be regret that such well-made knights should be disfigured in this way. The reason, I suggest, is that the image of the wild man, played with and manipulated in numerous texts, had by this time become totally amenable to chivalric discourse.

No such bargain, though, had been made with the female wild, and the revelation of Melusine's 'other' body precipitates disaster. The earl of Forest, Raymondin's brother, asks to see Melusine on a Saturday, and refuses to accept Raymondin's excuses, reading her absence another way entirely. In his opinion, she is either 'with another man in auoultyre' or 'a spyryte of the fayry, that on euery satirday maketh hir penaunce' (p. 296). The consequence is that Raymondin, his curiosity finally piqued, makes a hole with his sword point in an iron door and sees

melusyne within the bathe vnto her nauell, in fourme of a woman kymbyng her heere, and fro the nauel dounward in lyknes of a grete serpent, the tayll as grete & thykk as a barell, and so long it was that she made it to touche oftymes, while that raymondyn beheld her, the rouf of the chambre that was ryght hye. (p. 297)

It is the detail of the enormous, ceiling-touching tail that leads Susan Crane to conclude that Melusine 'could not have displayed herself more provocatively' (in *Partenay*, 'burlid' 'With siluer And Asure . . . Strongly the water ther bete, it flasshed hy', lines 2809–10). Yet there is no suggestion that Melusine is *displaying* herself for anyone. She is tending her body, pleasurably, and privately, communing with it. The tail which, especially in *Partenay*, seems to have a vitality of its own, almost constitutes an alternative companion for her—a reading concretized in an illustration in the Cambridge manuscript of Coudrette's *Mélusine* which shows it facing her, tipped with a small dragon's head.[49] It could be argued that what is shocking about the scene (from a male point of view) is not that Melusine is acting provocatively but that she is totally self-sufficient, needing no masculine presence to confirm her identity.

In any case, Raymondin has stumbled upon one of the absences which punctuate men's experience of women. He is, unsurprisingly, horrified, but, far from condemning Melusine for her deception, he blames first himself for breaking their 'covenant' and secondly his brother for his 'ryght fals admounestyng' (p. 297). The reading he imposes upon the situation is that prescribed by the code of promises and obligations through which he functions as a social being. It is almost as if the integrity of his wife's body rested with his obedience to such a code: 'by my venymous treson', he laments, 'I haue maculate your excellent fygure' (pp. 298–9). The iconography of the scene in illustrations to the French texts suggests that contemporary readers concurred in excusing Melusine.[50] Some versions omit the figure of the watching Raymondin, making us, as viewers, feel like voyeurs, spying on something that should properly remain private. Intriguingly, and contrary to the text, none of the pictures shows her combing her hair—a detail which might ally her with the figure of the siren, or with Venus as the avatar of lust. Instead she typically wears the elaborate headdress, the *hennin*, of a noble lady, and there are also visual allusions to Bathsheba, the innocent object of king David's sinful desires.

Raymondin is overwhelmed with anguish at the thought that, because of his broken promise, he is about to lose Melusine. He praises her as the ground and substance of all he has so far achieved: 'Farwel myn herte, my prowes, my valyaunce, For that lytel of honour whiche god had lent me, it came thrugh your noblesse, my swete & entierly belouyd lady' (p. 298). It is *his* identity, not hers, which has fractured—he continues to maintain her integrity, 'swete & entierly belouyd', while bitterly castigating his own falseness. As it

---

[49] Clier-Colombani, '*La Fée Mélusine*', Part III, fig. 16 (Cambridge University Library MS Ll. 2. 5).

[50] Ibid., figs. 14–20.

turns out, the crisis is not a crisis after all, for Melusine, fully aware that her husband has spied on her, decides to keep silent about it, and to forgive him, since he has not told anyone else about what he has seen. In structural terms, Raymondin's accusal of himself, and exoneration of Melusine, have been strongly painted in order to stand in contrast to the next major incident, when his attitude towards her will be dramatically reversed.

The event which at last forces the catastrophe is the burning of a number of monks in their abbey by Geffray, one of Raymondin and Melusine's sons. Geffray acts out of rage that his brother, Froimond, has become a monk—and Froimond is among those killed. Raymondin's reaction is one of horror and grief, and this time he has no compunction about blaming Melusine:

'By the feyth that I owe to god, I byleue it is but fantosme or spyryt werke of this woman and as I trowe she neuer bare no child that shal at thende haue perfection . . . by god, ye and wel I wote certayn it is som spyryt, som fantosme or Illusyon that thus hath abused me For the first tyme that I sawe her she knew & coude reherce all my fortune & auenture.' (p. 311)

The trust Raymondin had placed in Melusine as the foundress of his noble line suddenly dissolves when he is forced to confront its dismemberment through the awful sin of fratricide. It is only now, perhaps, that he really does 'see' her other body in all its disorienting alienness. 'Goo thou hens, fals serpente by god!', he declares (p. 314). Melusine swoons, Raymondin at once repents, but it is too late—the curse, uttered in front of the whole court, is now irrevocable.

In a long speech, Melusine accuses Raymondin of breaking faith, and describes the consequences for herself: now, instead of living the life of a mortal woman, she must remain in torment until doomsday:

'Halas, my frend! yf thou haddest not falsed thy feythe & thyn othe, I was putte & exempted from all peyne & tourment, & shuld haue had al my ryghtes, & hadd lyued the cours natural as another woman; & shuld haue be buryed, aftir my lyf naturel expired, within the chirche of our lady of Lusynen, where myn obsequye & afterward my annyuersary shuld haue be honourably & deuoutely don but now I am, thrughe thyn owne dede, ouerthrowen & ayen reuersed in the greuouse and obscure penytence, where long tyme I haue be in, by myn auenture: & thus I muste suffre &

bere it, vnto the day of domme & al through thy falsed but I beseche god to pardonne the.' (p. 316)

In effect, Melusine reconfigures the absences which, in the end, have destroyed their relationship—no longer excursions into female inaccessibility, they are now a part of the penance 'where long tyme I haue be in', absorbed into the Christian schema and time-frame which she insistently points to. She also (in *Melusine*, but not in *Partenay* at this point) explains why she has been condemned to spend every Saturday in serpent's form: the curse was placed on her by her mother, Pressyne, as a punishment for her role in imprisoning her father, king Elynas (who had caused Pressyne's disappearance, and the disinheritance of her three daughters, by looking on her in childbed).

In the immediate context, Melusine's bid for understanding is certainly effective. 'Ha, fals Fortune!' the barons lament. 'We shal lese this day þe best lady that euer gouerned ony land the moost sage most humble moost charytable & curteys of all other lyuyng in erthe' (p. 317). Melusine underlines her commitment to her husband's lineage by urging him to put the one completely evil son, Horrible, to death: she foresees that he will cause devastating harm if allowed to live. But there is nothing she can do to deflect the main weight of the curse which now descends on the house of Lusignan:

'Wete it, Raymondyn, that certayn after your lyf naturel expired, no man shal not empocesse nor hold your land so free in peas as ye now hold it, & your heyres & successours shal haue moche to doo and wete it shal be ouerthrawen & subdued, thrugh their foly, from theire honour & from theire ryght enherytaunce . . .' (pp. 317–18)

In *Partenay*, Melior, Melusine's sister, predicts that the last of the line will be called after the king of the beasts—a striking image of ultimate exile into marginality:

> And he which laste shall leue it, vnderstand,
> Of A beste the name shall he be bering,
> Which off all other is the brutall king.   (5626–8)

All of Melusine's parting words (and there are a great many of them) bond her, emotionally, to the life she is about to leave. Her piety, her solicitude for her children (apart from Horrible), and her grief all draw sympathy from those who listen to her. This sympathy

persists when she leaps from the window and is immediately transformed into a flying serpent (interpreted by the illustrators as a
draconopede). As she flies round the castle, the sounds she makes
are heard in two different ways, as both dreadful and piteous:

And the noble Melusyne so transffygured, as it is aforsaid, flyeng thre tymes
about the place, passed foreby the wyndow, gyuyng at euerche tyme an
horrible cry pyteous, that caused them that beheld her to wepe for pyte.
For they perceyued wel that loth she was to departe fro the place, & that it
was by constraynte.... And whan she had floughe about the Fortresse thre
tymes she lyghted so sodaynly & horrybly vpon the toure called poterne,
bryngyng with her such thundre & tempeste, that it semed that bothe the
Fortres & the toun shuld haue sonk and fall & therwith they lost the syght
of her, and wyst not where she was become. (pp. 320–1)

Although Melusine is now transformed into a completely alien—
and, by association, demonic—body she is still accorded subjectivity, so that reactions to her are curiously compounded of both fear
and pity. She is at once powerful—in her threatening of the founda-
tions of the fortress—and powerless, exiled as she is from any kind of
social intercourse.

Raymondin never sees Melusine again, and, although he lives for
a while longer, he is from this time a broken man. She returns daily
to the castle, though, to care for her two youngest children: an
extraordinary illustration in a French manuscript shows her with the
upper half of a young woman, tenderly cradling one of her babies
and feeding him at her breast, but with the lower body of a scaly
draconopede.[51] She also returns to portend the death of Raymondin, and of all subsequent heirs of Lusignan: 'For there was seen
vpon the batelments of the Castel a grete & horryble serpent the
which cryed with a femenyne voys, wherof all the peuple was
abasshed' (p. 354).

Melusine's story has been one of absences which, in the end,
bring her to catastrophe. Wholly present in so many ways—as
devoted mother, loyal wife, castle-builder, and city-founder—she
is finally undone by her husband's refusal to comprehend the peculiarly female rhythms which govern not only her life but those of

[51] Clier-Colombani, '*La Fée Mélusine*', Part III, fig. 26 (BN MS fr. 24383, fo. 30ʳ). The
iconography of Melusine when she returns to feed her children varies: she is sometimes
fully human, sometimes a fish-tailed siren, and sometimes half human and half dragon.
She is always, however, shown as a tender and attentive mother (ibid., figs. 37–9).

women everywhere. For although Melusine is a shape-shifter, a hybrid monster, she is more fundamentally the product of male ambivalence over women's role within society. As she is the ground upon which fortunes are built, and the fertile mother who will ensure dynastic continuance, she cannot be relegated to the periphery. Yet within her compliance with the dominant schema she appears to hide a secret dissidence, since there are times when she is simply *not there*, in mind or in body, not open to the male gaze. This is the moment of hybridization, when images from the edge—the dreadful dragon's tail—appear. It is close to the quality which Susan Crane, following Freud, illuminatingly describes as the *unheimlich*, or uncanny:

Uncanniness expresses particularly well the troubling oppositions that mark the feminine at the deepest levels of conception: we might say that shape-shifting naturalizes woman's contradictoriness, and that magical power essentializes her otherness. Feminine uncanniness is enfolded in intimacy as the *unheimlich* depends for its sense on the *heimlich*: woman once familiar and domestic now also disturbingly *unheimlich*—not at home, on the margins, undomesticated, unfamiliar.[52]

We can now attempt to answer Le Goff's question, 'What accounts for this tenderness toward a demonic woman?' Melusine is certainly demonic in her bodily form, but in the mixed responses which her *Unheimlichkeit* elicits, she becomes the carrier of a universal, rather than an exceptional, female experience.

[52] Crane, *Gender and Romance*, 164.

Conclusion

IN THE PREVIOUS chapters I have described some of the ways in which medieval people used the animal world as a resource when giving form to many of the concerns and values of their society. The bodies of animals are re-imagined, and made to participate in particular kinds of play, in order to generate social messages. Overall, the scolding of the fox for *not* being human, the flourishing of the clawed and horned beasts of heraldry, and the dismemberment and ingestion of the slain bodies of the deer may be seen as attempts to define and maintain a pristine selfhood, the *corps propre* of Julia Kristeva's phrase.[1] In *Powers of Horror* Kristeva identifies the 'abject' as that which has to be thrust aside for individuals and social systems to manifest their 'proper' selves, and she finds it present in 'those fragile states where man strays on the territories of *animal*'.[2] 'Fragile' is suggestive: the boundary between humans and animals is in one sense a site of play, richly productive of cultural enterprises, but it is also a danger area, a place where human identity—construed as difference from animal kind—may slip from one's grasp.

'Do you not see, therefore,' wrote the ninth-century philosopher John Scotus Erigena, 'that man is in all the animals and they are in him, but that man is above them all? Hence one can speak correctly of him both affirmatively and negatively by saying: "Man is an animal; man is not an animal."'[3] The undeniable 'animality' of humans infuses a number of the texts I have discussed, and can be seen as exerting a pressure within those texts for resolution. A memory of shared bodiliness haunts *Sir Gawain and the Green Knight*,

[1] In the English translation of *Powers of Horror: An Essay on Abjection* (New York, 1982), the translator, Leon S. Roudiez, renders this phrase as 'one's own clean and proper body', in order 'to preserve its full meaning' (p. viii).

[2] Ibid. 12.

[3] *De divisione naturae*, 4.5, trans. Myra L. Uhlfelder, *Periphyseon: On the Division of Nature* (Indianapolis, 1976), 220.

while in *The Knight's Tale* Theseus does his utmost to ratify the ascendancy that Palamon and Arcite have endangered through their involvement with states at the furthest limit of social functioning. In the wild man's various manifestations, we see him being subjected to tests which will settle his humanness one way or the other; and in the tales of the romance heroes who venture out into the wilderness and experiment with wild-man living we hear the reassuring message that humans can indeed walk to the edge, look over, and return, without compromising their absolute difference from the not-human.

My treatment has been eclectic, and there are many subject areas I have not touched on. For instance, I have said very little about religious texts or representations—a start might be made with a study of the role of animal lore and animal fables in collections of exempla. I have also largely ignored the 'grotesques'[4] in the margins of manuscripts, which are obvious examples of the blending of human and animal bodies. Michael Camille, in particular, has studied the relationship between centre and periphery which is expressed in the iconography of the margins, and has found there replications of the way society at large was organized.[5] How might the 'grotesques' fit into such a scheme? Are their gestures or activities associated with particular kinds of human bodies? How is their 'animal' element employed in visual renderings of marginality? Another line of approach would be to find out which animals appear most frequently in marginalia—why these and not others? Joyce E. Salisbury has looked at a large number of manuscripts from the thirteenth to the fifteenth centuries, and her analysis reveals that the creatures that predominate in marginal art are either those whose bodies are dialogically related to human ones (centaurs, apes, wild people) or those intimately linked to human interests or pursuits (dogs, foxes).[6] *How* are these bodies shown, how do they move,

[4] It is anachronistic to use the word 'grotesque' in a medieval context, hence the inverted commas. (The term originates in the humanistic archaeological enterprises of the late 15th cent. and is not recorded in English before the mid-16th cent.) I use it rather than 'hybrids' (a medieval equivalent would be 'babewyns') because it does incorporate, however imprecisely, the judgement of the viewer. So, a mermaid, or a horse with wings like Pegasus, would be a hybrid form but not necessarily a 'grotesque'.

[5] *Image on the Edge: The Margins of Medieval Art* (London, 1992).

[6] Joyce E. Salisbury, *The Beast Within: Animals in the Middle Ages* (New York and London, 1994), 135.

how interact—and how do they map on to the kinds of play between animals and humans which have been explored in this book?

These are all questions for another day. I would like to conclude by looking briefly at two more instances where the human–animal interface is an important thematic element, in a way shaping, and constraining, the kind of text which is produced. The first example is the romance of *William of Palerne*, and the second a group of written accounts of the Rising of 1381.

William of Palerne was translated from the French *Guillaume de Palerne* about the middle of the fourteenth century, at the command of Humphrey de Bohun, earl of Hereford.[7] The long and involved plot tells of the adventures of William, son of the king of Sicily. At the age of 4, William is snatched from his family by a werewolf and is subsequently adopted first by a humble cowherd and then by the emperor of Rome. He falls in love with the emperor's daughter, Melior, and much of the story is concerned with the fortunes of the two lovers after they have run away together. In their wanderings, they are helped and guided by the werewolf, who is really Alphouns, son of the king of Spain, placed under enchantment by his envious stepmother. (His motive in abducting William in the first place was to save him from being murdered by his uncle.) The story ends happily with the reunion of William and his mother (his father having died, so that William succeeds as king of Sicily), the disenchantment of Alphouns by his now penitent stepmother, and a clutch of marriages, including one between Alphouns and William's sister.

Alphouns as werewolf is, physically, a large and ferocious animal—he terrorizes a peasant in order to take from him his bag of food, and later advances angrily on his stepmother 'grisliche gapande with a grym noyse' (line 4343) so that she almost goes out of her mind with fear, and screams for help. Yet the text continually insists that he is no brute but wise and intelligent. His episodes of 'wolfish' behaviour (there is another when he steals the provost's little son in order to lead the pursuit away from William and Melior) are always carefully furnished with logical explanations: he needs to take the

---

[7] *William of Palerne*, re-ed. G. H. V. Bunt, Mediaevalia Groningana, 6 (Groningen, 1985), 14. Subsequent references are included in the text.

peasant's food in order to feed the lovers, while his fury when he sees the woman who has enchanted him is completely understandable. Although the spell made his outer shape a beastly one, 'his witt welt he after as wel as tofore' (line 142), the narrator explains. William and Melior frequently marvel at his benevolence and acuity, and in their prayers for his safety implicitly link him with Christ as one who undergoes suffering for others' sake.[8]

Clearly the author wishes to assure us of Alphouns's essential humanness. What is interesting is the *degree* to which he does this. His stress upon the werewolf's wit—*witty* is the adjective most commonly applied to him—infuses his fiction, to the extent that the qualities of William, the titular hero, are often downplayed. For example, after the lovers have escaped from the emperor's palace by disguising themselves in white bearskins, they hide in a den and fall asleep in each other's arms, oblivious to the hunting pack that has been loosed to track them down. It is left to the werewolf to draw the hounds away, endangering his own life in the process. William and Melior simply sleep on: they 'wisten no þing of þis werk þat hem was aboute' (line 2195), the narrator comments, in a line that is unique to his English version.[9] Elsewhere, he emphasizes the agency of the werewolf in shepherding the lovers along every stage of their journey: on board the ship which will take them across the strait of Messina to Sicily, he even directs them to hide behind some barrels (lines 2742–3)—a dodge which, we can't help feeling, they could have worked out for themselves. William's eventual transformation into the valiant champion who will rescue his people from the besieging Spanish forces is enabled by his adoption of a werewolf as his cognizance:

> 'Bi Crist, madame,' sede þe kniȝt, 'I coveyte nouȝte elles
> but þat I have a god schel of gold graiþed clene,
> and wel and faire wiþinne a werwolf depeynted,
> þat be hidous and huge, to have alle his riȝtes,
> of þe covenablest colour to knowe in þe feld;
> oþer armes al my lif atteli never have.'   (3215–20)

---

[8] See e.g. lines 2505–11: '"Now, sertes, for soþe | þis best has mannes kynde, it may be non oþer. | Se what sorwe he suffres to save us tweine; | and namli when we han nede, never he ne fayleþ | þat he ne bringeþ, wher we ben, þat to us bihoves. | He þat suffred for our sake sore wondes five, | he our buxum best save and hald us his live!"'

[9] Ed. cit., n. to line 2195.

It is as though William needs to have the werewolf constantly by his side in order to fill out his role as a knight.

The werewolf's identity as a noble human being is also expressed through his association with a number of discourses which, as we have seen, typically posit a distinction between people and animals. In Chrétien's *Yvain*, for example, the hero's journey back to complete social functioning was reflected in his improving diet. So, here, the werewolf demonstrates that he is an informed member of the human community by supplying the sort of food to William and Melior which properly reflects their shared status. We have seen that he first menaces a peasant and robs him of his bag, which contains 'bred . . . and fair bouf wel sode' (line 1849). The lovers eat their fill and are well satisfied—*they* find no deficiency in what is before them. But the narrator does, observing that they ate 'boute salt oþer sauce', and so, congruently, does the werewolf: realizing that he has not provided them with 'any semli drynk' (line 1882), he runs off and accosts a travelling clerk, forcing him to abandon the two flagons of fine wine he is carrying.

The werewolf is also involved in the activity of the hunt, offering himself as a quarry on two occasions so that William and Melior can evade capture. Accounts of hunts invariably foreground the capacity of the hunters, and their control over the beasts they pursue, but on these two occasions the tables are turned and the werewolf dictates both the rhythms and the outcome of the chase. In the first instance God gives him grace to flee with such speed 'þat [h]orse ne hounde for non hast ne miȝt him oftake' (line 2198); while in the second, after stealing the provost's little boy, he deliberately toys with the crowds who rush after him, piquing their hopes by waiting until they have nearly caught up before dashing away again. Later in the narrative, he hunts down and kills first a great hart and then a hind in front of William and Melior (lines 2568–73), playing to perfection the part of a courtly huntsman such as Ipomadon. (His motive is to provide deerskins with which the lovers can cover themselves, and here again the English translator has altered the French text to emphasize his initiative, for in the original the werewolf only kills the second animal after Guillaume has commented that if they had two skins they could change their disguise.[10])

[10] Ibid., n. to lines 2568–88.

Therefore the author of *William of Palerne* takes pains to remove all ambiguity from his description of the werewolf. He in fact overcompensates for the danger he has perceived, that the enveloping form of the huge and hairy beast might somehow contaminate the personhood of Alphouns, the noble prince, heir to the Spanish throne, for the 'witty' werewolf ends up being *more* human than the people who surround him—'For wel I wot witerli, and wel I have it founde, | þat he has mannes munde more þan we boþe' (lines 4122–3), William tells the king of Spain, who has just realized that the werewolf is in fact his lost son. Shortly before this, while the werewolf was paying one of his flying visits to the hall, dispensing unmistakably courtly gestures (kneeling at the king's feet and kissing them) before going on his way 'whider him god liked' (line 4021), the narrator tells us that 'some savage men' grabbed axes, swords, and spears, and would have set off after him to kill him if William had not intervened. The word *savage* makes clear how far we have been led—it is not the animal but the men who are the brutes here.[11]

If in *William of Palerne* an apparent animal is reconfigured as a human, in several of the extant accounts of the Rising of 1381 humans are re-imagined as animals.[12] The chroniclers of the Rising take as their backcloth the stable, hierarchical world of the Bestiary, in which every part sustains the whole by keeping to its appointed place. This backcloth—the fabric of society, to refocus the meta-

---

[11] Bunt (ed. cit.) glosses *savage* as 'valiant, intrepid', but the meaning intended here is surely the primary one of 'wild, fierce, uncivilized': Tobler-Lommatzsch, *Altfranzösisches Wörterbuch* (Wiesbaden, 1973), s.v. *sauvage*. Cf. also Marie de France's opening description of the werewolf in her tale of *Bisclavret*: 'Garualf, c[eo] est beste salvage . . .' (*Lais*, ed. A. Ewert (Oxford, 1965), p. 49, line 9).

[12] The accounts cited below are: Thomas Walsingham, *Historia Anglicana*, ed. H. T. Riley, 2 vols., Rolls Series, 28 (London, 1863–4); *The Anonimalle Chronicle, 1333 to 1381*, ed. V. H. Galbraith (Manchester, 1927; repr. with minor corrections, 1970); Henry Knighton, *Chronicon*, ed. J. R. Lumby, 2 vols., Rolls Series, 92 (London, 1889–95); *The Westminster Chronicle 1381–1394* (a continuation of the *Polychronicon* of Ranulph Higden), ed. and trans. L. C. Hector and Barbara F. Harvey (Oxford, 1982). These are all discussed, and their reliability assessed, in R. B. Dobson, *The Peasants' Revolt of 1381*, 2nd edn. (London, 1983), which also prints the relevant passages in translation. (It is important to point out that, since I am dealing with *textual* representations, I am not concerned with the accuracy, or otherwise, of the chroniclers' reports. It is known, for instance, that the social origins of the rebels were far more varied than they allow: see e.g. Rodney Hilton, *Bond Men Made Free: Medieval Peasant Movements and the English Rising of 1381* (London, 1973).) Texts from the 'other side'—the brief letters written by the rebels themselves—are considered in Steven Justice, *Writing and Rebellion: England in 1381* (Berkeley and Los Angeles, 1994).

phor—is very nearly torn apart by the 'cherles rebellyng'. In the texts produced by the chroniclers we find a bias towards particular sorts of animal comparisons—ones that reflect the homologies that have been explored in previous chapters.

One strand of imagery links the rebels who entered the city of London from Kent and Essex to domesticated animals such as pigs, sheep, and cattle. Henry Knighton, for example, likens Wat Tyler's followers after his death to 'forsaken sheep without a shepherd',[13] while Walsingham expands upon the same image when he describes the way in which the bands were hemmed in by the armed knights who galloped on to the scene at Smithfield:

They immediately surrounded the entire band of rustics with armed men, just as sheep are enclosed within a fold until it pleases the labourer to choose which he wants to send out to pasture and which he wants to kill.[14]

Here the comparison of peasants with sheep is developed with sinister complacency into an image of total control: they are compassed on every side, their lives hanging on a hireling's whim.

Earlier, when the rebels dragged archbishop Sudbury, and their other victims, out of the Tower of London to execute them, Walsingham took particular note of the noise they made:

When he [Sudbury] arrived there, a most horrible shouting broke out, not like the clamour normally produced by men, but of a sort which enormously exceeded all human noise and which could only be compared to the wailings of the inhabitants of hell. Such shouts used to be heard whenever the rebels beheaded anyone or destroyed houses, for as long as God permitted their iniquity to be unpunished. Words could not be heard among their horrible shrieks but rather their throats sounded with deafening bellowing, or, to be more accurate, with the devilish voices of peacocks.[15]

[13] 'quasi oves desolatas sine pastore' (*Chronicon*, ii. 138).
[14] 'repente circum cinxerunt omnem turbam undique rusticorum viris bellatoribus, velut cum oves caulis includuntur, usquedum mercenario complacuerit quas vult in pasturam emittere et quas vult morti deputare' (*Historia Anglicana*, i. 266; trans. Dobson, 179).
[15] 'Quo cum pervenisset, factus est clamor horrendissimus, non similis clamoribus quos edere solent homines, sed qui ultra omnem aestimationem superaret omnes clamores humanos, et maxime posset assimulari ululatibus infernalium incolarum. Qualibus etiam clamoribus usi in omni decapitatione cujuslibet, et prostratione domorum, quandiu Deus permisit eorum nequitiam impunitatam. Non tamen resonabant verba inter horrificos strepitus, sed replebantur guttura multisonis mugitibus, vel quod

The terrible howling of the frenzied crowds seems to have made a lasting impression on everyone who heard it: Gower devotes a whole chapter of his *Vox Clamantis* to it,[16] presenting it as a cacophony of beastly sounds—asses braying, wolves howling, bees buzzing—while Chaucer too preserves a memory, through the prism of purely animal catastrophe, in his *Nun's Priest's Tale*:

> So hydous was the noyse—a, benedicitee!—
> Certes, he Jakke Strawe and his meynee
> Ne made nevere shoutes half so shrille
> Whan that they wolden any Flemyng kille,
> As thilke day was maad upon the fox.   (3393–7)

Chaucer emphasizes the piercing nature of the cries. But Walsingham does not seem sure of their register. He first likens them to the deep, regular bellowing or lowing (*mugitibus*) of oxen, but then at once offers a correction: the shrieks now resemble 'the devilish voices of peacocks'. But why did he think of oxen in the first place? Surely because a prevailing strain of imagery associated the rebels with domesticated beasts. Such an accommodation achieved two ends: it implied that the rebels were acting against nature (since it is the function of oxen to submit to man and serve him), and it predicated their eventual defeat (oxen are no match for armed knights).

The rebels were also linked with other, less tractable creatures. Henry Knighton, for instance, describes the crowds literally overrunning the houses in the city: 'even when old and senile, the rebels climbed with extraordinary agility as though they were rats or carried aloft by some spirit'.[17] Knighton also compares the rebels to wolves, while in the continuation of the *Polychronicon* they are 'rabid dogs'.[18] The author of the Anonimalle Chronicle describes the Norfolk bands, after their defeat by the forces of the bishop of

---

est verius, vocibus pavonum diabolicis' (*Historia Anglicana*, i. 460; trans. Dobson, 173). I have made one change to Dobson's version: he renders 'multisonis mugitibus' as 'the bleating of sheep'; I have substituted what I think is a more accurate translation.

[16] *The Complete Works of John Gower*, ed. G. C. Macaulay, 4 vols. (Oxford, 1899–1902), vol. iv: *The Latin Works*, bk. 1, ch. 11.

[17] 'Domos quoque juratorum in civitate subverterunt, quas senes et quasi decrepiti, quod dictu mirum est, tanta agilitate ascenderunt, acsi essent ratones vel spiritu aliquo vecti' (*Chronicon*, ii. 135; trans. Dobson, 184).

[18] 'rabidissimi canes' (*Westminster Chronicle*, 2).

Norwich, scattering to hide themselves like hunted animals run to earth:

et le dit evesqe les fist confesser et puis decolere pur lour malveys faitz et issint les ditz comunes departerount par tute le pais pur defaute et meschieff et pur doute qils avoient de le roy et de les seignurs et soy mistrent en fuyt come bestes entapisone.[19]

The said bishop made them confess and then had them beheaded for their evil deeds. And so the said commons wandered throughout the country-side because of their crimes and mischiefs as well as their fear of the king and the lords; and they took to flight like beasts that run to earth.

The project here is not just to ally the rebels with animals that naturally inspire fear or disgust: it is rather to ensure that we associate them with 'borderline' creatures, which must be confined to their proper place in the system if the integrity of the whole—the entire articulated scheme of 'humanness'—is to be maintained. In the first book of *Vox Clamantis*, John Gower illustrates the kind of threat that the rebels posed when he describes former criminals as 'foxes', who leave their burrows to invade the houses of the nobility:

Qui suberat terra seruilis vulpis in aulas
Scandit, et hospicium liber vbique petit.[20]

The lowly fox, which used to live underground, climbed up into palaces and freely sought shelter anywhere.

The adjective *servilis*, 'lowly', fits the fox in a literal sense, since it lives underground, but it also has overtones of 'service', 'servility'. Just as foxes naturally live under the earth, Gower implies, so some people are naturally destined for lives of submission. It is as mon-strous to quarrel with your role in society as it would be for foxes to live in a different environment. (Gower would have been especially horrified by today's opportunistic urban foxes.) At the same time, Gower covertly extends the sense of repugnance associated with the fox—its bad smell and its filthy habits—to individual members of the rebelling peasantry.

[19] *Anonimalle Chronicle*, 151 (trans. Dobson, 237).
[20] *Vox Clamantis*, I. 487–8 (trans. Eric W. Stockton, *The Major Latin Works of John Gower* (Seattle, 1962)).

The first book of the *Vox Clamantis* contains the most extended literary response to the events of 1381. In many ways it is a Bestiary gone horribly wrong. Gower's narrator has a dream—or, rather, nightmare—vision in which he sees the curse of God descend upon the hordes of rebels and transform them into beasts. Nor are they changed into normal beasts, but into creatures whose evil nature appears either in hideous hybridization or in deeply aberrant forms of behaviour. One band, for instance, is turned into oxen with bears' feet and tails like dragons, who refuse to be yoked to the plough and exhale deadly sulphurous fumes. Another group become asses who scorn to carry loads and claim the horses' place for themselves. They despise the tail God gave them, considering it 'vile'. These asses then metamorphose into monsters with long horns in the middle of their foreheads—horns that cut and slash and run with blood. They can jump higher than leopards and have longer tails than the mighty lion himself. Here Gower introduces allusions from heraldry, another threatened 'noble' discourse—the lion and leopard are traditional devices, while the mutant asses with sawlike horns are parodies of the heraldic antelope.

Gower's monstrous creatures not only metamorphose in terrifying ways—they also act collectively to undermine the network of affinities and antipathies between different species. Foxes, formerly the enemies of the dogs who guarded their masters' homes, now make their peace with them and act in concert with them. Packs of hunting hounds refuse to chase the hare or the stag and snap at men's heels instead. And the owl, formerly shunned by other birds, now flies beside them.

Gower devotes particular attention to changes in the bird world—understandably, since, as I argued in Chapter 2, that world was so closely linked to expectations of stability and order. I have already mentioned his reductive characterization of Wat Tyler as a 'jay'; he also alludes to the traditional scale of ascent, from humble dunghill fowl to soaring eagle, to show the way values are being overturned:

> Qui residere domi que fimum calcare solebant,
> Presumunt aquile sumere iura sibi:
> Falconis rostrum rapuit sibi gallus et vngues,
> Ancer et ex alis sidera tacta cupit:
> Et sic de bassis succumbunt alta, que cara

Vilibus ex causis exule lege cadunt:
Nam quo non poterant animalia figere gressus,
    Vt predas capiant, hii super omne volant.[21]

Those which used to stay at home and tread on dung dared to assume the eagle's prerogative for themselves. The cock seized the falcon's beak and talons for itself, and the gander wanted to touch the heavens with its wings. And so the lofty birds sank down because of the lowly ones, and the valuable fell because of the worthless ones, since law and order were banished. And wherever the animals could not direct their steps to seize their prey, the birds swooped over everything.

The cock becomes a raven, the gander a kite, and both try to feed off human carcasses. In Gower's nightmare vision the bird world is no longer the mirror of order within human society—it has become horribly crazed and now reflects only chaos. Even the boundaries between individual species shatter as the gander mates with 'Coppa', the cock's wife.

Gower, and the other chroniclers of the Rising, make use of a shared tradition about animals, and their relationship to human society, to elaborate a deeply conservative thesis. In doing so, they also demonstrate the vitality of that tradition—its continuing life both as a pressure within texts and as an enabler of particular kinds of writing. Like other works that have been examined, their productions show that the boundaries of the human—that space where various bodies resort, and disport—had a richly generative influence upon medieval culture.

---

[21] *Vox Clamantis*, 1. 519–26 (trans. Stockton).

Bibliography

PRIMARY SOURCES

MANUSCRIPTS

London: British Library

Royal 10 E IV (the Smithfield Decretals)
Yates-Thompson 13 (the Taymouth Hours)

Oxford: Bodleian Library

Ashmole 1511
Ashmole Rolls 4
Bodley 264
Bodley 764
Digby 82
Douce 88
Eng. misc. d. 227
Laud misc. 247
Laud misc. 733
Rawlinson poet. 223

Oxford: Christ Church

E II (Treatise of Walter de Milemete)

PRINTED WORKS

ADAM OF USK, *The Chronicle of Adam Usk 1377–1421*, ed. and trans. C. Given-Wilson (Oxford, 1997).
AELFRIC, *Aelfric's Lives of the Saints*, ed. W. W. Skeat, EETS OS 94, 114 (1890; repr. in one vol. 1966).
ALBERT THE GREAT, *Man and the Beasts (De animalibus, Books 22–26)*, trans. James J. Scanlan (Binghamton, NY, 1987).
The Anonimalle Chronicle, 1333 to 1381, ed. V. H. Galbraith (Manchester, 1927; repr. with minor corrections, 1970).

AQUINAS, THOMAS, *Summa Theologiae* (Rome, 1962).

ARISTOTLE, *Historia animalium*, with English translations by A. L. Peck and D. M. Balme, 3 vols., Loeb Classical Library (London and Cambridge, Mass., 1965–91).

Aucassin et Nicolete, ed. F. W. Bourdillon (Manchester, 1970).

AUGUSTINE, ST, *City of God*, trans. Henry Bettenson, introd. John O'Meara (Harmondsworth, 1972).

The Avowing of King Arthur, ed. Roger Dahood (New York, 1984).

Bestiary (an English version of MS Bodley 764, with all the original miniatures reproduced in facsimile), trans. and introd. Richard Barber (London, 1992).

The Bestiary, being a reproduction in full of the manuscript Ii. 4. 26 in the University Library, Cambridge, ed. M. R. James, Roxburghe Club (Oxford, 1928).

BOCCACCIO, GIOVANNI, *The Decameron*, trans. and introd. G. H. McWilliam (Harmondsworth, 1972).

BOORDE, ANDREW, *A Compendyous Regyment, or a Dyetary of Helth* (1542), ed. F. J. Furnivall, EETS ES 10 (1870).

Boutell's Heraldry, rev. J. P. Brooke-Little (London, 1950).

CAXTON, WILLIAM, *The Book of the Knight of the Tower*, ed. M. Y. Offord, EETS SS 2 (1971).

—— *Caxton's Mirrour of the World*, ed. Oliver H. Prior, EETS ES 110 (1913).

—— *The Golden Legend or Lives of the Saints as Englished by William Caxton*, ed. F. S. Ellis (London, 1900; repr. New York, 1973).

—— (trans.), *The History of Reynard the Fox*, ed. N. F. Blake, EETS OS 263 (1970).

La Chace dou cerf, ed. Gunnar Tilander, Cynegetica, vii (Stockholm, 1960).

CHAUCER, GEOFFREY, *The Complete Works of Geoffrey Chaucer*, ed. W. W. Skeat, 6 vols. (Oxford, 1894).

—— *The Complete Works of Geoffrey Chaucer*, ed. F. N. Robinson, 2nd edn. (Oxford, 1974).

—— *The Riverside Chaucer*, ed. Larry D. Benson, 3rd edn. (Oxford, 1987).

—— *The Knight's Tale*, ed. Charles Moseley, Penguin Masterstudies (Harmondsworth, 1987).

—— *The Knight's Tale*, ed. A. C. Spearing (Cambridge, 1966).

The Chester Mystery Cycle, ed. R. M. Lumiansky and David Mills, 2 vols., EETS SS 3, 9 (1974, 1986).

Chevelere Assigne, in *Medieval English Romances*, ed. Diane Speed, 2 vols. (Sydney, 1987).

CHRÉTIEN DE TROYES, *Le Chevalier de la charrete*, ed. Mario Roques (Paris, 1960).

CHRÉTIEN DE TROYES, *Cligés*, ed. Stewart Gregory and Claude Luttrell (Cambridge, 1993).

—— *Yvain: Le Chevalier au lion*, text W. Foerster, introd. T. B. W. Reid (Manchester, 1942).

CLANVOWE, JOHN, *The Works of Sir John Clanvowe*, ed. V. J. Scattergood (Cambridge, 1975).

A Common-Place Book of the Fifteenth Century, ed. L. T. Smith (London, 1886).

CONDÉ, JEAN DE, *La Messe des oisiaus*, trans. B. Windeatt, in *Chaucer's Dream Poetry: Sources and Analogues* (Woodbridge, 1982), 104–19.

DUNBAR, WILLIAM, *The Poems of William Dunbar*, ed. James Kinsley (Oxford, 1979).

EADMER, *Historia novorum*, ed. Martin Rule, Rolls Series, 81 (London, 1884).

The Early South-English Legendary or Lives of the Saints, ed. Carl Horstmann, EETS OS 87 (1887).

EDWARD, SECOND DUKE OF YORK, *The Master of Game*, ed. W. A. and F. Baillie-Grohman (London, 1904).

English Hawking and Hunting in 'The Boke of St Albans', ed. Rachel Hands (Oxford, 1975).

English Historical Documents 1042–1189, ed. David C. Douglas and George W. Greenaway, 2nd edn. (London, 1981).

An English Medieval Sketchbook, No. 1916 in the Pepysian Library, Magdalene College, Cambridge, ed. M. R. James, Walpole Society, no. 13 (Oxford, 1925).

Firumbras, ed. Mary Isabelle O'Sullivan, EETS OS 198 (1935).

FROISSART, JEAN, *The Chronicle of Froissart*, trans. Sir John Bourchier, Lord Berners, introd. W. P. Ker, 6 vols. (London, 1901–3).

GEOFFREY OF MONMOUTH, *Life of Merlin*, ed. and trans. Basil Clarke (Cardiff, 1973).

GERALD OF WALES [GIRALDUS CAMBRENSIS], *De principis instructione*, ed. George F. Warner, Rolls Series, 21, vol. viii (London, 1891).

—— *Expugnatio Hibernica*, ed. and trans. A. B. Scott and F. X. Martin (Dublin, 1978).

—— *Itinerarium Kambriae*, ed. James F. Dimock, Rolls Series, 21, vol. vi (London, 1868).

GOWER, JOHN, *The Complete Works of John Gower*, ed. G. C. Macaulay, 4 vols. (Oxford, 1899–1902).

—— *The Major Latin Works of John Gower*, trans. Eric W. Stockton (Seattle, 1962).

GRAY, DOUGLAS (ed.), *The Oxford Book of Late Medieval Verse and Prose* (Oxford, 1988).

GUILLIM, JOHN, *A Display of Heraldrie*, 5th edn. (London, 1679).

HENRY OF LANCASTER, *Le Livre de seyntz medicines*, ed. E. J. Arnould, Anglo-Norman Text Society, no. 2 (Oxford, 1940).

HENRYSON, ROBERT, *The Poems of Robert Henryson*, ed. Denton Fox (Oxford, 1987).

Historical Poems of the XIVth and XVth Centuries, ed. R. H. Robbins (New York, 1959).

HOLLAND, RICHARD, *The Buke of the Howlat*, in *Longer Scottish Poems, i: 1375–1650*, ed. Priscilla Bawcutt and F. J. Riddy (Edinburgh, 1987), 43–84.

Ipomadon A, ed. Eugen Kölbing (Breslau, 1889).

ISIDORE OF SEVILLE, *Etymologiae*, bk. 12: *De animalibus*, in J.-P. Migne, *Patrologia Latina*, vol. 82, cols. 423–72.

JEROME, ST, *Vita S. Pauli primi eremitate*, in J.-P. Migne, *Patrologia Latina*, vol. 23, col. 23.

JOHN OF SALISBURY, *Policraticus*, ed. Clemens C. I. Webb (Oxford, 1909).

JOHN SCOTUS ERIGENA, *Periphyseon: On the Division of Nature*, trans. Myra L. Uhlfelder (Indianapolis, 1976).

JONSON, BEN, *Works*, ed. C. H. Herford and P. and E. Simpson, vol. vii (Oxford, 1941).

Julians Barnes Boke of Huntyng, ed. Gunnar Tilander, Cynegetica, xi (Karlshamn, 1964).

KNIGHTON, HENRY, *Chronicon*, ed. J. R. Lumby, 2 vols., Rolls Series, 92 (London, 1889–95).

LANGLAND, WILLIAM, *Piers Plowman: The B Version*, ed. George Kane and E. Talbot Donaldson, rev. edn. (London and Berkeley, 1988).

LE FÈVRE, JEHAN, *Les Lamentations de Matheolus*, ed. A.-G. Van Hamel, 2 vols. (Paris, 1892, 1905).

Legends of the Saints in Scottish Dialect, ed. W. W. Metcalfe, STS 13 (1896).

The Lisle Letters, ed. Muriel St Clare Byrne, 6 vols. (Chicago, 1981).

Les Livres du Roy Modus et de la Royne Ratio, ed. Gunnar Tilander, 2 vols., SATF (Paris, 1932).

Lybeaus Desconus, ed. Maldwyn Mills, EETS OS 261 (1969).

LYDGATE, JOHN, *Minor Poems*, ed. H. N. MacCracken, Part II, EETS OS 192 (1934).

—— *The Temple of Glas*, ed. J. Schick, EETS ES 60 (1891).

The Mabinogion, trans. Gwyn Jones and Thomas Jones, Everyman's Library, rev. edn. (London, 1989).

MACHIAVELLI, NICCOLÒ, *The Prince*, introd. Peter Bondanella, trans. Peter Bondanella and Mark Musa (Oxford, 1984).

MALORY, SIR THOMAS, *Works*, ed. Eugène Vinaver (Oxford, 1954).

MANDEVILLE, SIR JOHN, *Mandeville's Travels*, ed. M. C. Seymour (Oxford, 1967).

MANNYNG, ROBERT, *Robert of Brunne's Handlyng Synne*, ed. F. J. Furnivall, EETS OS 119, 123 (1901).

MAP, WALTER, *Du nugis curialium*, ed. M. R. James (Oxford, 1914).

MARIE DE FRANCE, *Die Fabeln der Marie de France*, ed. Karl Warnke (Halle, 1898).

—— *Lais*, ed. A. Ewert (Oxford, 1965).

The Medieval Bestiary, text and commentary by Xenia Muratova, trans. Inna Kitrosskaya (Moscow, 1984).

Melusine, ed. A. K. Donald, EETS ES 68 (1895).

Le Menagier de Paris, ed. G. E. Brereton and J. M. Ferrier (Oxford, 1981).

The Middle English 'Physiologus', ed. Hanneke Wirtjes, EETS OS 299 (1991).

Middle English Romances, ed. A. C. Gibbs, York Medieval Texts (London, 1966).

Mum and the Sothsegger, ed. Mabel Day and Robert Steele, EETS OS 199 (1936).

NECKAM, ALEXANDER, *De naturis rerum*, ed. Thomas Wright, Rolls Series, 34 (London, 1863).

Nomina et Insignia gentilitia equitumque sub Edoardo primo rege militantium . . ., ed. E. Rowe Mores (Oxford, 1749).

OVID, *Metamorphoses*, Loeb Classical Library, 2 vols. (London, 1916).

The Owl and the Nightingale, ed. E. G. Stanley (London, 1960).

The Parlement of the Thre Ages, ed. M. Y. Offord, EETS OS 246 (1959).

Partonope of Blois, ed. A. Trampe Bödtker, EETS ES 109 (1912).

Paston Letters and Papers of the Fifteenth Century, ed. Norman Davis, 2 vols. (Oxford 1971, 1976).

The Peterborough Chronicle 1070–1154, ed. Cecily Clark, 2nd edn. (Oxford, 1970).

The Prose Life of Alexander, from the Thornton MS, ed. J. S. Westlake, EETS OS 143 (1913).

Queen Mary's Psalter, introd. Sir George Warner (London, 1912).

A Revelation of Purgatory by an Unknown, Fifteenth-Century Woman Visionary, ed. Marta Powell Hartley (Lewiston, NY, 1985).

ROBERT OF BRUNNE *see* Mannyng, Robert

ROGER OF HOWDEN, *Chronica*, ed. William Stubbs, 4 vols., Rolls Series, 51 (London, 1868–71).

ROLLE, RICHARD, *English Writings of Richard Rolle*, ed. H. E. Allen (Oxford, 1931).

Rolls of Arms of the Reigns of Henry III and Edward III, ed. N. Harris Nicolas (London, 1829).

Le Roman de Renart, ed. Jean Dufournet and Andrée Méline, 2 vols. (Paris, 1985).

The Romance of Guy of Warwick, ed. J. Zupitza, EETS ES 25, 26 (1875, 1876; repr. 1966).

The Romans of Partenay, or of Lusignen, ed. W. W. Skeat, EETS OS 22 (1866).

Select Pleas of the Forest, ed. G. J. Turner, Selden Soc. 13 (London, 1901).

The Seven Sages of Rome, ed. Karl Brunner, EETS OS 191 (1933).

The Siege of Caerlaverock, ed. N. Harris Nicolas (London, 1828).

Sir Beues of Hamtoun, ed. Eugen Kölbing, EETS ES 46, 48, 65 (1885, 1886, 1894).

Sir Ferumbras, ed. Sidney J. Herrtage, EETS ES 34 (1879).

Sir Gawain and the Carl of Carlisle in Two Versions, ed. Auvo Kurvinen, Annales Academiae Scientiarum Fennicae, Series B, 71 (Helsinki, 1951).

Sir Gawain and the Green Knight, ed. J. R. R. Tolkien and E. V. Gordon, 2nd edn., rev. Norman Davis (Oxford, 1967).

Sir Orfeo see *Middle English Romances*, ed. Gibbs.

Sir Tristrem, ed. George P. McNeill, STS (Edinburgh, 1886).

SISAM, KENNETH (ed.), *Fourteenth Century Verse and Prose* (Oxford, 1921).

SKELTON, JOHN, *The Complete English Poems*, ed. John Scattergood (Harmondsworth, 1983).

Songs, Carols, and other Miscellaneous Poems from Balliol MS 354, Richard Hill's Commonplace Book, ed. Roman Dyboski, EETS ES 101 (1907).

The Sowdone of Babylone, ed. Emil Hausknecht, EETS ES 38 (1881).

SPENSER, EDMUND, *Prosopopoia, or Mother Hubberd's Tale*, in *Works*, ed. Edwin Greenland, Charles Grosvenor Osgood, Frederick Morgan Padelford, and Ray Heffner: *The Minor Poems*, vol. ii (Baltimore, 1947), 101–40.

A Thirteenth-Century Bestiary in the Library of Alnwick Castle, ed. E. G. Millar, Roxburghe Club (Oxford, 1958).

Three Fifteenth-Century Chronicles, ed. James Gairdner, Camden Soc., NS 28 (London, 1880).

TREVISA, JOHN, *On the Properties of Things*, trans. of Bartholomaeus Anglicus' *De proprietatibus rerum*, 3 vols. (Oxford, 1975–88).

Turbervile's Booke of Hunting 1576 (Oxford, 1908).

Two Early Renaissance Bird-Poems ed. Malcolm Andrew (Washington, 1984).

Two East Anglian Picture Books, ed. Nicholas Barker, Roxburghe Club (London, 1988).

Two Fifteenth-Century Cookery Books, ed. Thomas Austin, EETS OS 91 (1888).

Valentine and Orson, trans. Henry Watson, ed. Arthur Dickson, EETS os 204 (1937).

The Vulgate Version of the Arthurian Romances, ed. H. O. Sommer (Washington, 1908–16).

WALSINGHAM, THOMAS, *Historia Anglicana*, ed. H. T. Riley, 2 vols., Rolls Series, 28 (London, 1863–4).

WALTER DE MILEMETE, *The Treatise of Walter de Milemete De nobilitatibus, sapientiis, et prudentiis regum*, introd. M. R. James, Roxburghe Club (Oxford, 1913).

The Wars of Alexander, ed. H. N. Duggan and T. Turville-Petre, EETS ss 10 (1989).

The Westminster Chronicle 1381–1384, ed. and trans. L. C. Hector and Barbara F. Harvey (Oxford, 1982).

William of Palerne, re-ed. G. H. V. Bunt, Mediaevalia Groningana, 6 (Groningen, 1985).

WIREKER, NIGEL, *Nigel de Longchamps: Speculum stultorum*, ed. John H. Mozley and Robert R. Raymo (Berkeley and Los Angeles, 1960).

WYATT, SIR THOMAS, *Collected Poems*, ed. Joost Daalder (Oxford, 1975).

Ywain and Gawain, ed. Albert B. Friedman and Norman T. Harris, EETS os 254 (1964).

SECONDARY SOURCES

ABULAFIA, ANNA, 'Bodies in the Jewish–Christian Debate', in Kay and Rubin (eds.), *Framing Medieval Bodies*, 123–37.

ALEXANDER, J. J. G., 'Painting and Manuscript Illumination for Royal Patrons in the Later Middle Ages', in V. J. Scattergood and J. W. Sherborne (eds.), *English Court Culture in the Later Middle Ages* (London, 1983), 141–62.

ANDERSON, M. D., *Animal Carvings in British Churches* (Cambridge, 1938).

ANGLO, SYDNEY, *Spectacle, Pageantry, and Early Tudor Policy*, Oxford-Warburg Studies (Oxford, 1969).

ARDENER, EDWIN, 'Belief and the Problem of Women' and 'The "Problem" Revisited', in Shirley Ardener (ed.), *Perceiving Women* (London, 1975), 1–17, 19–27.

ATTENBOROUGH, DAVID, *The Life of Birds* (London, 1998).

—— *The Trials of Life* (London, 1990).

BACKHOUSE, JANET, *The Luttrell Psalter* (London, 1989).

BAILEY, MARK, *A Marginal Economy: East Anglian Breckland in the Later Middle Ages*, Cambridge Studies in Medieval Life and Thought, 4th ser. 12 (Cambridge, 1989).

BAKHTIN, MIKHAIL, *Rabelais and his World*, trans. Hélène Iswolsky (Bloomington, Ind., 1984).

BARTHES, ROLAND, *S/Z*, trans. Richard Miller (Oxford 1990; first pub. Paris, 1973).

BENNETT, J. A. W., *The Parlement of Foules* (Oxford, 1957).

BENSON, C. DAVID, 'O Moral Henryson', in Robert F. Yeager (ed.), *Fifteenth-Century Studies: Recent Essays* (Hamden, Conn., 1984), 215–35.

BENSON, LARRY D., *Art and Tradition in Sir Gawain and the Green Knight* (Cambridge, Mass., 1965).

BERGER, HARRY, Jr., 'The F Fragment of the *Canterbury Tales*: Part I', *Chaucer Review*, 1 (1966), 88–102.

BERGER, JOHN, review, *New Society* (25 Nov. 1971).

BERNHEIMER, RICHARD, *Wild Men in the Middle Ages: A Study in Art, Sentiment and Demonology* (Cambridge, Mass., 1952).

BLAMIRES, ALCUIN (ed.), *Woman Defamed and Woman Defended* (Oxford, 1992).

BOFFEY, JULIA, 'Women Authors and Women's Literacy in 14th- and 15th-Century England', in Carol M. Meale (ed.), *Women and Literature in Britain 1150–1500*, Cambridge Studies in Medieval Literature, 17 (Cambridge, 1993), 143–69.

BOSSUAT, R., *Le Roman de Renard* (Paris, 1957).

BOUTELL, C., *Heraldry, Historical and Popular*, 3rd edn. (London, 1864).

BROOK, LESLIE, 'Guigemar and the White Hind', *MÆ* 56 (1987), 94–101.

BULLOUGH, VERN L., 'Medieval Medical and Scientific Views of Women', *Viator*, 4 (1973), 485–501.

BURNLEY, DAVID, *Courtliness and Literature in Medieval England* (London, 1998).

BURROW, J. A., 'Henryson's *The Preaching of the Swallow*', *Essays in Criticism*, 25 (1975), 25–37.

BYNUM, CAROLINE WALKER, *Holy Feast and Holy Fast: The Religious Significance of Food to Medieval Women* (Berkeley and Los Angeles, 1987).

CADDEN, JOAN, *Meanings of Sex Difference in the Middle Ages: Medicine, Science, and Culture* (Cambridge, 1993).

CAMILLE, MICHAEL, *Image on the Edge: The Margins of Medieval Art* (London, 1992).

CAMPORESI, PIERO, *Bread of Dreams: Food and Fantasy in Early Modern Europe*, trans. David Gentilcore (Cambridge, 1989).

CARTELLIERI, OTTO, *The Court of Burgundy*, trans. Malcolm Letts (London, 1929).

CARTLIDGE, NEIL, 'The Source of John Lydgate's *The Churl and the Bird*', *Notes & Queries*, 242/1 (Mar. 1997), 22–4.

CASAGRANDE, CARLA, and VECCHIO, SILVANO, 'Clercs et jongleurs dans la société médiévale (xiie et xiiie siècles)', *Annales: économies, sociétés, civilisations*, 24/5 (1979), 913–28.

CAVE, C. J. P., *Roof Bosses in Medieval Churches* (Cambridge, 1948).

CHINCA, MARK, 'The Body in some Middle High German *Mären*: Taming and Maiming', in Kay and Rubin (eds.), *Framing Medieval Bodies*, 187–210.

CHRISTIE, A. G. I., *English Medieval Embroidery* (Oxford, 1928).

CLARK, WILLENE T., and MCMUNN, MERADITH T. (eds.), *Beasts and Birds of the Middle Ages: The Bestiary and its Legacy* (Philadelphia, 1989).

CLAXTON, ANN, 'The Sign of the Dog: An Examination of the Devonshire Hunting Tapestries', *Journal of Medieval History*, 14 (1988), 127–79.

CLIER-COLOMBANI, FRANÇOISE, *La Fée Mélusine au moyen âge: images, mythes et symboles* (Paris, 1991).

CLUTTON-BROCK, J., *Domesticated Animals from Early Times*, British Musuem (London, 1981).

COOPER, HELEN, *The Canterbury Tales*, Oxford Guides to Chaucer (Oxford, 1989).

—— 'Counter-Romance: Civil Strife and Father-Killing in the Prose Romances', in Cooper and Sally Mapstone (eds.), *The Long Fifteenth Century: Essays for Douglas Gray* (Oxford, 1997), 141–62.

CRANE, SUSAN, *Gender and Romance in Chaucer's 'Canterbury Tales'* (Princeton, 1994).

CROW, MARTIN M., and OLSON, CLAIR C. (eds.), *Chaucer Life-Records* (Oxford, 1966).

CUMMINS, JOHN, *The Hound and the Hawk: The Art of Medieval Hunting* (London, 1988).

CURTIUS, ERNST, 'Etymology as a Category of Thought', in *European Literature and the Latin Middle Ages*, trans. Willard R. Trask (London, 1953), 495–500.

DALTON, O. M., *Catalogue of the Ivory Carvings of the Christian Era of the British Museum* (London, 1909).

DAVENPORT, W. A., 'Bird Poems from *The Parliament of Fowls* to *Philip Sparrow*', in Julia Boffey and Janet Cowen (eds.), *Chaucer and Fifteenth-Century Poetry*, King's College London Medieval Studies, 5 (London, 1991), 66–83.

DEAN, RUTH J., 'An Early Treatise on Heraldry in Anglo-Norman', in Urban Tigner Holmes (ed.), *Romance Studies in Memory of Edward Billings Ham*, California State Publications, no. 2 (1967), 21–9.

DENNYS, RODNEY, *The Heraldic Imagination* (London, 1975).

—— *Heraldry and the Heralds* (London, 1982).

DICKSON, ARTHUR, *Valentine and Orson: A Study in Late Medieval Romance* (New York, 1929).

DIEKSTRA, F. N. M., 'The *Physiologus*, the Bestiaries and Medieval Animal Lore', *Neophilologus*, 69 (1985), 142–55.

DIGBY, GEORGE WINGFIELD, *The Devonshire Hunting Tapestries*, HMSO (London, 1971).

DIXON, LAURINDA S., 'The Curse of Chastity: The Marginalization of Women in Medieval Art and Medicine', in Robert R. Edwards and Vickie Ziegler (eds.), *Matrons and Marginal Women in Medieval Society* (Woodbridge, 1995), 49–74.

DOBSON, R. B., *The Peasants' Revolt of 1381*, 2nd edn. (London, 1983).

—— and TAYLOR, J., *Rymes of Robin Hood: An Introduction to the English Outlaw* (London, 1976).

DOLLIMORE, JONATHAN, *Sexual Dissidence: Augustine to Wilde, Freud to Foucault* (Oxford, 1991).

DONALDSON, E. TALBOT, *Chaucer's Poetry*, 2nd edn. (New York, 1975).

DOOB, PENELOPE, *Nebuchadnezzar's Children: Conventions of Madness in Middle English Literature* (New Haven, 1974).

—— *Purity and Danger: An Analysis of the Concepts of Pollution and Taboo* (London and New York, 1966).

DRACOPOLI, FELICITY, 'Wild Men in Suffolk', programme book of the 25th Aldeburgh Festival of Music and the Arts (1972), 12–15.

DRONKE, PETER, 'Poetic Originality in *The Wars of Alexander*', in Helen Cooper and Sally Mapstone (eds.), *The Long Fifteenth Century: Essays for Douglas Gray* (Oxford, 1997), 123–39.

DRUCE, G. C., 'The Amphisbaena and its Connexions in Ecclesiastical Art and Architecture', *Archaeological Journal*, 67/268 (Dec. 1910), 285–317.

—— 'Some Abnormal and Composite Forms in English Church Architecture', *Archaeological Journal*, 72 (1915), 135–86.

DUBOIS, PAGE, *Centaurs and Amazons: Women and the Pre-History of the Great Chain of Being* (Ann Arbor, 1991).

DUBY, GEORGES, *The Three Orders: Feudal Society Imagined*, trans. Arthur Goldhammer (Chicago, 1980).

DYER, C., *Standards of Living in the Late Middle Ages* (Cambridge, 1989).

ELLIS, H. D., 'The Wodwose in East Anglian Church Decoration', *Proceedings of the Suffolk Institute of Archaeology and Natural History*, 14/3 (1912), 287–93.

ELLIS, HENRY, 'Enumeration and Explanation of the Devices formerly borne as Badges of Cognizance by the House of York', *Archaeologia*, 17 (1814), 226–7.

EVANS, GEORGE EWART, and THOMAS, DAVID, *The Leaping Hare* (London, 1972).

EVANS, JOAN, *English Art 1307–1461* (Oxford, 1949).

FINLAYSON, JOHN, 'Arthur and the Giant of St Michael's Mount', *MÆ* 33 (1964), 112–20.

FIRTH, RAYMOND, *Symbols Public and Private* (London, 1973).

FLINN, J., *Le Roman de Renard dans la littérature française et dans les littératures étrangères au Moyen Age* (Toronto, 1963).

FLORES, NONA C. (ed.), *Animals in the Middle Ages: A Book of Essays* (New York and London, 1996).

—— '"Effigies Amicitiae... Veritas Inimicitiae": Antifeminism in the Iconography of the Woman-Serpent in Medieval and Renaissance Art and Literature', in Flores (ed.), *Animals in the Middle Ages: A Book of Essays*, 167–95.

FOX-DAVIS, A. C., *A Complete Guide to Heraldry*, rev. and annotated J. P. Brooke-Little (London, 1969).

GEREMEK, BRONISŁAW, *The Margins of Society in Late Medieval Paris*, trans. Jean Birrell (Cambridge, 1987; first pub. Warsaw, 1971).

GORDON, DILLIAN, *The Wilton Diptych*, National Gallery: Making and Meaning (London, 1993).

GOULD, STEPHEN JAY, review, *New York Review of Books*, (3 Mar. 1988).

GRAY, DOUGLAS, *Robert Henryson* (Leiden, 1979).

GREEN, R. H., 'Classical Fable and English Poetry in the 14th Century', in Dorothy Bethurum (ed.), *Critical Approaches to Medieval Literature* (New York, 1960), 110–33.

HANAWALT, BARBARA, 'At the Margins of Women's Space in Medieval Europe', in Robert R. Edwards and Vickie Ziegler (eds.), *Matrons and Marginal Women in Medieval Society* (Woodbridge, 1995), 1–17.

—— 'Men's Games, King's Deer: Poaching in Medieval England', *Journal of Medieval and Renaissance Studies*, 19 (1988), 175–93.

HARWOOD, BRITTON J., 'Language and the Real: Chaucer's Manciple', *Chaucer Review*, 6 (1972), 268–79.

HASSIG, DEBRA, *Medieval Bestiaries: Text, Image, Ideology* (Cambridge, 1995).

HAZELTON, RICHARD, 'The Manciple's Tale: Parody and Critique', *JEGP* 62 (1963), 1–31.

HELTERMAN, JEFFREY, 'The Dehumanizing Metamorphoses of the Knight's Tale', *Journal of English Literary History*, 38 (1971), 493–511.

HERBERT, J. A., *The Sherborne Missal*, Roxburghe Club (Oxford, 1920).

HILTON, RODNEY, *Bond Men Made Free: Medieval Peasant Movements and the English Rising of 1381* (London, 1973).

HOLSINGER, BRUCE W., 'Pedagogy, Violence, and the Subject of Music: Chaucer's *Prioress's Tale* and the Ideologies of "Song"', in

Wendy Scase, Rita Copeland, and David Lawton (eds.), *New Medieval Literatures 1* (Oxford, 1997), 157–92.

HONEGGER, THOMAS, *From Phoenix to Chauntecleer: Medieval English Animal Poetry*, Swiss Studies in English, 120 (Tübingen and Basle, 1996).

HOPE, W. H. ST JOHN, *A Grammar of English Heraldry*, 2nd edn., rev. Anthony Wagner (Cambridge, 1953).

HOUWEN, L. A. J. R. (ed.), *Animals and the Symbolic in Mediaeval Art and Literature*, Mediaevalia Groningana, 20 (Groningen, 1997).

—— 'Flattery and the Mermaid in Chaucer's *Nun's Priest's Tale*', in Houwen (ed.), *Animals and the Symbolic in Mediaeval Art and Literature*, 77–92.

HUSBAND, TIMOTHY, *The Wild Man: Medieval Myth and Symbolism* (New York, 1980).

HUTCHINSON, G. EVELYN, 'Attitudes towards Nature in Medieval England: The Alphonso and Bird Psalters', *Isis*, 65 (1974), 5–37.

INGHAM, MURIEL, and BARKLEY, LAWRENCE, 'Further Animal Parallels in *Sir Gawain and the Green Knight*', *Chaucer Review*, 13 (1979), 384–6.

JONES, E. J., *Medieval Heraldry* (Cardiff, 1943).

JUSTICE, STEVEN, *Writing and Rebellion: England in 1381* (Berkeley and Los Angeles, 1994).

KARRAS, RUTH MAZO, 'Holy Harlots: Prostitute Saints in Medieval Legend', *Journal of the History of Sexuality*, 1 (1990), 3–32.

KAY, SARAH, and RUBIN, MIRI (eds.), *Framing Medieval Bodies* (Manchester, 1994).

KEAN, P. M., *Chaucer and the Making of English Poetry*, vol. ii: *The Art of Narrative* (London, 1972).

KEEN, MAURICE, *The Outlaws of Medieval Legend* (London, 1961).

KENAAN-KEDAR, NURITH, 'The Margins of Society in Marginal Romanesque Sculpture', *Gesta*, 31/1 (1992), 15–24.

KLINGENDER, FRANCIS, *Animals in Art and Thought to the End of the Middle Ages*, ed. Evelyn Antal and John Harthan (London, 1972).

KNIGHT, STEPHEN, *Geoffrey Chaucer* (Oxford, 1986).

KRISTEVA, JULIA, *Powers of Horror: An Essay on Abjection*, trans. Leon S. Roudiez (New York, 1982).

LANE, HARLAN, *The Wild Boy of Aveyron* (London, 1979).

LAQUEUR, THOMAS, *Making Sex: Body and Gender from the Greeks to Freud* (Cambridge, Mass., 1990).

LEACH, EDMUND, 'Anthropological Aspects of Language: Animal Categories of Verbal Abuse', in Pierre Maranda (ed.), *Mythology* (Harmondsworth, 1972), 39–67.

LE GOFF, JACQUES, *Medieval Civilization: 400–1500*, trans. J. Barrow (Oxford, 1988).

LE GOFF, JACQUES, *The Medieval Imagination* (Chicago and London, 1988; trans. of *L'Imaginaire médiéval: Essais*, Paris, 1985).

—— 'Melusina: Mother and Pioneer', in *Time, Work and Culture in the Middle Ages*, trans. Arthur Goldhammer (Chicago, 1980), 204–22.

LÉVI-STRAUSS, CLAUDE, *La Pensée sauvage* (Paris, 1962), translated as *The Savage Mind* (London, 1966).

—— *Totemism*, trans. Rodney Needham, introd. Roger C. Poole (Harmondsworth, 1969).

LOMPERIS, L., and STANBURY, S. (eds.), *Feminist Approaches to the Body in Medieval Literature* (Philadelphia, 1993).

LONDON, H. STANFORD, 'The Greyhound as a Royal Beast', *Archaeologia*, 97 (1959), 139–63.

LOOMIS, R. S., 'A Phantom Tale of Feminine Ingratitude', *Modern Philology*, 14 (1917), 751–5.

MCCALL, JOHN P., *Chaucer among the Gods: The Poetics of Classical Myth* (University Park, Pa., 1979).

—— 'The Squire in Wonderland', *Chaucer Review*, 1 (1966), 103–9.

MCCLURE, PETER, 'Gawain's *Mesure* and the Significance of the Three Hunts in *Sir Gawain and the Green Knight*', *Neophilologus*, 57 (1973), 375–87.

MCCULLOCH, FLORENCE, *Mediaeval Latin and French Bestiaries* (Chapel Hill, NC, 1962).

MCDONALD, CRAIG, 'The Perversion of Law in Robert Henryson's Fable of the Fox, the Wolf, and the Husbandman', *MÆ* 49 (1980), 244–53.

MCFARLANE, K. B., 'Bastard Feudalism', *Bulletin of the Institute of Historical Research*, 20 (1945), 161–80; repr. in *England in the Fifteenth Century: Collected Essays* (London, 1981), 23–43.

MALSON, LUCIEN, *Wolf Children* (London, 1972).

MATHEW, GERVASE, *The Court of Richard II* (London, 1968).

MEAD, W. E., *The English Medieval Feast* (London, 1931).

MEALE, CAROL M., '. . . alle the bokes that I haue of latyn, englisch, and frensch: Laywomen and their Books in Late Medieval England', in Meale (ed.), *Women and Literature in Britain, 1150–1500*, Cambridge Studies in Medieval Literature, 17 (Cambridge, 1993), 128–58.

MELLINKOFF, RUTH, *The Mark of Cain* (Berkeley and Los Angeles, 1981).

—— *Outcasts: Signs of Otherness in Northern European Art of the Late Middle Ages*, 2 vols. (Berkeley and Los Angeles, 1993).

Middle English Dictionary (Ann Arbor, 1956–).

MOORE, R. I., *The Formation of a Persecuting Society* (Oxford, 1987).

MORGAN, G., 'The Action of the Hunting and Bedroom Scenes in *Sir Gawain and the Green Knight*', *MÆ* 56 (1987), 200–16.

MORSON, JOHN, 'The English Cistercians and the Bestiary', *Bulletin of the John Rylands Library*, 39 (1956), 146–70.

MURATOVA, XENIA, 'Workshop Methods in English Late Twelfth-Century Illumination and the Production of Luxury Bestiaries', in Clark and McMunn (eds.), *Beasts and Birds of the Middle Ages: The Bestiary and its Legacy*, 53–68.

MUSCATINE, CHARLES, 'Form, Texture, and Meaning in Chaucer's *Knight's Tale*', *PMLA* 65 (1950), 911–29.

NEUBECKER, OTTFRIED, *Heraldry: Sources, Symbols, and Meaning* (London, 1976).

NEUSE, RICHARD, 'The Knight: The First Mover in Chaucer's Human Comedy', *University of Toronto Quarterly*, 31 (1962), 299–315.

NOVAK, MAXIMILLIAN E., 'The Wild Man Comes to Tea', in Edward Dudley and Maximillian E. Novak (eds.), *The Wild Man Within: An Image in Western Thought from the Renaissance to Romanticism* (Pittsburgh, 1972), 183–221.

OGGINS, ROBIN S., 'Falconry and Medieval Views of Nature', in Salisbury (ed.), *The Medieval World of Nature: A Book of Essays*, 47–60.

ORTNER, SHERRY B., 'Is Female to Male as Nature is to Culture?', in Michelle Zimbalist Rosaldo and Louise Lamphere (eds.), *Woman, Culture and Society* (Stanford, Calif., 1974), 67–87.

OWST, G. R., *Literature and Pulpit in Medieval England*, 2nd edn. (Oxford, 1961).

PÄCHT, OTTO, and ALEXANDER, J. J. G., *Illuminated MSS in the Bodleian Library, Oxford*, vol. iii (Oxford, 1973).

PATTERSON, LEE, *Chaucer and the Subject of History* (London, 1991).

PEARSALL, DEREK, 'Hunting Scenes in Medieval Illuminated Manuscripts', *Connoisseur*, 196/789 (Nov. 1977), 170–81.

—— *Lydgate* (London, 1970).

PEVSNER, NIKOLAUS, *The Buildings of England: North-West and South Norfolk* (Harmondsworth, 1962).

POPE, ROBERT, 'A Sly Toad, Physiognomy and the Problem of Deceit: Henryson's *The Paddok and the Mous*', *Neophilologus*, 63 (1979), 461–8.

POPPE, ERICH, and ROSS, BIANCA (eds.), *The Legend of Mary of Egypt in Medieval Insular Hagiography* (Dublin, 1996).

PUTTER, AD, *'Sir Gawain and the Green Knight' and French Arthurian Romance* (Oxford, 1995).

RANDALL, LILIAN M. C., *Images in the Margins of Gothic Manuscripts* (Berkeley and Los Angeles, 1966).

RÉAU, L., *Iconographie de l'art chrétien*, 6 vols. (Paris, 1955–8).

REMNANT, G. L., *A Catalogue of Misericords in Great Britain*, with an Essay on their Iconography by M. D. Anderson (Oxford, 1969).

RIDDY, FELICITY, 'The Speaking Knight: Sir Gawain and Other Animals', in Martin B. Schichtman and James P. Carley (eds.), *Culture and the King: The Social Implications of the Arthurian Legend: Essays in Honor of Valerie M. Lagorio* (Albany, NY, 1994), 149–62.

RILEY, DENISE, *Am I That Name? Feminism and the Category of 'Women' in History* (Basingstoke, 1988).

RITVO, HARRIET, *The Platypus and the Mermaid, and Other Figments of the Classifying Imagination* (Cambridge, Mass., 1997).

ROONEY, ANNE, *Hunting in Middle English Literature* (Woodbridge, 1993).

—— 'The Hunts in *Sir Gawain and the Green Knight*', in Derek Brewer and Jonathan Gibson (eds.), *A Companion to the 'Gawain'-Poet* (Woodbridge, 1997), 157–63.

SALISBURY, JOYCE E., *The Beast Within: Animals in the Middle Ages* (New York and London, 1994).

—— (ed.), *The Medieval World of Nature: A Book of Essays* (New York, 1993).

SALTER, ELIZABETH, *Chaucer: The Knight's Tale and The Clerk's Tale* (London, 1962).

SCAGLIONE, ALDO, *Knights at Court: Courtliness, Chivalry, and Courtesy from Ottonian Germany to the Italian Renaissance* (Berkeley and Los Angeles, 1991).

SCATTERGOOD, V. J., *Politics and Poetry in the Fifteenth Century* (London, 1971).

SCHAMA, SIMON, *Landscape and Memory* (London, 1995).

SCOTT-MACNAB, DAVID, 'A Re-examination of Octovyen's Hunt in *The Book of the Duchess*', *MÆ* 56 (1987), 183–99.

SHAHAR, SHULAMITH, 'The Old Body in Medieval Culture', in Kay and Rubin (eds.), *Framing Medieval Bodies*, 160–86.

SHATTUCK, ROGER, *The Forbidden Experiment: The Story of the Wild Boy of Aveyron* (London, 1980).

SPEARING, A. C., *Medieval Dream-Poetry* (Cambridge, 1976).

SPEIRS, JOHN, 'Sir Gawain and the Green Knight', *Scrutiny*, 16 (1949), 274–300.

SPERBER, DAN, *Rethinking Symbolism*, trans. Alice L. Morton, Cambridge Studies and Papers in Social Anthropology (Cambridge, 1975).

SPRUNGER, DAVID A., 'Wild Folk and Lunatics in Medieval Romance', in Salisbury (ed.), *The Medieval World of Nature: A Book of Essays*, 145–63.

STALLYBRASS, PETER, and WHITE, ALLON, *The Politics and Poetics of Transgression* (London, 1986).

STEVENS, JOHN, *Music and Poetry in the Early Tudor Court* (Cambridge, 1979).

STORM, MELVIN, 'The Tercelet as Tiger: Bestiary Hypocrisy in the *Squire's Tale*', *English Language Notes*, 14 (1976–7), 172–4.

THIÉBAUX, MARCELLE, 'The Medieval Chase', *Speculum*, 42 (1967), 260–74.

—— *The Stag of Love: The Chase in Medieval Literature* (Ithaca, NY, 1974).

THOMPSON, E. P., *Whigs and Hunters: The Origins of the Black Act* (London, 1975).

TRACHTENBERG, JOSHUA, *The Devil and the Jews: The Medieval Conception of the Jew and its Relation to Modern Antisemitism* (New Haven, 1943; repr. Cleveland, 1961).

TRISTRAM, E. W., *English Wall Painting of the Fourteenth Century* (London, 1955).

TURNER, FREDERICK, 'A Structuralist Analysis of the *Knight's Tale*', *Chaucer Review*, 8 (1974), 279–96.

TURNER, VICTOR, *Dramas, Fields and Metaphors: Symbolic Action in Human Society* (Ithaca, NY, 1974).

—— *The Ritual Process: Structure and Anti-Structure* (Chicago, 1969).

VAN MARLE, RAIMOND, *Iconographie de l'art profane au Moyen-âge*, 2 vols. (The Hague, 1931–2).

VARTY, KENNETH, 'The Death and Resurrection of Reynard in Medieval Literature and Art', *Nottingham Mediaeval Studies*, 10 (1966), 70–93.

—— 'The Pursuit of Reynard in Mediaeval English Literature and Art', *Nottingham Mediaeval Studies*, 8 (1964), 62–81.

—— 'Reynard the Fox and the Smithfield Decretals', *Journal of the Warburg and Courtauld Institutes*, 26 (1963), 347–54.

—— *Reynard the Fox: A Study of the Fox in Medieval English Art* (Leicester, 1967).

WAGNER, ANTHONY, *Heraldry in England* (Harmondsworth, 1946).

—— 'The Swan Badge and the Swan Knight', *Archaeologia*, 97 (1959), 127–38.

WHITE, HAYDEN, 'The Forms of Wildness: Archaeology of an Idea', in Edward Dudley and Maximillian E. Novak (eds.), *The Wild Man Within: An Image in Western Thought from the Renaissance to Romanticism* (Pittsburgh, 1972).

WHITE, T. H., *The Book of Beasts* (London, 1954).

WHITING, B. J., *Proverbs, Sentences, and Proverbial Phrases from English Writings Mainly Before 1500* (Cambridge, Mass., 1968).

WILLIAMS, CHARLES ALLYN, 'Oriental Affinities of the Legend of the Hairy Anchorite, Part I: Pre-Christian', *University of Illinois Studies in Language and Literature*, 10 (1925).

WILLIAMS, CHARLES ALLYN, 'Oriental Affinities of the Legend of the Hairy Anchorite, Part II: Christian', *University of Illinois Studies in Language and Literature*, 11 (1926).

WOKLER, ROBERT, review, *Times Literary Supplement* (17 Sept. 1993).

WOODFORDE, CHRISTOPHER, 'Some Medieval English Glazing Quarries Painted with Birds', *Journal of the British Archaeological Association*, 3rd ser. 60 (1944), 1–11.

YAMAMOTO, DOROTHY, 'Heraldry and the *Knight's Tale*', *Neuphilologische Mitteilungen*, 93 (1992), 207–15.

YOUNG, CHARLES R., *The Royal Forests of Medieval England* (Leicester, 1979).

ZUCKERMAN, S., 'Apes Я Not Us', *New York Review of Books* (30 May 1991), 43–9.

INDEX